SO-AWZ-507

William S. Phillips has created the
paintings for the covers of most of the
Air & Space books. He described himself as
specially interested in painting
the B-47, which Tex Johnston test-piloted.
Artists interested in aviation subjects
sometimes are moved to create a portrait of a
plane that captures the character
of the particular aircraft.

The detail from the above painting that
appears on the cover of this edition is used by
courtesy of The Greenwich Workshop.

I unbuckled my belt and started forward to the cockpit. On the way, the perturbed chief stewardess grabbed my arm and said, "The captain wishes to see you." I opened the cockpit door. The airplane was on autopilot, the control wheel oscillating right and left with the Dutch roll. The coatless captain, shirt wet with sweat, hands clenching the seat armrests, was almost in shock. The copilot and flight engineer were in a similar state.

I slid into the jump seat as the captain asked, "What can we do?"

"Disconnect the damn autopilot," I said.

"No, no," he said. "We'll lose it."

"There is nothing wrong with the airplane. The autopilot is misrigged," I said. "Disengage it."

"Could you fly it?" he asked.

"Sure," I said, "let me in there."

He stood watching as I fastened my safety belt and reached for the autopilot disconnect button. He grabbed my arm. "We'll lose it," he cried.

"Sit down," I said. "Let me show you something." As he eased into the jump seat, I grasped the control wheel, pushed the autopilot release, and with two slight control movements we were flying straight and level, altitude 35,000 feet.

THE BANTAM AIR & SPACE SERIES

To Fly Like the Eagles . . .

It took some 1800 years for mankind to win mastery of a challenging and life-threatening environment—the sea. In just under 70 years we have won mastery of an even more hostile environment—the air. In doing so, we have realized a dream as old as man—to be able to fly.

The Bantam Air & Space series consists of books that focus on the skills of piloting—from the days when the Wright brothers made history at Kitty Hawk to the era of barnstorming daredevils of the sky, through the explosion of technology, design, and flyers that occurred in World War II, and finally to the cool daring of men who first broke the sound barrier, walked the Moon and have lived and worked in space stations—always at high risk, always proving the continued need for their presence and skill.

The Air & Space series will be published once a month as mass market books with special illustrations, and with varying lengths and prices. Aviation enthusiasts would be wise to buy each book as it comes out if they are to collect the complete Library.

TEX JOHNSTON
JET-AGE TEST PILOT

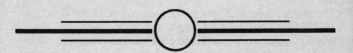

By A. M. "Tex" Johnston
with Charles Barton

BANTAM BOOKS
NEW YORK • TORONTO • LONDON • SYDNEY • AUCKLAND

*This edition contains the complete text
of the original hardcover edition.*
NOT ONE WORD HAS BEEN OMITTED.

TEX JOHNSTON

*A Bantam Falcon Book / published by arrangement with
the author*

PRINTING HISTORY
The Smithsonian Institution Press edition published 1991
Bantam edition / July 1992

ISBN 0-553-29587-X

Published simultaneously in the United States and Canada

PRINTED IN THE UNITED STATES OF AMERICA

OPM   0 9 8 7 6 5 4 3 2 1

This book is dedicated to my parents, Alva Merril and Ella Viola Johnston, whose loving support helped give me wings, and to my ever-beautiful bride and partner for fifty-five years, DeLores Honea Johnston, whose long-suffering patience and understanding enabled me to pursue dreams of experimental flight test on the frontiers of aviation development.

Contents

Foreword

Tex Johnston tells the thrilling and factual story of the developmental flight testing of America's first jet airplanes. But more than that, he tells how in the space of one man's career aviation has progressed from wooden, fabric-covered biplanes to mammoth jet transports and rockets to the moon. I well recall my first solo flight in the mid-twenties in an OX-5 Travel Air, a two-cockpit, fabric-covered biplane that flew slightly over 100 mph. And when I was a kid, a train trip from coast to coast, which we took often, consumed four days. Today jet planes make it in roughly four hours.

On March 11, 1957, I flew with Tex Johnston on a recordbreaking flight of 3 hours and 48 minutes across the continent from Seattle to Baltimore on the Boeing prototype 707 jet airliner, the 367-80. As I said in my newspaper column on March 17, 1957, "We knew darn well that we were participating in a giant step forward in the evolution of the airplane."

In the first place, I got a definite feeling of tremendous power and, for the first few thousand feet, of tremendous speed. Some of you may recall that in the old propeller-driven airplanes, after you were up, say, to a thousand feet, the ground below seemed to go by quite slowly. Not so with the 707. We climbed at the rate of 2,000 feet per minute, and even at that rate our speed was around 500 mph. Looking out the window I could see that we were covering the ground much faster than ever before.

The plane was not as fully soundproof as commercial airliners would be. Even so, from over the wing forward to the cockpit the noise was considerably less than in the reciprocating-engine transports.

The outstanding difference, though, was in its total lack of vibration. This we proved to ourselves by balancing pencils and cigarettes and even standing coins on edge on the tables. We did not appreciate the great importance of the lack of vibration until the trip was over, when we realized that none of us felt any fatigue whatever.

The plane was much bigger and roomier than any of the commercial airliners of that day. And with its additional speed, we knew it was the dawn of a new age for commercial air transportation.

More recently, I have flown half a dozen or so times in the supersonic Concorde, which cruises at better than twice the speed of sound. So, at age 82, I think that I have seen as big a jump forward in one lifetime as anyone could expect. Tex Johnston has lived through and participated in this phenomenal development of the jet age. His story is a fascinating account of how it came about.

William Randolph Hearst, Jr.

1

First Flights

In younger years friends called me "Al" Johnston, but that name changed when I became a test pilot for the Bell Aircraft Company. In the dim light of a wintry morning in early January 1943, I hung my Stetson on the wall of the company's P-39 fighter plane flight-line office in Niagara Falls, kicked off my overshoes, and polished the toes of my cowboy boots on the leg of my trousers. The mechanic standing by with the Form One said, "Get your chute, Tex. You get the first one today."

Smiling, I put on helmet and goggles and picked up my chute. "Come on, pardner," I said. "Let's see if she's a live one."

The story of that arrival quickly spread from flight line to plant. Within a week my name became "Tex" Johnston and remains so today, 47 years later.

In October 1944, I arrived at Bell Aircraft's Muroc Flight Test Base in California's Mojave Desert, as base manager and project test pilot of the Bell XP-59A, the first jet-powered airplane to be built in the United States.

General Electric, the maker of the plane's jet engines, and Wright Field, headquarters for Army Air Corps research and development, had reviewed the data from earlier low-altitude test flights. Both were eager for maximum-altitude performance information. So I was not surprised one morning to see that the day's plan of test called for a full-throttle climb to 46,000 feet, a stabilized full-throttle run at that altitude, followed by another level run at reduced power.

After my preflight preparations and briefing, I suited up, strapped in, and taxied out to takeoff from Muroc Dry Lake, the future site of Edwards Air Force Base. In position, with takeoff checks completed, I advanced the throttles and released the brakes. As usual for early jets, the acceleration was slow at first but built up as the takeoff progressed. The complete absence of vibration and the low noise level were welcome changes from the sound and fury of a propeller-driven takeoff. Flying alternate headings, I climbed away from the wooden mess hall, barracks, and Quonset-type hangar of the test base, leveled off at 46,000 feet, and entered a shallow turn to 90 degrees. Engine temperatures and pressures were normal, pressurized cabin altitude 25,000 feet, cockpit temperature comfortable, outside temperature –55 degrees Fahrenheit.

The called-for high-speed run started over the slate gray of the Pacific with the California coastline just ahead. The plane raced eastward with throttles still against the forward stops. The absolutely smooth air, the absence of airframe and engine vibration, the comforting whine of the engine compressors, and the infinite visibility were as though I was suspended in space. I felt a surge of joy and exhilaration. "Here I am in one of the most advanced airplanes in the world, flying in a totally new environment. Most important, I'm the only person in the United States up here."

Over western Arizona, run completed and data logged, I slowly retarded the throttles. Surprise. The engine rpm remained at 20,000. The plane still charged ahead at full power. I eased the throttles back to idle—no effect. Engine rpm remained the same. I turned left to 270 degrees and raised the nose slightly. Airspeed slowly decreased 1, 2, 3, 4, 5 miles per hour. Suddenly, a slight tremor—a low-speed stall warning. I dropped the nose to level flight and checked the altimeter—46,000 feet. As airspeed slowly increased, the stall warning tremor ceased. I lowered the nose a bit more. Slowly the airspeed built up—1, 2, 3, 4, 5, 6 mph. At plus 7 mph, altitude 45,700 feet, a high-frequency tremor alerted me to new danger.

I remembered an N.A.C.A. (National Advisory Committee

for Aeronautics) article describing high-speed buffet due to airflow separation over the wing that can occur in level flight when airflow reaches the critical speed for a particular airfoil section. It appeared to fit my situation. I raised the nose.

Here I was, practically trapped at altitude because I couldn't throttle the engines and had only a 12-mph speed corridor between low- and high-speed stalls. With limited fuel remaining, a descent shallow enough to preclude the high-speed buffet and possible loss of control would require too much time. If fuel ran out I would lose cabin pressurization and heat.

I called Muroc. "I hesitate to extend flaps or gear," I said. "I don't know what effect a change in airflow over the wing may have. I plan to shut down the left engine. The right engine pressurizes the cabin seal tube and provides cabin heat. A fifty-percent reduction in power will result in a satisfactory descent rate." The test engineers on the ground agreed. I closed the left engine fuel valve. The tail-pipe temperature dropped, and the engine rpm drifted down to an approximate 2,000-rpm windmill speed. Airspeed decreased. A stable 700-feet-per-minute descent was established with the right throttle remaining at idle. As the plane descended through 35,000 feet, the right engine rpm slowly decreased. I logged the data.

Returning to base in a relatively steep single-engine dive, I came across the ramp 100 feet off the deck, pulled up in a chandelle, extended gear and flaps, landed, and rolled up to the hangar ramp. A postflight conference with local General Electric and Bell reps concluded with a conference call to G.E. Engineering at Lynn, Massachusetts.

G.E. contacted the Woodward Company of Chicago, which produced the first jet-engine altitude-compensating fuel regulator. Subsequently, I flew the developmental and proof testing of that unit. The final product provided satisfactory throttling throughout the altitude range and significantly reduced the transient high temperatures during engine starts and rapid power accelerations.

The data from the 46,000-foot altitude high-speed performance tests submitted to Wright Field and General Electric assured the future of jet aircraft. Those flights in the XP-59A in 1944 were my indoctrination to seventeen years of developmental engineering flight testing of turbojet-powered aircraft, a period that saw the most significant advances in airframe and engine development in the history of aviation.

In 1946 I became chief test pilot at Bell. In 1948 I was employed by Boeing as project pilot for the six-jet Boeing XB-47, the first swept-wing bomber. In 1952 I was project pilot for the eight-jet Boeing XB-52 bomber that became the backbone of the Strategic Air Command. From 1954 to 1961 I was chief of flight test and project pilot for the Boeing 367-80, prototype 707, the 707 series aircraft, and the KC-135 tanker, a version of the 707 design. It was thus that I was present at the creation of the jet age.

It all started in 1925. I was eleven years old. I still remember the warmth of the Midwestern sun on my back and the smell of the aroma-laden spring air slightly tainted with odors of oil and burned carbon. Father had removed the head from our Model T engine. I chipped and scraped at encrusted carbon while he ground and refaced intake and exhaust valves. Gradually an unfamiliar sound grew louder. I ran to the south side of the house and looked at the sky. "It's an airplane," I shouted.

The plane headed toward us, then tilted left and headed west. We watched in silence, thinking it had left. Then I saw it start down. "Dad! It's going to land!"

"Why would he land here?" my father replied.

"Come on," I cried. "Please, let's go see."

When we got to the landing site, the airplane sat gracefully on green pasture near a barbed-wire fence. Several buggies, spring wagons, and two other Model Ts were parked along the dirt road. The men wore bib overalls, the ladies nearly ankle-length cotton dresses. Small children hung to their mothers' skirts, halfway hiding behind them.

The pilot leaned on the fence. His well-worn but beautiful English riding boot rested on a lower strand of barbed wire. He was a bit over six feet tall with a tapering black mustache, friendly blue eyes, and square jaw. He wore slightly flared English riding breeches with chamois knee patches, a well-worn soft brown leather jacket over a soldier's shirt with a pocket on each side, a soft brown leather helmet with goggles pushed up, and a long white scarf around his neck. He was trying to make conversation, but everyone was so awestruck he got only a few questions, such as: "How fast does she go?" and "Bet it burns a lot of gas."

Just then, another Model T arrived and another "Mr. Bibs" stepped out and headed for the pilot. "This is my land and I don't want that airplane on it," the new Mr. Bibs said. "You'll have to move it."

"Okay, but I was going to sell rides and was hoping we could work out a deal."

"No," the landowner said with finality. "You can't use this pasture."

With that, another Mr. Bibs spoke up, "That's my pasture across the road. You can use it if you wish."

"Thanks," said the pilot. "Come on. Get in. You can ride along."

The man who had offered the use of his land stared for a moment in stunned surprise, then smiled weakly. "No, that's not necessary," he said.

"Okay," said the pilot. "Anyone else want to ride across the road for free?"

All the men studied their shoes or looked for someone down the road while the women attended to their hair or looked off into the sky.

"Come on, Dad. Let's go," I cried, pulling his hand. The pilot was turning toward the airplane and I tried again. "Please, Dad, let me go. Ask the pilot if I can go."

The pilot had taken several steps when Dad finally called, "Hey, Mister. Can the boy go?"

The pilot turned and looked at me. I stood as tall as I could and said, "Please, Mister. I just have to fly."

Looking at my father, the pilot asked, "Don't you want to come along?"

"No, I guess not. But the boy wants to go."

The pilot held the strands of wire apart, and in an instant I was beside him. He took me by the hand, and as we walked to the plane he said, "It'll be a little noisy and a little breezy." He pointed to a rough area about twelve inches wide on top of the lower wing alongside the fuselage. "That's the catwalk," he said. "If you step outside that rough area you'll tear a hole in the wing." He put me in the front cockpit and fastened the safety belt. I was so short I couldn't see over the side. I wriggled upward under the belt until I got my knees on the seat.

The pilot set the cockpit switches, walked around the wing to the prop, and pulled it through. Engine noise, prop wash, and vibration all started up together. As the pilot slid down into the rear cockpit, he smiled slightly and winked a clear blue eye.

As we turned to takeoff heading, the throb of the engine increased to a roar, the slipstream became a constant rush, the irregular bumping of the wheels over the uneven ground smoothed out and ceased completely as the cockpit seat tilted upward. I peered over the edge of the cockpit. The ground fell away. We were flying!

Rising higher on my knees, I saw the patchwork pattern of the fields below. White houses and red barns looked very small. As the left wing moved down in a turn, I saw Emporia, Kansas, looking about the size of the top of my school desk. Another left turn and I saw the Neosho River where Dad, Mother, and I frequently went fishing.

The throb of the engine decreased; the airplane tilted downward. I could barely see over the nose through the propeller's blur. Another left descending turn, then the wings returned to level, and through the windshield I could see the buggies and cars parked alongside the road. The people and wagons flashed past, the throb of the engine became a purr, the nose came up, a solid thud, and the wheels once again rolled on the pasture surface. When we stopped near the fence, I stood up in the cockpit and saw the waiting group waving and laughing. I jumped to the ground and grabbed the pilot's hand. "I love you and I'm going to be just like you."

"I believe you liked it," Dad said with a happy smile.

The spectators gathered around. "Please go for a ride," I said. "It's wonderful."

As we climbed into the Model T, we could hear the pilot's convincing voice. "Come on, folks. See your hometown from the air. Only one dollar."

The following morning in Sunday school, the teacher spoke of David and Goliath. "The message here, boys, is that throughout your lifetime you will encounter major obstacles that appear to block your path—Goliath problems in your job or business and with your own family.

"Remember that David appeared small and insignificant in comparison to Goliath. Success is achieved through self-confidence, dedication to your objective, and perfection in your field of endeavor."

At home, I lay with my hands behind my head on the warm fresh grass that was decorated with the springtime beauty of Kansas dogtooth violets. I looked at the white puffball clouds floating in the dimensionless sky. Yesterday, I'd been there. Words from Mr. Moon's Sunday school lesson flashed back: "Dedication to your objective and perfection in your field of endeavor." Now it all came together. "Starting today—no—yesterday, my objective is to be a pilot. I must study, observe, and learn about airplanes and engines and somehow, someday, learn to fly."

I covered the walls of my bedroom with airplane pictures from the Waco Airplane Company in Troy, Ohio; the Travel Air, Swallow, and Knoll companies in Wichita, Kansas; American Eagle in Kansas City; Alexander in Colorado Springs; and Monocoupe in St. Louis. Occasionally, I found aviation magazines on the drugstore news rack and learned the names of airplane components: fuselage, ailerons, stabilizers, rudder, elevators—I rolled the magic words around on my tongue. I built model airplanes in my father's shop and suspended them on wires from the eaves around Mother's back porch.

At fifteen I began delivery of the daily Kansas City newspapers, a first step in financing my dreams. The monthly cost to the subscriber was 65 cents, which I collected the first of each month. After paying the district agent each month, I received 20 cents per subscriber. My average monthly gross was around $32. Through careful saving I first bought a second-hand bicycle. The following year I advanced in prestige with the purchase of my first motorcycle, a beautiful Excelsior Super-X with a V-twin-cylinder, 37-cubic-inch engine.

One evening when I arrived home from the paper route, Carl Jacobs, a classmate and close friend who studied airplanes with me, was waiting. "I found us a glider," he yelled as I switched off the Super-X. "The flying club cracked up their old Cessna primary. It's dismantled and leaning against a chicken house out by the city waterworks. We can buy it for twenty-five dollars.''

The next day we rode the Super-X out to see it. The single-frame fuselage was intact except that the seat had failed from the hard landing. The wings and tail units had broken ribs and ripped fabric. Although rain had entered the wing, the spars appeared to be okay. The flying and landing wires that held the wings in position were broken and would have to be replaced.

''How much money do you have?'' I asked.

''Five bucks,'' he replied.

I gave him ten dollars, my gas money for the bike, and said, ''Offer them fifteen dollars. If they won't take it, tell 'em I'll have the other ten bucks by the fifth of next month.''

We worked on it nights, Saturdays, and Sundays whenever we had money to buy necessary materials. We reglued all the ribs and varnished the ribs and spars before recovering the wings and tail surfaces. By spring the glider was ready for assembly.

Father got permission from the Maddocks to assemble the glider in a long-abandoned T-hangar on their farm and to use their pasture for takeoffs and landings. The hangar had no door, so we strung strands of barbed wire across the opening to keep the cows out.

When the glider was ready, we still had to wait for the Kansas wind to weaken. Finally, conditions were right for our first practice session. With the help of friends we moved the glider out of the hangar, a man on each wingtip, one holding the tail, and two pulling the towrope. After the glider was headed into the wind, Carl and I took turns at the controls, keeping the wings level with the ailerons, moving the nose left and right with the rudder, and lifting the nose slightly with the elevators. In that way, we continued practicing in winds of increasing velocity until we were confident that we could control the glider while being towed two or three feet above the ground by Father's Model A. On the great day of our first flights most of our buddies turned out to watch. Carl won the toss to fly first.

He strapped into the seat mounted on the central skid—a

bit like riding a broomstick—and, when all was set, with towrope connected, gave the high sign. I eased out the clutch of the Model A and gradually increased the speed while watching the towed glider in the rearview mirror. Two friends ran alongside the wingtips to keep the wings level until Carl achieved aileron control. At first he overcontrolled the elevators and climbed to about five feet in erratic steps. Then he got the feel and flew level for a short distance before pulling the towline latch. The glider descended, touched, made one little skip, then skidded to a stop.

Now it was my turn. When set, I gave the high sign. The towrope tightened, and the glider moved ahead into the wind. As the speed increased, the glider controls became increasingly effective. I raised the nose. The ground began falling away—how smooth, how quiet, how wonderful. The simple craft flew effortlessly. As the Model A neared the far end of the pasture, I pulled the towline release and lowered the nose slightly. Approaching the ground, I applied slight back stick. The nose slowly came up, the single center skid touched down, and the glider slid to a stop. My first solo flight had ended.

Carl and I flew many times after that. We learned to fly higher, to make ten- or fifteen-degree turns before releasing the towline, and then to make gliding turns back into the wind for landing.

One Sunday morning while returning from my paper route, I saw an airplane circle town and head toward Maddock's pasture. Wheeling my ol' Super-X around, I roared out to the field in a cloud of dust. Two men stood by the wing of a Waco three-place open-cockpit biplane.

"I saw you over town," I said. "My name's Al Johnston."

"Glad to meet you," the pilot said. "I'm Toy Franklin, and this is my student Bill Miller."

I showed them the glider in the T-hangar, and Toy briefed me on the Waco. "How much for flight instruction?" I asked.

"Twenty-five dollars an hour," Toy said.

"I can't afford an hour at a time."

"That's okay. I'm going to stay in Emporia for some time with Bill at his folks' home."

"Can I take a lesson now? How long a flight for ten dollars?"

"To get you started, I'll make it thirty minutes today."

Toy explained how dual instruction would proceed and then gave some advice: "Never think of moving the rudder, ailerons, or elevators. Think in terms of pressure: right and left pressure on the rudder pedals for directional control, side pressure on the stick for roll, and fore-and-aft pressure on the stick to move the nose towards you or away from you— don't think of nose up and nose down. That way when you advance to acrobatics and get on your back you won't be confused.

"During taxi, takeoff, and climb, keep your toes on the rudders, right hand on the stick, and left hand on the throttle. Just follow me through; don't resist my actions as I fly the airplane. When I shake the stick, you take control. I won't be on the controls; I'll allow you as much time as possible to correct, then I'll assist you. You read?"

"You bet," I replied. "I'll get my helmet and goggles from the bike."

That day in 1929 marked the beginning of a great friendship among the three of us. Later, when I was at the Spartan School of Aeronautics, Toy joined Northwest Airlines. He retired as a senior captain soon after I joined the Boeing Company, when Northwest was flying DC-6's and DC-7's. Bill Miller became a Department of Commerce (now the F.A.A.) inspector based in Kansas City until his untimely death from medical problems.

Because of my limited finances, all my flight training from Toy was accumulated in ten- to twenty-minute flights over a period of two years. He was a knowledgeable pilot and a patient and thorough instructor.

One Saturday morning, the Super-X and I arrived at Maddock's pasture expecting to find Toy and Bill. Their car was there, but the Waco was gone. About to leave, I heard an unfamiliar engine. A high-wing monoplane circled the field, landed, and taxied to the T-hangar. The prop ticked to a stop, the cabin door opened, and there stood the first female pilot I'd ever seen. "I've been flying since seven this morning," she said. "I saw the car and was hoping for a ride to town. I'm starving."

"I'm sorry," I said. "It's not my car, but if you don't mind a little breeze I'll take you on my bike."

She looked at the X, then smiled at me. "That'd be great."

As I was about to step on the kick starter, I turned, stuck out my hand, and said, "I'm Al Johnston."

"My name's Amelia," she said.

During lunch at Emporia's Coney Island Cafe on Sixth Avenue, Amelia said her last name was Earhart and that she was flying daily to accumulate hours on a prototype engine for the manufacturer. That explained why the engine sound was new to me.

The Earhart name had no significance for me at the time. She was not beautiful, but her easy conversation and pleasing, radiant personality made a deep impression. The two hours we spent together was the only time our flight plans in life intersected. Later, seeing her name in headlines, I thought of our chance meeting at Maddock's pasture.

Emporia's Fourth of July celebration was an important yearly event drawing people from miles around. To take advantage of it, Inman's Flying Circus arrived over Emporia at midmorning on July 2 with four airplanes: a Ford Tri-motor, a Stinson monoplane, an OX-5 Waco, and an OX-5 Travel Air. By the time I arrived at Maddock's pasture on my newly acquired Harley-Davidson 74, which had replaced the old Super-X, the planes were parked and the gear unloaded.

I had made contact with Inman's advance man about three weeks before and had handled the delivery of handbills and the display of posters and signs. Now I arranged with Art Inman to sell tickets, gas planes, and clean them up after the show each day. I learned a lot about barnstorming during the show's stay at Emporia and during subsequent shows in Herington, Kansas, where in addition to ticket sales, fueling, and grease-monkey chores, I slept with the planes at night as an on-site guard.

In rural areas during the early thirties, few residents had seen an airplane on the ground and never a trimotor. Consequently, people traveled long distances to see them, particularly when an air show was scheduled. Airplanes were considered somewhat miraculous, and many people were frightened of them. So during barnstorming days it was always difficult to sell the first tickets. In fact, if one could

Ford Trimotor

persuade someone to go for a free ride, it was well worth the effort and the cost, particularly if the first passenger was enthusiastic after landing.

I was maturing faster than most Emporia teenagers, what with my paper route, glider, flying lessons, a summer of varied experience learning the ways of the world with a traveling carnival and riding my Super-X on the vertical wall of a motordrome, my first experiences with Inman's Flying Circus, a trip to the West Coast that included wheat harvesting in western Kansas, a visit to the Boeing Aviation School in Glendale, California, a visit to the gaming tables of Reno, farm work in Oregon, and the winning of a preliminary bout as an amateur prizefighter in Portland, Oregon. My senior year of high school in 1932 was particularly gratifying. Relationships were changing. Teachers became advisors and consultants.

Meanwhile, pilot training progressed as my financial condition permitted. Father had not yet made a commitment to invest in my flying career, but I was confident that somehow something would work out. I was determined to go to an accredited flying school, preferably one of the three with the best reputations: Parks Air College in Marshall, Missouri; Spartan School of Aeronautics in Tulsa, Oklahoma; or Boeing in Glendale. Although the cost of such a school was probably more than my folks would consider, I hoped to make a deal to work part-time at whatever school I attended. That hope was dashed at the Boeing School. During my visit in Glendale the school manager had said such an arrangement was not possible. "First, the ground school requires the student's full time, and second, only professional people are employed by the school."

Nothing had been resolved by the fall after my high school graduation, so I enrolled at the Kansas State Teacher's College in Emporia. Then, one Friday, a week before the end of my second semester at Teacher's College, just as we were finishing our evening meal, Father said, "Your mother and I have decided we should visit the Spartan School at Tulsa." Visions of flight instruction, a pilot's license, a flying career, flashed through my mind. But Father continued, "We believe an airplane mechanics course would prepare you for a good job."

Mother smiled happily and added her bit. "We believe mechanical training would be of great value to you in an aviation career."

I was devastated at the thought of not flying but delighted at the opportunity for formal technical training, so I managed a heartfelt thank-you despite my reservations. A visit to Tulsa by the three of us sealed the deal, and I enrolled at Spartan.

I found the mechanics course extremely interesting and challenging. The airframe (fuselage, wings, tail assembly, and landing gear) portion of the curriculum was conducted in the Spartan Airplane Factory, half a mile from the school. The factory manufactured three-place open-cockpit airplanes equipped with Walter radial air-cooled engines for the commercial market and the Mexican government. Following initial instruction, we acquired actual experience on the production line constructing, assembling, and painting the entire airplane.

Because of my mechanical aptitude, I enjoyed a good relationship with Jess Green, flight instructor and director of the ground school. Jess introduced me to Vance Vassacheck, the maintenance foreman of the Spartan government-approved airplane repair station. Vance was known from coast to coast as a fine mechanic, so the Spartan shop was continually filled with engine and airframe work. Vance suggested I come to the shop in my spare time and on Saturdays to help. I did so and was soon doing routine work on the metal machining lathe. Vance and I became good friends and frequently visited a German friend of his for talk and home brew. One evening, near the finish of my mechanic's course, I told Vance I wanted to get my pilot's license. "Do you think there's a chance for a job in the maintenance shop after graduation, taking flight instruction instead of pay?" Vance suggested I talk with Ed Hudlow, the school's administrator.

After I made my pitch to Hudlow, he replied, "How are you going to handle room and board? You know the time required to complete a limited commercial flight course and the cost. Vance says you're a good apprentice mechanic and he could use you, but the pay wouldn't come near paying those costs." He hesitated, then continued. "However, if you can arrange financing, we'll provide a job in the shop and credit your account with your earnings."

Filled with excitement, I wrote home. Shortly, Mother and Father arrived in Tulsa unannounced. For two long hours they talked with Hudlow while I waited impatiently in the rec room. When they finally reappeared, Mother was radiant. Father was his usual formal self. "You're now enrolled in the limited commercial pilot's course," he said.

Now, a new life started. Toy Franklin's basic flight instruction paid off. After two weeks, fellow students Byron Wing and Ernie Lum from Oakland, California, sponsored my unforgettable solo party at one of Tulsa's popular Chinese restaurants. As my piloting skills increased, shop assignments provided experience on all types of aircraft. Then, that year of 1933, a revolutionary new transport airplane indirectly widened my horizons still farther.

The Boeing 247, widely regarded as the first modern airliner, ushered in a new age of all-metal, internally braced, low-wing monoplanes. The main wing spar passed through the forward passenger cabin, the two engines were mounted in streamlined nacelles that merged smoothly with the leading edges of the wings, the main landing gear retracted into the engine nacelles—a basic layout that still exists in many planes today.

In addition, the aircraft's two radial, air-cooled Pratt and Whitney Wasp engines were equipped with the new Hamilton Standard variable-pitch propellers, enabling the pilot to change the pitch for optimum performance as required by changes in altitude, speed, and power. That important advance, in conjunction with retractable landing gear, a clean streamlined design, and improved engines, enabled the 247 to climb on either engine after the failure of the other, a heretofore elusive goal.

The scheduled arrival and display of the Boeing 247 at the Tulsa Municipal Airport had received much publicity, so on the appointed day a large crowd waited at the airport. Right on schedule, the sleek monoplane approached the field, made two low-level passes with landing gear retracted, extended the gear, landed, and taxied to the ramp to be officially welcomed by local dignitaries.

A short time later, to the surprise and pleasure of the crowd, famed one-eyed aviator Wiley Post and beloved humorist Will Rogers made an unannounced arrival in the *Winnie Mae,* the high-wing Lockheed Vega that Post flew solo around the world in 1933. After the *Winnie Mae* parked adjacent to the 247, fans and well-wishers surrounded the two men as they deplaned. It was common knowledge that Post relied on Vance for his maintenance, and Vance had told me that Rogers and Post were friends of Hudlow's, so I was not too surprised the next day when Hudlow came through the shop, stopped at my lathe, and said, "We're having a stag party for Bill and Wiley. Would you like to come along?"

The party included most of the business and professional leaders of Tulsa. Ed Hudlow seemed to know everyone on a first-name basis and introduced me as we worked the crowd. When dinner was announced, Ed said, "Come on, we're going to sit with Bill and Wiley." As I shook hands with the two famous men, it crossed my mind, "Mother and Dad are not going to believe this."

The mayor welcomed Rogers and Post, recognized the 247 pilots seated at an adjacent table, praised the airplane, thanked the pilots for including Tulsa in their tour, then turned to Rogers. "Will, tell us what's going on in Washing-

"Winnie Mae"

ton.'' With a mixture of wit, humor, and seriousness, Will Rogers talked of the military's catastrophic attempt to fly the airmail, of Congress, and of international problems. He praised the new Boeing 247, spoke of the necessity for a national network of commercial air routes, and concluded with humorous anecdotes about Wiley Post.

On the way back to the barracks I thanked Ed for including me. "I'm glad you came along, Al," he said. "The aviation industry is destined for major and, I believe, rapid expansion. Vance and John Carroll [chief flight instructor] tell me you are making good progress. I believe Spartan is providing the background you need, and it's good to meet the people who are major contributors in this business."

It was difficult to go to sleep that night. The events of the evening, the new 247, and the much-publicized conflict between industry and government over operation and control of the fledgling but ambitious air transport industry occupied my thoughts to the exclusion of sleep.

I had progressed in my flying to the cross-country stage and had asked my instructor, Jess Green, if I could make mine to Emporia and remain overnight with my parents. Meanwhile, when not flying, I overhauled a Walter nine-cylinder radial air-cooled engine under the watchful eye of Vance Vassacheck, completed the required engine test runs on the ground-test stand, and reinstalled the engine in *Che-Che*, one of the school's single-engine trainers. Upon completion, Jess said, "You overhauled that engine. Are you prepared to fly it?"

"Yes, sir," I said emphatically.

"Okay, get your chute and put an hour on it."

I looked at Vance for confirmation. With a slight nod and a quick wink, he walked back to the hangar with Jess.

After the flight, Jess inspected the engine. "How much time did you put on the engine?" he asked.

"An hour and ten minutes—two takeoffs, one at the practice field, full takeoff power, climb power, and cruise throttle during the airwork."

"Looks good," he said. "No leaks. Cowl it up. This airplane is ready for cross-country. Hudlow has okayed your flight to Emporia."

Early next morning, zero wind conditions permitted a north takeoff, so after clearing the field boundary I continued climbing directly on course, heading 355 degrees. At 3,500 feet, I leveled off. The tachometer held constant at 1,800 rpm, oil pressure at 60 pounds. I watched the patchwork fields and farm buildings appear ahead and then slide away behind. My world was perfect.

I made shallow turns left and right just to reassure myself that this was real, that I was really in command and flying home. I believed then, and still believe, that the personal triumph and satisfactions a pilot receives in accomplishing his missions in the limitless sky are similar, if not identical, to the emotions of all those who see the successful fruition of study and commitment in their chosen fields of endeavor, whether it be in the arts, sciences, or technology.

I could see Emporia when I was fifteen minutes out, a sprawling little city of 12,000 inhabitants on a table-top-flat landscape. I buzzed the hangar at Maddock's farm to see that there were no cows in the landing area, did a 360 over a girlfriend's place, then picked up a heading for home. I came in from 1,500 feet in a shallow dive, passed over the house at 100 feet, made a full-power, climbing right turn, rolled back to a left bank, and came in for another pass. There they were, Mother and Dad, standing in the back yard waving. I wobbled my wings and headed for the pasture. I knew they'd have the ol' Pontiac on its way immediately.

The next morning, Bill Price drove his gas truck to the field. Gasoline was ten cents a gallon, and airplanes got a refund of the two-cents-a-gallon road tax from the state tax office. The *Che-Che* took 35 gallons.

The return flight to Spartan was sheer joy. My classmates were full of questions about the trip, but I couldn't spend much time in talk. The maintenance shop was loaded with work and receiving daily calls from pilots and owners scheduling airframe, engine, and relicensing activity. Many nights I worked until midnight helping to meet schedules.

One morning Ed Hudlow visited navigation class and announced that the Spartan Dawn Patrol had been invited to a fly-in party at Vinita, Oklahoma. The name derived from the filming at Spartan of a movie about a World War I fighter squadron. We were to be Saturday guests of the Vinita Country Club, culminating in a dinner dance that night. Members of the Dawn Patrol would be paired up as house guests with country-club members.

The following morning the list of pilot and passenger assignments on the barracks' bulletin board included "Al Johnston, pilot; Bob Humbert, passenger." We flew to Vinita in one of three 3-ship V formations. After parking the *Che-Che*, Bob and I met our hosts on the hangar ramp. When we arrived at their lovely home, we were given the keys to their pickup to use during our stay.

Golf, tennis, and swimming were followed by the Saturday evening dinner dance. As I circulated among predinner conversational groups with a lovely young lady named Louise, we encountered Will Rogers. I was about to introduce them when it became obvious they were old friends. "I hear you've been flying all over Oklahoma and Kansas," Rogers said. "The airplane has a great future, and this country needs good pilots like you boys."

Several days after the Vinita trip, I had a check ride with John Carroll, who then scheduled me for a ride with U.S. Department of Commerce flight inspector Alcorn. Alcorn had a reputation for toughness, and I developed a case of "inspec-toritis." I dearly wanted that limited commercial pilot's license. When we deplaned at the hangar after the check, Alcorn said, "That was a good flight, Johnston. I thought you were going to get a little slow on that nose-high slip, but you lowered it just right."

I was now nineteen years old, an aircraft and engine mechanic with a valid limited commercial pilot's license number 29948. It was a beginning, but to progress I needed flight time in a variety of aircraft under operational conditions. I closed my barracks room door, sat at the desk where I had spent many study hours, and listed the possibilities. 1. I could continue to work for Vance in the shops with no flying unless I purchased flight time. 2. Walter Beech was starting full-time production in Wichita of his negative stagger-wing Beechcraft, a beautiful, technically advanced plane, with retractable landing gear, the fastest executive aircraft in the United States. The Beechcraft factory was hiring mechanics, but again, all mechanical work, no flying. 3. Of the flying operators I knew, only the Inman brothers seemed to offer an immediate opportunity for flying different types of airplanes.

The next morning I told Vance my plan. "I hate to see you go," he said, "but John and Jess say you're a good pilot, and I know that's where your interest lies."

Ed Hudlow was sitting behind his desk. "I didn't think you'd be picking up those tools long after you got that ticket in your pocket," he said. "I hate to see you go, Al, but we've done about all we can for you here. There's a great future out there. Go out there and get with it."

Two days later, after a wingding going-away beer bust, I said my last good-byes. Emotions I had never experienced before swelled in my chest. I was leaving something dear behind. But the limitless sky, the far horizons, and the great unknown future called.

2

Barnstorming

In Coffeyville, Kansas, I called Art Inman's airport number from the bus station. He was surprised to hear I was in town. "Just stand still. I'll be there in ten minutes," he said. He arrived bareheaded in the white Auburn Speedster with the top down. I showed him my pilot's license, and he smiled broadly. "Now you're cookin'. Get in. Everyone wants to see you."

He drove directly into the hangar and parked under the wing of the Ford Tri-motor. They were nearly all there: Mae, Art's beautiful blonde wife; his brother Don, who flew the Stinson; Virgil Smith, who had the red Travel Air; Rawley, Art's elder brother, an executive pilot who flew a Spartan six-place cabin monoplane for an oil company supply organization; and Carl Moore, the chute jumper. Only Jim Kantril and his Waco were missing. He was due the following week.

"Guess what," Art said. "Al graduated from the Spartan aircraft and engine school and has his pilot's license."

At that, Rawley grabbed a wrench from the workbench and handed it to me. "Come on, let's go to work."

When the laughter subsided I said, "That's why I'm here."

"Come into the office and bring me up to date," Art said.

An hour later I had a deal to sell tickets and maintain the engines on the Ford and Stinson. Compensation would be five cents per ticket sold, fifty cents a day for night watch of the planes, and flight instruction in the Ford en route from

Travel Air

show to show. The pay was small, but how many pilots with fifty hours total time could log trimotor flight time? That plus the operational experience would be worth it.

That night, I walked home with Rawley to occupy their spare bedroom. Rawley whistled as he led the way to the back door of their airport home. Out of the shrubbery bounded Thor, Rawley's pet full-grown male lion, complete with shaggy mane and a mouthful of impressive teeth, his tether sliding along a clothesline cable. He stood on his hind legs with his front paws on Rawley's shoulders and glared at me eyeball to eyeball. When he and Rawley fell to the ground with Rawley's arms around him, Thor broke free in one quick move and bounded over to sniff my pant leg. I stood very still.

"Pet him nice and easy," Rawley instructed, laughing from his position on the ground. "I believe he likes you."

"Rawley, are you sure he's had supper?"

On Friday morning as Art and I finished checking the Ford before departure, Art said, "Okay, let's get airborne. You're copilot." As I stepped through the cabin door I was greeted once again by Thor, my traveling companion from then on. "Thor likes to fly," Art said.

In the cockpit, Art grasped a husky lever rising from the floor between the pilot seats. "This is the wheel brake control. Pull straight back for both brakes and right and left for respective individual wheels. It takes muscle. Give it a try." I grasped the lever with my left hand and moved it back. He was certainly correct. "It's more work taxiing this machine than flying it," Art said.

In the climb after takeoff Art said, "Hold this heading at seventy-five miles per hour and level off at fifteen hundred feet." This was new to me. Never before had I flown with an airspeed meter to show how fast I was flying.

As we leveled off, Art said, "Set cruise power and trim her to hold altitude hands off." Another first—longitudinal trim control that relieved the pilot from holding constant elevator pressure. I was moving up in the world.

Maintaining airplanes, fueling, selling tickets, loading passengers, and babysitting the airplane and lion at night resulted in long days, but Thor was good company. He liked me and displayed aggression only when hungry or frightened by a sudden unfamiliar noise. Consequently, I was fastidiously punctual regarding his mealtime.

Occasionally, I envied his diet. He always enjoyed red meat, which Art or Mae provided every day, while I ate "rainbow trout" (canned sardines) or bologna and crackers. He loved to share my food but displayed a selfish disposition regarding his. Despite that drawback, he was an ideal companion and guard, aware of anyone or anything that came within a city block of the airplane.

In good weather, Thor and I slept on the ground under the wing with Thor's chain attached to the landing-gear strut. During rainstorms, we slept in the aisle between the seats, with me forward by the cockpit door, Thor aft by the entrance door. During the day Thor sat in the rumble seat of the Auburn. He especially enjoyed trips to town with Mae. He would snarl, display his fangs, and slap playfully at passing autos. A white Auburn roadster, top down, driven by an attractive blonde, with a handsome lion in the rumble seat and lettering on each door identifying Inman's Flying Circus, was great advertising.

During my time with Inman's Flying Circus, the Depression was at its height. It was disheartening to watch people with their faces grim from worry, their clothing threadbare, meticulously counting the change in their pockets to come up with a dollar for an airplane ride. But their eyes were bright with the anticipation of flying—a bit of joy, if only for a few minutes. Throughout my barnstorming days I cannot recall a passenger's ever saying he or she did not enjoy the experience, and there were many repeat customers.

Our show at Maryville, Missouri, was extremely successful but exhausting for me. In addition to regular daylight operations we flew until eleven o'clock each night. I was lucky to finish fueling and maintenance by three-thirty in the morning. But Art was a square shooter. He gave me an extra twenty dollars that week and allowed me to shoot some unassisted takeoffs and landings in the Ford. Those takeoffs and landings were worth more than gold to me.

At our next stop, the advance man arranged for us to use a pasture near Plattsburg, Missouri, that had an apple orchard adjoining to the south. Business was good. On Sunday afternoon at about four o'clock, I had loaded the Ford with passengers. The left and center engines were idling as I stood below the right engine and hand-cranked its inertial starter to maximum speed. I gave Art the signal and engaged the starter. The engine turned one revolution and locked. Art signaled he'd cut the switch. I tried to move the prop. No luck. It wouldn't move in either direction. I drew my finger across my throat, and Art shut down the other two engines. As I walked to let the passengers deplane, I saw people running toward the orchard. Art was first out. "Smitty crashed," he whispered, and rushed off.

The ambulance arrived while I was refunding ticket money. Art and Don returned from the crash site. Don had witnessed the accident as he waited his turn to take off. "Smitty's takeoff was okay," Don said, "but his engine apparently failed over the apple orchard. He didn't have enough altitude to clear it, so he tried to turn back. His plane stalled, fell off in a left spin, made less than half a turn, and went in nose down in the orchard."

"Smitty's passengers, a man and his small son, walked away uninjured," Art said. "Smitty's alive, but his head hit that damn steamboat compass he had on the panel." Art turned to me. "Al, what's wrong with the number three engine?"

"It's locked up, won't turn either way. I would guess a keeper ring came off one of the master rod knuckle pins, allowing the pin to slip out and hang up on a crankcase reinforcing web. We'll have to remove and dismantle the engine to know for sure."

"This is bad," Art said. "There's apt to be trouble. We have to get these airplanes out of here. If the sheriff attaches them we'll be tied up all summer. Al, will the Stinson engine go on the Ford?"

"Yes, sir."

"Can you remove the number three engine in the dark?"

"You bet."

"Okay, Don, fly the Stinson to Kansas City and get Brado Hilliard's shop to pull the engine. Al will have the number three engine there in the morning and return with the Stinson engine and install it tomorrow night."

Don in the Stinson and Kantril in his Waco took off to go their separate ways. It was getting dark, and the last of the onlookers left. Art turned to me again. "What do you need to get this engine off?"

"We'll need four twelve-foot four-by-fours, eight six-foot two-by-fours, a sack of spikes, a thousand-pound chain hoist with a tripod hanger chain, two lanterns, two flashlights, and a dozen spare batteries."

"Let's go to town," Art said. "I'll drop you at the hotel. Tell Mae the plan. Eat something and get a little rest. You're going to need it."

Mae had talked with the emergency ward. Smitty's head had been sewn up. Although he had a concussion, he'd be okay in a few days.

Art woke me at 10 p.m. As we headed toward the pasture with the necessary equipment in a rented pickup with a trailer in tow, the town was quiet. When we arrived we found a sheriff's property-attachment form tied to the Ford's door latch. Working in lantern light and racing the clock, I pulled the engine. Mae drove up in the Auburn just as we lowered it into the trailer. By 2:30 a.m. it was tied down and the trailer attached to the Auburn.

Art handed me fifty dollars. "Call me at the hotel and give me your expected return time," he said. "But remember, it has to be after dark. I'll meet you here. I want to be off before sunup."

Even with the tow, the Auburn drove like a dream. I was at the gate when Hilliard's opened at 7 a.m. Don and I loaded the Stinson engine for the return trip while the shop mechanics stripped the Ford's number three engine and removed the nine cylinders. When they removed the forward section of the engine case, they found the problem. It was as I had guessed.

Back at the pasture on schedule, I backed the trailer under the winch. By 4 a.m. that ol' J-5 came to life again. We let her idle to keep the noise level low. With temperature up and all checks made, Art cut the engine, and I installed the cowling. Mae and Art were watching as I installed the last piece.

"Al, you've done a hell of a good job," Art said.

"I enjoyed it," I said, "but not as much as flying."

"I know," he said. "Believe me, I know. I'm sorry I have to leave. You're ready to solo this bird, and I wanted to make it happen."

"I totally understand," I replied. I produced the pilot's logbook from my duffel bag and held a flashlight while Art signed my trimotor time—fourteen hours and fifty minutes— a real asset a few years later. That was the last time I saw Art Inman until we met again many years and flight hours later at a gathering of the Ancient Order of Quiet Birdmen in Hollywood.

As the ol' Tri-motor, exhausts flaring blue, roared off into the early morning darkness with Thor as copilot, Mae said, "Let's get this trailer to town before they attach me." We both laughed.

At the bus station, when I pulled my things from the rumble seat, it was hard to say good-bye without choking up. How do you say good-bye to so many things at one time— dear friends, the Ford, the Auburn, Thor, the glamour of the show, and the flying? My days with the Inmans were over. I was grounded.

New Plans

I arrived home with duffel bag, tool kit, and new plans for a flying future. For several days Mother, Dad, and I talked it over. We filled sheets of paper with financial calculations that littered the kitchen table. We discussed the pros and cons. Finally it was agreed, and we drove to Tulsa in search of an airplane.

The reunion at Spartan was a happy one. I was proud to learn that Rawley had spread the word about my progress in flying the Ford Tri-motor and of my mechanical skills in after-hours maintenance. As to what kind of airplane I wanted, my experience with Inman's indicated that a three-place biplane powered by a radial engine would be most appropriate for my purpose, which was barnstorming.

Ed Hudlow, Vance, John Carroll, Jess Green, and a few of my remaining classmates soon provided lists of airplanes for sale that might fit my dollar and configuration requirements. By mid-afternoon of the second day I was the owner of a Command-Aire biplane powered by a Curtiss Challenger. It was equipped with new low-pressure balloon tires, just the thing for rough pastures. It also had wheel brakes, the first I had encountered on small planes, an airspeed indicator, a compensated compass, and a clock, plus all the usual engine instruments.

We built a new hangar on the north side of the old T-hangar on Maddock's pasture, and after the Command-Aire was installed in its new home, Harris "Dinty" Moore, a friend of mine and a fellow student of Toy Franklin's, arrived. "I hear you're going barnstorming. How about going with you? I'll sell tickets, help gas and maintain the airplane, and pay my own expenses in return for flight time between towns."

"Dinty," I said, "you've got a deal."

The traditional Midwest fall fairs would start in a few weeks. Dinty called the local newspapers of the towns we planned to work for fair dates. The passenger tickets I had ordered arrived, but before leaving on our barnstorming tour, we worked our hometown of Emporia from Maddock's pasture. It was a Sunday. I flew twenty passenger flights and one elementary acrobatic demonstration, which included chandelles, lazy eights, barrel rolls, and loops, the results of Jess Green's extracurricular instruction.

The following morning, Mother drove us to the hangar for departure. We dressed the part in English riding boots, whipcord riding breeches, leather flight jackets and helmets, white scarves, and the standard transport aviator goggles. I'd never forgotten the appearance of the Hisso-Standard pilot who first inspired me to fly. When the plane was loaded and our farewells were said, I climbed into the rear cockpit; Dinty swung the prop and climbed in the front cockpit. As we taxied away, Mother waved a tearful good-bye.

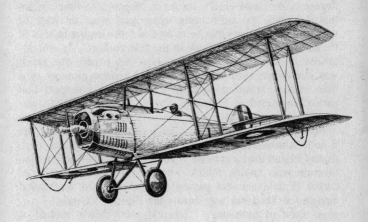

Hisso Standard

Business was good in the western Kansas towns of Hays and Goodland, but I felt the lure of the Rockies and opted to fly farther west. At Colorado Springs I first experienced the reduced power and performance of high-altitude operations.

One day while flying passengers over the spectacular Royal Gorge and the highest suspension bridge in the world, I saw level rangeland just to the east. The following day, Dinty and I returned to the area and landed. The surface was okay.

I made two more trial takeoffs and landings and was convinced the Command-Aire could safely carry passengers from this 6,000-foot-high field. As I climbed from the cockpit, I saw several cars parked to the side of the Royal Gorge Bridge highway, which ran past our field. Dinty walked over to sell tickets while I unloaded our gear. It was a profitable decision. Passing tourists were eager to see the gorge from the air. At 4 p.m. Dinty remained with the gear while I flew to Canon City for fuel.

For three days we operated from the field, carrying two passengers per flight provided their combined weight didn't exceed three hundred pounds. If I underestimated that critical information, it was soon revealed by reduced performance during takeoff and climb, the most inopportune time. When that occurred, the enthusiastic passengers were unaware of the rapid calculations that went on under the leather helmet of the nineteen-year-old aviator in the rear cockpit. My weight-estimating expertise increased rapidly with experience, but it was sometimes difficult to eyeball the female member of a pair without arousing hostility in the male. I suspect that particular hazard of the early days of flying has been overlooked by aviation historians.

Flying over the rugged terrain, I was keenly aware of the serious consequences of engine failure. Throughout each flight I maintained a constantly revised emergency action plan to cope with engine failure whenever and wherever it occurred. Frankly, I was somewhat relieved when we headed east and worked our way across the Kansas flatlands.

As cash accumulated, I worried about being robbed at night. Under the cover of darkness, I would remove a wheel cover, place the currency in the space, and reinstall the cover. I slept better after that.

Occasionally, a night thunderstorm forced us to sleep in the cockpit with snap-on covers secured. At such times, the high winds often loosened the tie-down ropes, and I would have to leave the dry cockpit, retie the ropes, and return drenched to the skin to anxiously await the break of day.

Hartford, Kansas, was known for its traditional fall fair and accompanying carnival. Our operations there were a tremendous success. That was where I met Wilma Caldwell, who became our star ticket seller for the duration of the barnstorming season.

It started after a successful day at Hartford, when Dinty and I went to the Friday night dance. At the dance hall, the brassy tones of the lead trumpet brought a slight pang. I had played trumpet in high school and later formed a combo that played for dances. Flying was my number one priority, but music was number two. Later, as I returned a dance partner to the sidelines, I noticed an unusually attractive blonde. She sat with her mother and a striking brunette who appeared to be her sister. Making my way through the crowd, I approached her and said, "Hi, may I have the next dance?"

"With the consent of my mother," she said with an attractive smile.

Her mother evaluated me with a skeptical eye and looked hard at my jacket and boots. I knelt in front of her and said, "I'm Al Johnston. May I dance with your daughter? I fly the airplane you saw over town today. We travel light, so we have only our flying gear."

"Where are you from?" she asked.

"Emporia," I replied.

"Oh, that's not far away. I thought you might be from Kansas City." Seventy-five miles appeared to make a difference, because as I rose to my feet, she said, "Yes, I guess it will be all right." Later, I introduced Dinty. By good luck the Caldwells knew Dinty's folks, which further eased Mrs. Caldwell's reservations regarding out-of-town strangers.

The Caldwells had a farm about nine miles northeast of town with a large alfalfa field that had just been harvested, so I arranged to pay a fly-in visit. The morning after the fair, Dinty and I flew at low altitude, following the road Wilma had described, until we spotted their white house and red barns. As the plane roared over the house, Wilma appeared, waving a towel as I had suggested. When I cut the engine and climbed out, the entire Caldwell family was standing at the wingtip. After being introduced to Mr. Caldwell, we were invited to share a delicious roast-beef dinner. Mr. Caldwell, a slim man with friendly blue eyes, asked, "How do you spell your last name?"

"With a *t*," I replied.

"I know a Masonic Lodge member in Emporia named Alva Johnston. Met him in Topeka at a Masonic convention."

"That's my father," I replied. What luck—one more chance relationship that helped pave the way to a most unusual business arrangement.

After dinner Mrs. Caldwell suggested we remain overnight, as it was getting late. We were delighted; it was the first bed Dinty and I had seen in more than two months.

The next day I gave Mr. and Mrs. Caldwell their first airplane ride, and when some of their friends and neighbors came by to see the airplane, I took them flying, too, in return for fifteen gallons of farm gasoline for each ride. After the friends and neighbors had departed, I gave the two girls a nice long, conservative flight. Lucille only said, "It was fun," but Wilma was infatuated with flying.

After our second night at the Caldwell's I proposed that Wilma barnstorm with us as a ticket seller for fifteen dollars a week plus room and board. The Caldwells were hesitant until I explained that Wilma would stay in private homes. In the days before motels became common, many private homes in towns throughout the Midwest displayed room-for-rent signs. And that was how the Caldwells, typical conservative Midwesterners, came to give permission for their high-school-age daughter to go barnstorming.

After our departure from the Caldwell's farm, our first day in business as a threesome (at Ottawa, Kansas) was slow, so Wilma and I hitched a ride to town and bought her three snug-fitting sweaters—a subtle red, a robin's-egg blue, and a white—with coordinated skirts. We also bought colorful ribbons to emphasize her long blonde hair. It was an irresistible combination. When she would walk up to a car, lean forward on the car door, smile, and say, "I know you boys want tickets for the next airplane flight," the boys would reach for their wallets. Dinty sold a lot of tickets, but Wilma became the new champion.

During refueling at Iola, Kansas, a man walked up and asked, "Are you Alvin Johnston?"

That got my attention. No one ever called me Alvin. "Yes, sir," I said. "What can I do for you?"

"You move around a lot. My name's Inderton, U.S. Commerce Department." I was flying with a limited commercial pilot's license, which allowed me to fly for hire only within a twenty-mile radius of my home base, so every time I arrived in a new town I mailed a letter to the Commerce Department notifying them of my new address: General Delivery in the respective town. "Why haven't you gotten a transport pilot's license?" he asked.

"Just haven't had the opportunity," I replied.

"Let me see your logbook," he said. He leafed through the log and said, "Well, you have almost three hundred hours. You need only two hundred for a transport license, and I don't remember anything in the law that says you can't move. However, you do seem to move rather frequently. You ready to take your transport flight test?"

"Yes, sir," I replied.

The flight required 45 minutes. Upon return to our loading area, he said, "Where'd you learn to fly?"

"Spartan," I replied, "with John Carroll and Jess Green."

"That's a first-class operation down there. That was a good flight, Johnston, and I like the way you handle the throttle, smooth and easy on the engine. You're now a transport pilot, and you won't have to move so much." We shook hands and he departed.

When the 1934 barnstorming season ended, I could look back on our adventures and accomplishments with considerable satisfaction. I had sent Dad money orders totaling $1,500, and I had a little more than $400 in my pocket. I had 525 flying hours and a transport pilot's license. The Command-Aire was performing well and required only routine maintenance.

But I knew that barnstorming belonged to an era that would soon be over. The airplane was destined to revolutionize the transportation business, and I wanted to be part of it. That year, United Airlines had been formed from the merger of Boeing Air Transport, National Air Transport, and Varney Airlines and was flying the new ten-seater Boeing 247 on a coast-to-coast schedule in about twenty hours. My interest was in the development of aircraft. To get into the field, I needed more education. I wanted to return to college and study mechanical and aeronautical engineering and really understand the science of flight. So after one last hurrah—flying with wing-walker Page Winchester at consecutive weekend air shows in Oklahoma at Enid, Ponca City, Shawnee, and Lawton and a final weekend show at Wichita Falls, Texas— I flew home and sold the Command-Aire and prepared to return to college.

Boeing 247

The additional barnstorming with Winchester and the sale of the Command-Aire prevented my enrollment for the fall semester at Kansas State University. To occupy my time and earn money for the return to school, I practiced the trumpet and reorganized a portion of my old music group. We were booked every Friday and Saturday night.

Beginning in my sophomore year in high school I had occasionally dated DeLores Honea, an attractive blonde from Emporia. Now I ran into her again at a party, and we began to date again, more and more frequently, often double-dating with old high school pals. On June 5, 1935, we became husband and wife. As a more stable and secure alternative to the music business, we became motion picture exhibitors, running first the Rialto Theater in Lyndon, Kansas, and then the 1,400-seat New Bays Theater in Blackwell, Oklahoma. On September 23, 1937, our first baby, Judy Marie, arrived.

It was eight one evening, with things running normally at the theater, when Dad called from Emporia. "There's a gentleman in town from Kansas City who has several theaters in the Kansas City area and wants to buy the Rialto."

"Does he have any money?" I asked.

"Yes, and we can make a few bucks. Do you want to sell?"

Here, finally, was my chance to return to my real career. "Sell," I said.

"What are your plans?"

"College, Kansas State at Manhattan."

"Good. I'll go ahead with the deal."

I returned home at my usual time, 2 a.m., and broke the news to DeLores.

"I know you're not interested in returning to Lyndon," she said, "but there must be something else that makes you so enthusiastic."

"I don't like this business," I replied. "I just do it to take care of us. We're going to Manhattan, and I'm going back to school."

"Okay," she said. "I know you'll never be happy until you're back in aviation. When do we leave?"

I was pleased with her reaction. I knew it was going to be rough taking care of my family responsibilities in addition to school. But my business was airplanes, and I'd already wasted almost three years. I was going to give it my best shot.

3

Instructing and Ferrying

Kansas State University, although generally known as an agricultural college, had an excellent engineering department with an aeronautical option. My courses were mathematics, engineering drafting, shop and foundry, and compulsory·history and literature. I quickly learned I had a lot of catching up to do. I had been away from school for a long time.

We found a combination living room, bedroom, and study area with adjoining bath in the attic of the home of Mr. Hartell, a widowed physics professor. We paid half the grocery bill, and DeLores prepared the morning and evening meals for Hartell and ourselves and kept the house in return for our use of the attic.

I worked at a filling station for three hours after classes each day, which produced a small amount of cash but resulted in late study hours. Early on, I had severe problems with math and needed a tutor. But that paid off, and by mid-semester I was handling it on my own. The second year was easier, and I was happy with my progress.

It was 1938. Europe was moving from crisis to crisis. In March Hitler, through threats, bluster, and the presentation of impossible demands, achieved *Anschluss,* incorporation of Austria into Germany. Two weeks later, he targeted Czechoslovakia and began provoking a succession of war scares on the pretext of protecting the rights of Czechoslovakia's Sudeten German minority. In September he made open demands for the annexation of the Sudetenland. On September 30,

1938, Britain's prime minister Chamberlain, believing he had achieved "peace in our time," signed away Czechoslovakia's rights at Munich and cleared the way for Hitler's further aggression.

During that sorry period, Hitler's war machine, which earlier could have been stopped with less cost, continued to grow and develop, emphasizing mobility and air power. As early as 1936, Charles Lindbergh had made a much-publicized inspection of the German Luftwaffe and was so impressed with its unprecedented technical advance and the size and quality of the organization that he thought it invincible.

The condition of the U.S. Army Air Corps, on the other hand, was appalling. To help alleviate the severe shortage of pilots, the Roosevelt administration launched the Civilian Pilot Training (CPT) program to finance the training of civilian pilots at contractor-operated flight schools. Many of the schools were near colleges and universities. A Pan American Airways captain, Frank Selken from Miami, Florida, got the CPT contract for Manhattan, Kansas. The day I read of the local program in the paper, I cut class and hitchhiked to the airport. Captain Selken was seated at his desk in a small office next to a dilapidated corrugated-metal hangar. "I understand you need a flight instructor," I said as I introduced myself and laid my transport license and logbook on his desk.

"Sit down," he said, and thumbed through my logbook. "You have some good flight time. However, you need an instructor's rating."

"Where do I get it?"

"Joe Jacobson has an instruction program at Kansas City Municipal Airport." That was great information. I knew Joe. "I have six new Porterfields arriving in about two weeks," Selken said. "Can you be ready?"

"What does the job pay?"

Selken didn't look up, just said, "Six hundred per month."

I nearly fell from the seat but managed to say quickly, "I'll call Joe and make arrangements."

My professors approved my requested ten-day absence with the provision that I make up their classwork after I returned. I called Mother and gave her the good news—and the bad news: "Send money."

She laughed. "This is wonderful. Dad will be delighted."

The day I arrived in Kansas City, I started ground school and took my first flight in one of Joe Jacobson's Warner-powered Fleet biplanes. The government had converted the old transport pilot license to a commercial license, so I elected to combine a commercial license with the instructor rating and took both written exams the same day. The next morning my name was on the flight-instructor check ride list. I was delighted to see that the inspector was Otto Inderton, who had given me my transport check ride in Ottawa, Kansas. "I'm glad to see you're keeping your ratings current," Inderton said with a smile. I returned to the Manhattan Airport with the new commercial license and flight instructor rating in my wallet. Selken's manager put me on the payroll and said the Porterfields would start arriving Monday.

It required some mighty long hours to catch up in my classes, but in three weeks I was again current. DeLores had located a rental four-bedroom home in good condition with kitchen stove and refrigerator. We made a deal with Russ Blessing, an old high school friend who was also attending Kansas State, and three of his buddies to rent rooms from us. The next month we were clearing $100 per month on the house plus my $600 from flight instructing—a happy change from our previous impecunious life-style.

The Porterfields arrived two at a time, ferried in by company pilots, one of whom was my friend Bill Miller, Toy Franklin's old student from Emporia. After student-pilot classes were set up, I was assigned four students who turned out to be college classmates. I began flying every day.

On a south takeoff I could see the foundations of the old World War I Camp Funston, where 22 years before I had shivered in the frozen ruts of the dirt road in 10-degree weather while Dad talked through the wire fence with his brother, my uncle Frank, quarantined by the flu epidemic. I'll never forget the row upon row of dead bodies frozen stiff and piled like cordwood five feet high, waiting for burial when the ground thawed. As I flew over that area, I considered the progress since that day when Mother had waited in a side-curtained Model T touring car with a quilt over her feet and legs that retained the feeble heat of a kerosene lantern. The roads were frozen mud, 90 percent of the vehicles were horse-drawn, and there was no electricity or running water or indoor facilities. Here I was flying over that same area at 90 mph in a closed-cockpit airplane warmed by a cabin heater. The roads were now paved, not a single horse-drawn vehicle could be seen, and electricity, hot and cold running water, and indoor facilities were standard—all accomplished in roughly twenty years. Looking ahead, I believed that the coming war would spark research and development and technical achievement at an even faster rate, a rate never before experienced. Here I sat in a cockpit of an airplane at 2,000 feet, a first meager step into that future.

On my second payday, I bought DeLores a Russian caracal fur coat with matching hat and muff. She was dazed but beautiful as she looked in the shop mirror at what our new prosperity had wrought.

In 1940 the Army Air Corps expanded its flight training program and needed experienced instructors, particularly pilots with flight time in large, multi-engined craft. I felt that I now had enough engineering to satisfy my future objectives and had gone as far as I could go in primary instructing in small, single-engine equipment. Near the end of the semester, I posted a letter to Bill Long in Dallas, a retired major who operated several contract military pilot training schools in Texas. The following week, I received an offer of employment as a primary flight instructor at Hicks Field, a reactivated World War I flight training field near Fort Worth, with a salary of $700 per month. The location was fortuitous. DeLores's father was from Fort Worth and her mother from nearby Cleburne.

The day after receiving the offer, I submitted my resignation to Frank Selken at the Manhattan Airport CPT office and traded my 1935 Ford V8 convertible roadster for a '39 Plymouth four-door sedan. Within two weeks, at semester end, we turned the rental house over to Russ and his housemates, loaded the Plymouth with our baggage, and hit the open road for Texas.

Hicks Field was a beehive of activity, with a flight line of thirty low-wing, Ranger-powered Fairchild primary trainers. I was assigned three students. From then on, my days began with a 0700 check-in at the instructors' ready room, followed by separate daily flights with each student.

Early in 1941, all flight instructors at Hicks were invited to apply for basic flight instructor training at Randolph Field and reassignment to a basic training base. I was one of the first to sign up. Soon DeLores, daughter Judy, now going on four, and I were San Antonio–bound. The basic flight instructor training program remains one of my most interesting, challenging, and productive experiences. It introduced me to the North American BT-14 basic trainer with a 300-hp radial engine, all-metal construction, full cockpit instrumentation, radio communication, instrument and formation flying, advanced aerobatics, and night cross-country missions.

Upon graduation from the instructor course, we were assigned to Curtis Field, a new facility at Brady, Texas. It was the Johnston family's fifth move in as many years. Our arrival at Brady caused DeLores considerable concern when she learned of a gunfight at the Cattleman's Restaurant the day before. We rented a duplex, and I settled down to the new routine. We instructors flew the new Vultee BT-15 basic trainers with four students each.

One night on a cross-country flight, the instructor and student failed to allow for increasing ground elevation and flew into the deck at cruising speed. Fortunately, the unplanned landing was on fairly smooth open range. Even so, what surface irregularities there were caused the landing gear to fail, the prop to hit the ground, and the engine to rip from the fuselage. The gearless, engineless airplane slid to a stop. Instructor and student opened their canopies and stepped out uninjured, except for damaged pride. On two other night flights, individual students experienced failure of the engine crankshaft at the thrust bearing, which allowed the suddenly detached propeller to spin away into the night. Both students successfully landed their propellerless aircraft.

One day the flight commander introduced a new flight instructor. I needed no introduction. It was Dinty Moore, from Emporia, whom I had soloed in my Command-Aire biplane just before it was sold.

I found basic flight instruction much more challenging than primary flight instruction. In addition, my flight time was building at the rate of 100 hours per month. The quality of life also greatly improved. Brady lay in the middle of the best deer and turkey hunting in Texas, there was fishing in the

Llano River, and, last but not least, there was dove hunting in season. As December approached, mornings were chilly but daytime temperatures balmy. We had a lot to be thankful for at Thanksgiving besides venison and wild turkey.

Ten days later the Japanese attack on Pearl Harbor shocked the world. Flight training was accelerated, and the student-pilot washout policy was modified to allow a weak student to be transferred to a second and third instructor, giving the third instructor the washout responsibility. That intelligent and welcome change reduced the percentage of students who failed to complete flight training.

After Pearl Harbor, President Roosevelt announced the immediate escalation of military aircraft production to 50,000 aircraft on a 24-hours-a-day, year-round manufacturing schedule. Soon, in ever-increasing numbers, new aircraft clogged the manufacturers' delivery ramps. There was an acute shortage of ferry pilots qualified to fly single- and multi-engine aircraft, trainers, fighters, bombers, transports, everything in the military inventory. To solve the problem, the Air Corps created the Ferry Command, a war-time organization commanded by the military and manned with civilian pilots. Ferry Command bases were established at strategic airports throughout the United States. Nearest to us was the Fifth Ferry Group at Hensley Field, Dallas. Three fellow instructors and hunting partners—Jack McNiece, Paul Cary, Fred Williams—and I drove to Dallas to check it out. We found that the salary would be the same as we were making, we would draw per diem while away from Dallas, all flights would be within the continental United States and Canada, and in the Ferry Command we would be flying the most sophisticated airplanes in the world. We surveyed the array of airplanes to be delivered and unanimously elected to sign up. We presented our pilot licenses and logbooks and were all accepted, to report for duty in four weeks.

The major reviewing my qualifications asked, "Where did you get the Ford Tri-motor time?"

"Barnstorming," I replied.

"I'm glad to see that," he said. "We need multi-engine pilots."

That triggered McNiece. "You're going to check us out on multi-engine equipment, aren't you?"

"Oh, sure," the major said, "but it will take a while. Don't worry, you'll get all you can handle."

And he did. Mac ended up based in Karachi, Pakistan, flying B-24 tankers and cargo models over the Hump into China. Two years later I ran into him in the Beverly Hills Hotel bar one night and asked, "How's the Hump, Mac?"

"Rougher than a bull's ass sewed up with a log chain," he said. There were a lot of pilots who agreed with him.

On the return trip to Brady in DeLores's new 1942 Oldsmobile, we picked up a couple of GI hitchhikers who helped polish off a jug of Scotch. Soon everyone was asleep but the driver. As I drove along enjoying the music of Harry James, I smelled something burning. Slamming on the brakes, I shouted, "One of you guys is on fire." The car was still moving when they started bailing out. They were okay, but the back seat of the new car was smoldering. Mac quenched it with a bottle of mix, and we were on our way.

The first month in the Ferry Command was disappointing. All we did was deliver primary trainers. On one such mission we picked up five primary trainers at Langley Field, Virginia, for delivery to a new training base at Fort Morgan, Colorado. Mac got a chuckle from the Langley dispatch officer when he said, "Hell, these putt-putts will be wore out by the time we get to Fort Morgan."

Plagued with boredom, we were flying a loose V formation in central Kansas, our landing gear barely clearing the tops of green five-foot-high corn. Suddenly, Mac pulled up in tight formation on my right wing and pointed behind us. I made a climbing left turn and saw two of our group flying in circles about a mile back. As we flew nearer, I saw the fifth airplane on its back in the cornfield with the pilot standing alongside and waving. I saw he was okay, rocked the wings for the other three to join up, and we continued on our way. The pilot we left behind had allowed his wheels to hit the tops of the corn and failed to react in time when the drag on the wheels caused the plane to nose down and overturn.

Upon my return to Dallas, the duty officer handed me a form and said, "Present this at the flight line for multi-engine checkout."

At the flight line, the young captain glanced at the form

and said, "Come on, take me for a ride in this Beech D-18."
After a cockpit briefing that included engine-start procedure,
he said, "Fire her up. Let's go."

Later, as we lifted off, I retracted the landing gear, set
climb power, and retracted the flaps. As the flaps reached
full retraction, the instructor pulled the number two throttle
to idle to simulate a right-hand engine failure. I held course
with left rudder, dropped the nose, and added power to number one to maintain adequate single-engine speed, and said,
"If number two was out I'd feather the prop" (the D-18
didn't have feathering, but I was reciting procedure), "close
the mixture control, and call for an emergency landing."
After being cleared for landing, I carried an extra 5 mph
above approach speed and put her on the first hundred feet
of runway.

"Okay," he said, "let's go to the ramp." As we deplaned,
the captain said, "You didn't learn those procedures in a
Ford Tri-motor."

"Not all of them," I replied. "I've been studying multi-
engine procedures, and I had a briefing from two multi-
engine-rated friends."

"Pick up your multi-engine credentials from the duty office
in the morning. I'm approving you for all multi-engine aircraft. We have a lot of airplanes to fly."

My next trip was with four guys I didn't know to pick up
five more single-engine trainers for dear old Fort Morgan.
Five days later, when I arrived back in Dallas, Mac, Fred,
and Paul had all completed their multi-engine ground school
and checked out on all twin-engine trainers. The next morning the duty officer called our names and gave us our orders:
"Proceed to flight operations at Cessna and Beechcraft facto-
ries in Wichita for twin-engine trainer delivery flights."

Throughout the thirty-day period in Wichita, we alternated
between Cessna deliveries to Winnipeg, Canada, and Val-
dosta, Georgia, and Beechcraft deliveries to Bakersfield, California, a bombardier training base. At Beechcraft I received
a truly pleasant surprise; the chief test pilot was Vern Car-
stairs, a friend from barnstorming days. Vern had piloted
Martin and Osa Johnson's Sikorsky amphibian on an African
big-game hunt that had been made into a movie. After I
introduced my three friends to Vern, he said, referring to me,

"I hired him to fly the number two amphib on the next expedition. We were all set to go. Martin departed for Los Angeles to complete financial arrangements. Unfortunately, his United Airlines flight terminated in the side of a mountain."

"A real tragedy," I said. "However, Vern, you're better off here than chasing lions."

Our flights to Winnipeg required an R.O.N. (remain overnight) stop at Sioux Falls, South Dakota, for refueling and filing of a multiplane international border crossing flight plan. After hotel check-in on our first R.O.N. at Sioux Falls we arrived at an elegant club suggested by the hotel bell captain. As the elderly bartender mixed our drinks, he said, "You gentlemen are a bit early. Business begins around five-thirty." At 5:35 the door opened and several young ladies arrived and sat at a table near the dance floor. Small groups of females continued to arrive.

Mac called the bartender and said, "Pardner, what are you puttin' in these drinks? I don't believe what I'm seeing."

"You're seeing okay. Practically all the eligible males have been drafted."

Soon there were 25 female customers and only 11 males. Mac slid off the bar stool, put a couple of dollars in the Wurlitzer, pushed all the numbers available, and selected a cute little brunette at one of the tables. The party was under way.

When the word got out at home base, everyone was maneuvering for the Winnipeg flights.

The Beechcraft bombardier trainer was an all-metal twin-engine airplane with two 450-horsepower radial engines. The airplanes were equipped with top-secret Norden bombsights, so when we ferried the planes we were issued 45-caliber automatics and had to obtain armed guards for the airplanes during our R.O.N. stops.

On a five-ship flight to Bakersfield, we landed at Luke Field to R.O.N. in Phoenix, taxied in, parked in the designated area, and requested armed guards for all five airplanes. The guard and the fuel truck arrived at my plane at the same time. While I talked with the guard, the fuel-truck driver unreeled the fuel hose, walked to the side of the airplane,

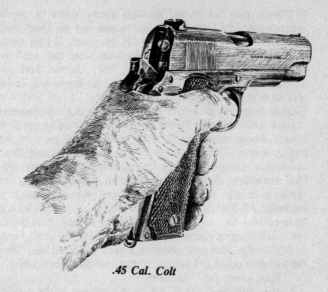

.45 Cal. Colt

opened a small inspection door, stuck in the nozzle, and began to pump fuel. Soon 100 octane was running out the belly. "What you doing?" I shouted. "The fuel tanks are in the wing."

After properly instructing the fuel boy, we departed via staff cars. As we entered our Phoenix hotel's lobby dressed in Air Corps trousers, shirts, and leather flight jackets, with .45 automatics strapped to our hips, the bellboy looked puzzled. "Which motorcycle gang are you guys with?"

Here we were, responsible for five twin-engine aircraft with top-secret equipment, wearing the uniform of the U.S. Army Air Forces, and he thinks we're a motorcycle gang. Mac was standing next to me. "Where's the bar? Let's have a drink on that one."

Bakersfield, California, was a remote location in 1943, so as soon as our delivery paperwork was completed we went by staff car to Burbank to arrange a return airline flight to Dallas. The Burbank Airport was completely camouflaged with painted patterns on the buildings and camouflage nets suspended over areas in between. From Burbank we traveled by streetcar to Hollywood through several miles of countryside occupied by farm homes and orange groves. Harry James was at Hollywood's Paladium with long lines of fans waiting to get in. All the clubs on Sunset Strip were full, each with famous entertainers—Lena Horne, Earl Garner, and other greats, vocalists, comedians, combos, and big bands. In fact, at that time, cities coast to coast in the United States and Canada were jammed with people looking for entertainment.

Back once more in Dallas operations, two other pilots and I were issued orders to proceed to Miami to pick up three Pan American DC-3's and deliver them to the Long Beach, California, Douglas factory for modification. We arrived at Pan American, signed for the aircraft, found the line crew chief, gave him the tail numbers, and were directed to the airplanes. While my friends had coffee, I talked with the crew chief. "We need a cockpit check, a briefing on the fuel system, emergency gear extension, et cetera," I said. He just looked at the floor and shook his head in disbelief. "We're multi-engine pilots," I said. "We just haven't flown DC-3's."

"Okay, come on," he said.

I sat in the pilot's seat, the crew chief sat in the copilot's seat, and my buddies watched through the cockpit door. He produced a DC-3 pilot's manual and took us through the checklist system by system. At the conclusion he said to me, "Start number one."

I set the parking brakes, turned the fuel valve to tank-to-engine, set the throttle, actuated the primer, turned the mag switch to both, and engaged the starter. When she fired, I moved the mixture control to full rich and checked the fuel, oil, and hydraulic pressures and generator output. As I moved the mixture to idle cutoff, I said, "Let's get out of here."

As we deplaned, the crew chief, still in a state of wonderment, said, "Where's your copilots?"

"We don't have any," I said.

He stopped dead still and shook his head again. "I don't believe this," he said.

All three planes were full of fuel and oil, so we filed our flight plans, climbed aboard, secured the entrance doors, and proceeded to start engines. I called the tower and got taxi clearance for the three of us, and we taxied to takeoff position. After run-up, we were cleared to take off in sequence.

When I leveled off at 5,000, my buddies pulled up in a loose V formation and we headed for Oklahoma City, our first fuel stop. When we refueled at Oklahoma City and Tucson, ground personnel asked, "Where are your copilots?"

I gave them a story to tell their friends. "They were on a party last night and didn't show up, so we left them in Miami."

In Long Beach, the staff car driver who met the planes said, "Where's your copilots?"

"Don't have any," I replied. As we entered operations I looked back. He was still staring after us.

During the time of that Miami-California trip, Mac, Paul, and Fred qualified in C-47's, the military version of the DC-3, and were approved for all twin-engine airplanes. Soon thereafter, Mac and I received orders to pick up two Douglas A-20's at Chicago for delivery to Douglas Long Beach for overhaul, and believe me, they needed it. When we arrived at the parked aircraft, oil lay in large pools under each engine and dripped from the engine cowlings.

The A-20 was a fast, twin-engine medium bomber with a single-pilot cockpit like a fighter. We read the handbooks but could find no one who knew anything about the airplanes. The two planes had bomb-bay tanks installed for long ferry missions. "Mac," I said, "we won't need much, if any, fuel in these bomb-bay tanks. I suspect our problem will be oil stops, not fuel." And so it was. During flight, oil ran from the engine cowlings while oil smoke spewed from exhaust stacks. At every fuel stop, airport personnel were bitter about ramp conditions when we left. Nevertheless, we enjoyed the trip. The A-20 was a fine high-performance airplane. The cockpit fit the pilot like a fighter, visibility was good, and control forces and airplane reaction to control were excellent.

After delivery, Burbank operations had orders for us to pick up a C-47 at Burbank and deliver it to Hensley Field, Dallas. The plane was on the maintenance ramp with engines uncowled and mechanics conducting a periodic check. "The aircraft will be on the flight line at one a.m.," the crew chief said. We grabbed the streetcar to Hollywood. When we returned at midnight, we were told we'd be taking a load of troops to Dallas. We completed our preflight check as the G.I. bus arrived. The driver was in a bad mood. We understood why when the G.I.s, some black and some white, staggered off the bus. Most were drunk and had bottles in their coat pockets. "Damn," Mac said. "How we goin' to get that booze away from them?"

"We're not," I said. "It's impossible. Just herd them aboard. Everything will be okay."

It required fifteen minutes to load the troops, who were laughing and having a ball. I told them to remain in their seats as we had to fly without lights until east of Palm Springs. Mac held the cockpit door open enough to observe the passengers as I taxied out. Many were standing. It was impossible to persuade them to remain seated with belts fastened. Field lights were at a minimum, but we found our way to the runway without using landing lights. After engine run-up and clearing for takeoff, I applied full power and roared down the runway and into the night. During the climb out, we locked the cockpit door to keep our passengers from sticking their heads in the cockpit and waving bottles in our faces. I had to adjust longitudinal trim continually as our partying passengers moved fore and aft in the cabin. As we climbed through 10,000 feet, I put on my oxygen mask. Mac looked at me. "Now I know what your plan is." At 12,000 feet things began to quiet down. At 16,000 there wasn't a sound all the way to Dallas.

The Ferry Command flight schedule was rugged—we flew every day and many nights—but it was a pilot's dream. Although early in the program we had attended officer's training classes and were told that we could qualify for commissions, I had decided against it. I loved flying the many types of airplanes, but I thought that the way the war was going we would eventually be assigned to specific areas for specialized flying. That is exactly what happened to Mac when he was assigned to Pakistan. For my part, I still wanted to become involved in aircraft developmental flying. I had developed my piloting technique. I had the basic engineering. It was decision time.

4

Test Pilot Beginnings

I prepared three application letters: one to Pan American, which had a government contract delivering B-24's to Europe, salary $1,200 per month; one to Bell Aircraft in Niagara Falls, New York (a fighter manufacturer), as a test pilot; and one to Martin in Baltimore (manufacturer of medium bombers), also as a test pilot. Two weeks later I returned from a delivery flight and found four letters waiting. The Army Air Forces offered a commission as second lieutenant. Pan Am offered an interview in Miami. Bell offered a job as production test pilot, $10,000 per year. Martin offered an interview in Baltimore.

The next morning I wired Robert M. Stanley, chief test pilot at Bell, and accepted the offer as production test pilot. In a following letter I requested payment of moving costs and gasoline ration stamps to enable me to drive to Niagara Falls. Bell responded affirmatively.

DeLores didn't know where Niagara Falls was. "Isn't it cold there?" she asked.

"Yeah, but they have some great airplanes. We'll ship everything, then drive to Emporia. You guys can stay with the folks. I'll drive to Niagara Falls, get a house, and you and Judy can come by train."

Niagara Falls was 1,500 miles from our families and friends. Judy, now nearly six years old, was depressed about leaving her school friends. DeLores was expecting in February. I understood, but I needed to move on. I had accumulated pilot time and technique in every type of aircraft—trainers, cargo, fighters, and bombers. There was no school at that time (or today) where pilots could accumulate that kind of experience. Now, with my engineering background and piloting skills, I was prepared for the position I had worked and prayed for since I first started to fly: engineering test pilot. Production test pilot at Bell was a step in the right direction.

It was a dark 5:30 p.m. in heavy traffic when I arrived in Niagara Falls. Snow packed the streets and was piled in dirty hummocks along the curbs. The temperature was 5 degrees Fahrenheit, quite a change from the balmy 65 in Dallas. The next morning, after a tow to a heated garage for an oil change and an engine start, I drove to the Bell Aircraft Company's corporate offices and factory. Identifying myself at the reception desk, I was escorted to the office of the chief test pilot.

Robert M. Stanley was a well-built man with dark, slightly wavy hair and bushy eyebrows. "I was expecting you after Christmas," he said as we shook hands. "The plant closes after second shift today and will reopen first shift December twenty-seventh, but I'll show you around and introduce you." He took me through the experimental flight-test hangar, then returned to the flight-test section and pointed out the various areas and departments: flight-test planning and analysis engineering, data transcription, and the test instrument department. Finally we entered the pilots' lounge. "I want you fellows to meet Al Johnston, a new pilot," Stanley said.

I shook hands with Jay Denning, Joe Cannon, and Harold Dow, former flight instructors at a Canadian military base near Toronto, Ontario; Ed Hensley and Bob Garrill, former military flight instructors from civilian-contract schools in Oklahoma; and Floyd and Milt Carlson. All were production test pilots except Floyd Carlson. The former P-39 experimental test pilot had recently transferred to the new Bell helicopter division to conduct preliminary flight testing of the company's first helicopter. During our conversation, Harold Dow invited me to accompany him to Toronto to spend Christmas with his family.

On December 27, 1942, I officially became a Bell Aircraft Company production test pilot, at $10,000 per year with company-provided flight insurance. On December 28 I began the P-39 service school with Stanley's admonition fresh in my mind: "It is mandatory to know in technical detail each and every part and system of the airplane and the interface relationship of all systems."

A most unusual feature of the airplane was the installation of the twelve-cylinder Allison behind the pilot. A driveshaft encased in a tunnel extended forward under the pilot's seat and through the cockpit and nose section to the lower section of the reduction gearbox bolted to the nose structure of the airframe. A 37-millimeter cannon, a lethal antitank and train weapon, fired through the gearbox and hollow propeller shaft and hub, an ingenious design that proved very reliable. I learned that empty 37-mm shell casings were too large and heavy to jettison without risking damage to the airframe. Although pilot and shop manuals directed that the airplane not be flown on noncombat missions without ballast in the nose section equivalent to a combat load, violations of the regulations caused numerous crashes, and the airplane suffered much criticism.

The P-39 was well designed for low-level strike and ground-support missions, but it did lack versatility for high-level combat roles because its single-stage, gear-driven engine supercharger could not maintain the required power above 12,000 feet.

Early in P-39 school I rented a three-bedroom, two-bath, two-story brick home in North Tonawanda, about fifteen minutes from the plant. Shortly thereafter DeLores and Judy arrived at the Buffalo station on a train crowded with wartime travelers and G.I.s. I was pleased that their delight in our new home made up for the miseries of the trip.

The morning after I completed P-39 ground school, I cranked up my first P-39. The various fighters I had flown in the Ferry Command had cockpits that the pilot entered from the top. To enter the P-39, I climbed up on the wing and entered the small, well laid out cockpit through a door in the side of the fuselage.

After taxi tests to familiarize myself with the airplane and its brakes, I ran up the engine, received takeoff clearance, and lined up between deep snowbanks so high in places that I could not see over them from the cockpit. It was going to

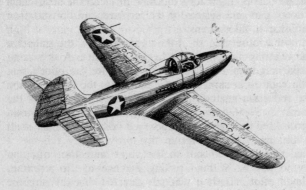

P-39

be like flying out of and landing in a ditch. Nonetheless, that first P-39 flight shall forever remain in my memory. All airplanes are great, but the P-39 was a dream. I leveled out at 6,000 feet and flew to Rochester, New York, acquainting myself with landmarks. After a 180-degree turn over Rochester I applied full power, 55 inches of mercury, and 2,000 rpm. In five minutes there was Niagara Falls just over the nose. I pulled the power back, set the rpm at 1,800, nosed down and flashed over Niagara Falls and the Rainbow Bridge at 375 mph, pulled up in a loop, and rolled out on top at 7,000 feet altitude with the Grand Island Bridge across the Niagara River directly below and Buffalo over the nose. "This is what it's all about," I thought.

The following day I began flight testing new P-39's fresh off the assembly line. Occasionally we would get a "one-hopper," one that required only one test flight, but on average it took three hops per airplane before delivery. Operating three shifts a day, seven days a week, the factory produced twenty airplanes a day. Consequently, inclement weather resulted in severe airplane parking problems compounded by snow removal.

The production flight tests included firing all the armaments at a floating target anchored in a designated area offshore on Lake Ontario. Pilots were instructed to fire the guns at high speed while observing the tracer pattern from the guns for proper sighting alignment and to make a turn before passing over the target to avoid being struck by bullets ricocheting off the water. On several occasions pilots, too intent on the target and ammo patterns, continued on course. Postflight inspections revealed aircraft damage from their own ammo. After one such flight across the target the aircraft crashed in Lake Ontario, killing the pilot.

One morning I returned to the flight-line office after an early morning flight and was given a message to report to Stanley's office. There I was introduced to Jack Woolams, the company's senior experimental test pilot, who had been out of town since my arrival. Woolams, handsome, well-built, and over six feet tall, shook hands and said, "Hear you were in the Ferry Command. What type equipment were you flying?" We talked about that for a while and about airplanes and my engineering background.

Two days later, Stanley again wanted to see me. "Inspection has found a production airplane on the delivery line with one and a half degrees of permanent set in the wings." I could think of no comment and waited for him to continue. "The acceptance flight was conducted by a junior-grade Air Force pilot. I want you to obtain assistance from engineering, quality control, and the service department and inspect and evaluate the damage to the airplane. Then discreetly see what you can learn regarding the lieutenant's piloting skill and general attitude, and finally talk to him personally. Then prepare a detailed report and submit it to this office. You are relieved of flight duties for the period required."

In the pilot's lounge, I considered the assignment. Was this an exercise to investigate any talent, other than flying, I might possess? I considered the known facts: 1. The wing of the subject airplane had one or two degrees of permanent set (bend). 2. The pilot was a junior-grade officer with pilot skills, technical knowledge, and judgment unknown. 3. The

XP-39 ("X" meaning "experimental," the designation of the original test airplane) had satisfactorily completed its structural integrity testing, including 9-G pullouts (a G is a unit of force equal to the force of gravity) at maximum speed. Conclusion: The airplane had been subjected to structural loads in excess of 9 Gs.

Investigation tasks: 1. Determine extent of damage to the airplane. 2. Investigate the lieutenant's piloting skills. 3. Discuss the maneuver that overstressed the airplane with the lieutenant. 4. Submit report.

Using transects and supporting equipment, the inspection team that I recruited from the various departments verified that each wing had an increased positive dihedral angle (the angle with the horizontal that the wingspan makes where it joins the fuselage) of 1.5 degrees. From careful inspection the team concluded that structural integrity had not been affected. The aircraft was satisfactory for delivery.

Conversations with company pilots indicated the lieutenant was a satisfactory pilot, he enjoyed flying, and he had flown more hours than many of his colleagues. However, two company pilots had observed him unsuccessfully attempting complicated aerobatics that terminated in steep dives and hard pullouts. The next morning I visited the delivery flight line and introduced myself to the lieutenant. After some preliminary conversation I told him that inspection had found a 1.5-degree permanent set in the wing of an airplane he had flown. He gave me a hostile look. "Lieutenant," I said, "I'm not criticizing you. My purpose is to provide information."

"Such as?" he interrupted.

"The subject P-39 has been subjected to loads exceeding nine G. A fraction higher acceleration would have failed the structure. Maneuvers involving loads in excess of five G cause pilot blackout" (failure of sight as blood is drained from the brain by high G forces). "Lieutenant, I believe you were blacked out for a period during the maneuver."

He hesitated, then said, "Yeah, I've been blacked out several times."

"You were lucky this time."

His attitude changed as we continued a discussion of aerobatic maneuvers and control techniques for about thirty minutes. At the end, he said, "I'm glad you came over. I appreciate the information and explanation."

Some time after I turned in the report to Stanley's office, Jack Woolams came into the flight-line office and said, "Let's go to lunch."

"You convinced me. Where are we going?"

"The Green Lantern. You'll like it. It has a history going back to prohibition days, and it's the Bell pilots' home away from home."

The place was packed. Many greetings and calls from the crowd attested to Woolams's popularity. A buxom lady with beautiful white hair gave him a peck on the cheek. "Trixie, meet Tex Johnston, our new test pilot. Tex, this is Mrs. Grimmer, owner of this establishment, a good friend to have, and someone you need to know." Clasping her hand in both of mine, I expressed my pleasure. She led us to a carpeted private dining room where we could talk and lunch in private. This one-on-one opportunity gave each of us a more in-depth knowledge of our respective educational and flying backgrounds. We found that we were both pursuing the same objective, the development and expansion of performance and mission capability of high-performance aircraft.

During lunch, a partially gray, slightly rotund gentleman joined us. "Tex, meet Fran Grimmer, he runs this place for his mother." Fran and his mother were destined to become close friends with DeLores and me.

It had been a productive day; I had accepted five airplanes. Returning to the pilots' lounge, I found a letter from Stanley in my mailbox requesting me to report to his office at eight the next morning. When I arrived, Stanley leaned back in his swivel chair, his eyes intense under bushy eyebrows. "Woolams needs another experimental test pilot," he said. "I'm assigning you to Experimental for sixty days. At the end of the period, providing your work is satisfactory and you want the position, I will transfer you to Experimental." He stood, shook my hand, and said, "There's a lot to learn. We'll talk again in sixty days."

At the experimental hangar, Harry Cleveland, who ran Flight Equipment, issued my equipment and assigned me a locker in the experimental pilots' locker room. Then I went to Jack Woolams's office.

"I'll brief you on your activity for the next sixty days," Jack said. "Better take notes." Jack said that although the XP-39 had satisfactorily met contractual specifications prior to production, Allison had increased the engine's power, so new performance data were needed. Acquiring such data would require the utmost in precision piloting. During three-minute level-flight, stabilized-speed tests, the airspeed must be held within one mile per hour of a particular speed and the altitude within five feet of a particular height. Sawtooth climb testing, which determines the best climb speed at increments of 5,000 feet throughout the operational altitude range of the airplane, would require even more precise piloting skill because of the variables involved.

"The industry needs more sophisticated data-recording instrumentation," Jack said. "But for now, it is the pilot's responsibility to locate proper atmospheric conditions, perform the tests within rigid tolerances, read and record the data, navigate, avoid other traffic, and simultaneously monitor the operation of the aircraft and special test systems."

"A big order," I thought. But engineering flight testing was the answer I had been searching for. The piloting technique and precision required were not only an invigorating challenge but resulted in deep inner satisfaction and pride.

Jack next spoke of potential emergencies. "The emergency bailout procedure must be automatic," he said. "There will be no time to search for switches, controls, and hatch or door releases in an emergency. In full flight gear, board an airplane in the hangar. Make all equipment connections and close the cockpit as in flight. Have an observer with a stopwatch give a bailout signal, then disconnect everything necessary, jettison the cockpit door, and roll, step, or leap out in minimum time. Practice until you develop a consistent, automatic, minimum-time escape routine. That way, you'll feel a lot more comfortable when you're gyrating around after a structural failure and can't tell up from down. Comprendo?"

"Damn right," I said.

Ben Hamlin, chief flight-test engineer, and his group of capable and dedicated engineers indoctrinated me in the rigors of test planning, data acquisition, transcription, and analysis.

Unknowingly, I was the guinea pig in the development of a curriculum for a new flight-test engineering indoctrination program for experimental test pilots. Later I learned that Stanley had suggested the curriculum and guidelines that Hamlin and Dexter Rosen, Hamlin's lead test engineer, used in developing and implementing the program. The Bell Aircraft engineering test pilot curriculum was the first in the industry. Colonel Albert Boyd, chief of the Wright Field flight-test organization in Dayton, Ohio, was concerned by the increasing need for adequately trained engineering test pilots. He monitored the Bell program and subsequently sparked the establishment of the now prominent Edwards Air Force Base test pilot school.

During one session with two of the test engineers, I noticed an unusual dark piece of graph paper containing a trace. They explained that it was a sheet of smoked graph paper recovered from the revolving cylinder of a power-driven barograph in the aft fuselage of my flight number six. As the cylinder rotated, a stylus had scribed a graphic time and altitude history of my entire flight.

"You didn't know about it because your test traces were well within limits," one of the engineers said. I thought it was a bit sneaky, but it was proof that the flight had accurately fulfilled test conditions and I did not violate their confidence.

Onboard instrumentation in the early forties was crude by today's standards. A pyrometer mounted on the ship's instrument panel provided various temperature data as selected by the pilot. The pilot manually recorded airspeed, altitude, engine rpm, manifold pressure, and pyrometer data while simultaneously maintaining the stabilized test condition.

Calendar time flashed by. Each day brought new challenges. A special one occurred on February 27, 1943, with the arrival on flight plan time of son Gary Alva Johnston.

Testing the Focke-Wulf Fw 190

The Army Air Force captured three damaged German Focke-Wulf Fw 190 aircraft in Europe. Wright Field contracted with Bell Aircraft to rebuild one airworthy aircraft from the remains of the three damaged machines and to conduct a complete performance test program. During the rework and assembly operations, Stanley discovered that the hydraulically controlled variable-pitch propeller was an exact copy of the one he had designed and patented before World War II. As project pilot, I learned the ship's systems as they were disassembled, inspected, repaired, and reassembled.

Focke-Wulf Fw 190

From those studies, taxi tests, and engine run-ups, I learned what I could about the aircraft on the ground. Now it was time to try it in the air. The takeoff was normal for a high-performance tail-dragger. The ground fell away, and I retracted the landing gear. Suddenly, the airspeed indicator became inoperative. I continued the climb to 6,000 feet. Although many of the tests programmed for this first flight could not be conducted without airspeed indication, I wanted to see how the aircraft handled.

The cockpit was comfortable and well designed and had good inflight visibility. Flight control effectiveness was excellent, control forces ideal. When I flew simulated combat maneuvers, the aircraft responded beautifully—truly a fighter pilot's airplane.

Still at 6,000 feet, I set up landing configuration with gear down and full flaps. Slowly I retarded the throttle, keeping the nose slightly above the horizon. As the speed dropped, a slight vibration warned of stall approach. About five seconds later, the wing did stall and the aircraft's nose fell below the horizon. Continuing to hold the stick back during the stall, I was able to maintain constant heading and keep the wings level. When I applied full throttle and forward stick, the aircraft readily resumed normal flight. Although flight characteristics, stall warning, and stall recovery were all satisfactory, without an airspeed indicator I could accomplish no more. I returned to the field, made a normal landing, and taxied in.

Postflight inspection revealed the airspeed static pressure line had been misrouted. The landing gear had pinched it closed during retraction.

Subsequent tests proved the Fw 190 to be comparable to the North American P-51 and Bell P-63. It was a terrific aerobatic airplane. In simulated dogfights I had no difficulty getting into firing position on the tail of our guys in P-39's and the Curtis boys in their P-40's.

When Colonel Albert Boyd visited Bell during the Fw 190 test program, I briefed him on the test procedures, airplane performance, and flight characteristics. His questions showed keen intelligence and extensive knowledge. I was impressed by his manner, bearing, and no-nonsense aura of authority. At the time, I was unaware of the influence he would have on my subsequent career.

The probationary assignment to experimental flight test had lapsed almost to the hour when I received a call to report to Stanley's office. Effective immediately I was assigned to Woolams as experimental test pilot at a salary of $11,000 per year. Woolams greeted me as I returned to Flight Test. "This requires a celebration at Grimmer's."

At 5 p.m., twelve test pilots descended on the Green Lantern. A dozen or so flight-line mechanics already waited at the bar. In another fifteen minutes, flight test and service department engineers and secretaries arrived. I telephoned

DeLores. She understood. ''Have a ball,'' she said. She knew that the festivities marked the culmination of dreams and efforts first inspired in an eleven-year-old boy by a long-ago barnstormer in a Kansas cow pasture.

The XP-63

The Bell XP-63, a new interceptor, was larger than the P-39 but had the same mid-engine configuration. However, its laminar-flow wing and two-stage engine supercharger gave it a high-altitude capability. Stanley and Woolams did the preliminary testing.

During early flights, Woolams encountered diminishing stick forces when maneuvering above 6 G. Such decreasing stick forces at high G loads not only don't feel right but also can lead to overcontrolling with resultant structural damage or failure. On the other hand, increasing stick forces at higher G loadings help the pilot anticipate the approach of critical load conditions. Bell corrected the problem by adding a relatively simple bob-weight mechanism to the elevator control. I flew the developmental tests and final demonstration of that fix to 9 G with satisfactory stick forces throughout the speed, altitude, and center-of-gravity ranges.

Wright Field, in an attempt to reduce airframe weight and improve performance, contracted with Bell to design, build, install, and flight test a V tail on the P-63. The V tail's movable control surfaces, called rudavators, were linked by an integrated control system to provide both directional and longitudinal control. During high-speed taxi tests, takeoff, and climb to 18,000 feet, I found that the V-tail aircraft handled the same as the standard airplane except for reduced directional stability in rough air. All aerobatic maneuvers could be performed but required constant attention to compensate for reduced directional stability. That problem was slightly improved by the installation of a ventral fin on the underside of the aft fuselage. Climb and high-speed performance were the same as those of the standard airplane.

When it was time for the critical stall and spin tests, a spin recovery chute was installed on the aft starboard side of the fuselage as a precautionary measure. Stanley flew chase in a

P-39. At 15,000 feet, I performed power on and off stalls and found I needed excessive directional control to maintain constant heading during both the stalls and recoveries.

Just before the first spin test, I pressed the transmit button on the throttle knob and said, "Stanley from Tex, spin entry on one-hundred-eighty-degree heading, right spin, three turns."

Stanley "Rogered" and I proceeded with the test while holding the transmit button down and giving a running description of control application and response: "Throttle closed. Increasing up elevator. Nose slightly above horizon. Increasing up elevator. Excessive rudder required to maintain heading. Slight buffet. Full back stick, stall, full right rudder. Nose descending, right bank increasing, bank angle eighty degrees. Nose rising to the horizon, bank angle decreasing. Nose falling, bank angle increasing. An oscillatory spin, nose down almost vertical. Estimate roll rate two hundred fifty degrees per second. Three turns, applying full left rudder, full forward stick. Spin stopped, altitude ten thousand feet, neutralizing controls.

"Damn. The airplane has reentered the right spin, nose straight down, airplane rolling around the longitudinal axis—similar to a slow roll. Controlling with the spin, full back stick, full right rudder. No change. Full left aileron, no change. Full left rudder, full back stick, no reaction, estimate roll rate three hundred degrees per second. Controls in neutral position, no change. Full forward stick, full left rudder, no effect. Altitude six thousand, pulling spin chute."

As my fingers closed on the spin chute T handle, the airplane quit rolling. I was in a vertical dive. As I pulled the nose up and added power, the altimeter read 3,600 feet. "Old girl," I said, "I thought you weren't going to make it."

The V-tail project engineers were on the ramp with sober faces as I opened the cockpit door and released the safety belt. "Back to the drawing board, boys," I said. "This mother gets a little hairy."

Aerodynamics had no explanation for the unorthodox spin and control response. I tried unsuccessfully to duplicate the condition but completed the spin program with only normal recoveries. In my 26 years of engineering flight testing, that one V-tail spin is the only unorthodox and unexplained flight condition I ever experienced.

As a result of our performance tests, Wright Field lost interest in the V tail. The weight saved was insufficient and the decreased directional stability unacceptable.

The P-47

For some time, military pilots of the Republic P-47 had been reporting violent lateral control stick oscillation at 6 G and above. They called it stick snatch. Bell Aircraft responded to a Wright Field bid request and received the contract to investigate the problem. I became the P-47 test program pilot.

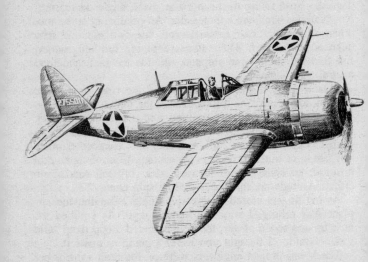

Republic P-47

The P-47, familiarly known as the Jug, was a large single-engine, conventional landing gear (tail dragger) fighter, powered by a double-row (eighteen-cylinder) Pratt and Whitney Wasp turbocharged engine. The cockpit was huge. The only cockpit visibility on the ground was to either side, so frequent S turns were necessary while taxiing to clear the area ahead.

When I first looked into the cockpit, I noted the switches

for the electrically controlled propeller and made a mental note to check their setting with special care before takeoffs and landings.

I enjoyed the airplane. That turbocharged P&W could haul you right up to 36,000 feet. On the first flight, I climbed to 15,000 to see what stick snatch was. At 6 G, I soon found out. At the approach to high-speed stall, the stick suddenly jerked from my hand and rapidly banged the inboard sides of both my knees. Wiser, I took a firmer grip on the stick and repeated the maneuver. Again the stick went berserk; my firm grip could only slightly restrain the motion. Obviously, stick snatch during combat could ruin a fighter pilot's whole day. Changes in the dynamic balance of the ailerons and modified sealing of the wing aileron cavity corrected the problem.

While entering the parking gate the morning after the modified aircraft was ready for return to Wright Field, I observed the takeoff roll of the lieutenant making the delivery. Well past the runway midpoint, he was still on the ground. "He should be airborne by now," I thought. As he passed from view, there was an explosive sound and an eruption of white dust upwind of the field. I backed out the gate and sped down a side road beside the airport.

The lieutenant, barely airborne at the end of the runway, had flown across the road and through an abandoned wooden building. The aircraft hit just below the roof eaves, pulverized the plasterboard partitions, and collapsed the roof, blasting white powder into the air. The P-47 rested on its belly slightly beyond the debris. The cockpit was open. The lieutenant was standing beside the road in a daze.

Making my way through the debris, I stepped up on the wing and looked in the cockpit. The electric propeller selector switch was in the high-pitch position. That was a major problem with electric propellers. If the switch was accidentally left in the high-pitch, low-rpm position, the aircraft required a hell of a long takeoff roll.

The P-51

In mid-1944, newspapers reported alarmingly high combat losses of P-51 fighters from wing failures during combat maneuvers. Wright Field selected Bell to investigate the problem, and again, I got the job.

The airplane delivered to us for testing was the original configuration A model with trunk-type cockpit access. On my first flight, while setting up for the test, what seemed to be an explosion in the cockpit got my attention. I quickly closed the throttle and pulled up the nose to kill the speed and made a quick check. The aft starboard cockpit window adjacent to my ear had blown out.

With a new window installed, I continued the tests. They showed a stick force problem similar to that encountered on the XP-63, diminishing elevator stick force above 6 G, which became more severe with aft CGs (centers of gravity).

A report supported by flight-recorded data was submitted to Wright Field. Subsequently, the P-51, with an elevator-control system modification, became the number one Air Force fighter, a significant factor in the Allied victory.

5

The First U.S. Jet

Responding to a call, I arrived at Stanley's office and met three men I'd never seen before. "Bell Aircraft has a top-secret program," Stanley said. "These gentlemen have investigated your family and personal history and conclude you are eligible for top-secret clearance. If you agree to become involved, you will be assigned to a remote location. Your position will be base manager and project test pilot."

"I'm honored to be chosen," I said.

"Will your family agree?" one of the gentlemen asked.

"Absolutely," I replied. "They give me complete support."

I was sworn to secrecy, signed the previously prepared papers, and received my security credentials. The next morning, Stanley handed me a travel voucher and told me to report to Colonel Gagge, chief of the Aeromedical Laboratory at Wright Field, Dayton, Ohio, for special training and indoctrination on new equipment.

During my initial briefing at the laboratory, Colonel Gagge told me that although the airplane I would be testing had a pressurized cabin, the use of an experimental pressurized oxygen system was mandatory for survival should cabin pressure fail. The subsequent high-altitude training I received at the aeromedical center included the use of that new system at 50,000 feet in an altitude chamber. The laboratory also introduced me to "grunt breathing." By initially holding your breath while straining to exhale, you can work to increase oxygen pressure in the lungs. This emergency technique can sustain life for brief periods at high altitudes should the pressure oxygen system fail. At the completion of the course, I was issued my own high-altitude survival gear, including a personal oxygen mask fabricated to fit my face.

In five days I was back in Niagara Falls being welcomed to the new program by Jack Woolams. DeLores was shocked that evening when I told her I was being assigned to another base and test program and I still didn't know where I was going. Five days later Woolams revealed my destination: Muroc Dry Lake on the Mojave Desert northeast of Lancaster and east of Rosamond, California. "Our base is on the edge of a dry lake," he said. "It's a bit primitive, but knowing you" (we had hunted and fished together), "I believe you will like it."

In late November 1943, with temperatures in the twenties and snow and ice on the highways, I departed Niagara Falls in the family Oldsmobile bound for Muroc via Emporia, to see the folks. Reaching Rosamond after a nostalgic overnight stay at the Hollywood Roosevelt Hotel, I stopped for gas and directions. It was a bleak, sandy, small desert town with tumbleweeds banked against the buildings by dry winds. The Standard Oil station attendant pointed east down a narrow road in the desert sand. "Keep on goin' past Rosamond Dry Lake 'til you come to Williams Lake," he said. "Everyone calls it Muroc Dry Lake. You can't miss it. It's ten or twelve miles wide and twenty miles long."

"Where's the Bell Aircraft Base?"

"There'll be a barbed-wire fence running along on your right. Keep goin' til you come to a gate with an old phone booth for a guard shack. Just open the gate; there's no guard. You'll see the buildings at the end of the road on the edge of the lake bed."

I reached the base at 11:30 a.m. Two wooden buildings and a Quonset-style hangar were set in a landscape of sand and sagebrush that merged with a flat, smooth lake bed stretching into the distance. The smaller building was a mess hall, the other a barracks. I intercepted two guys in blue jeans who had emerged from the hangar and headed for the mess hall, my first meeting with Bob Wheelock, flight test engineer, and Don Buttons, chief instrumentation engineer. "Come along," they said. "It's chow time."

Inside, a dozen or so men sat at a long table. I loaded a tray and was about to join them when there was a sudden swish and a roar overhead. "What the hell was that?" I asked.

"Come on," someone said. Outside, I spotted the plane coming in for another pass. As it swooshed by, I understood. No prop. I had just witnessed my first jet-propelled airplane.

Jet propulsion had come just as reciprocating aircraft engines and propeller-driven aircraft were reaching their limits in size, weight, complexity, and performance. Achieving higher speeds and higher altitudes required a new kind of engine. The birth of the jet engine cannot be ascribed to any one individual, nor did it take place at any one place or time. Both England and Germany developed jet-propelled aircraft in the early years of World War II.

In England, former R.A.F. fighter pilot Frank Whittle first became interested in the problems of aircraft propulsion while a cadet at R.A.F. College Cranwell in 1926. Later, his vital contribution was to use a gas turbine not to drive a propeller but simply to produce a jet of hot gases that when exhausted through a suitable nozzle would produce thrust. After heart-breaking years of courteous refusals from an apathetic establishment, he borrowed enough money to set up his own company, Power Jets.

The success of the company's first experimental engine in April 1937 led to a contract to power a small Gloster research aircraft that first flew on May 15, 1941. Subsequent test results prompted George Carter to hurriedly design the twin-jet Gloster Meteor fighter. Shortly thereafter, General H. H. "Hap" Arnold, chief of staff of the U.S. Army Air Corps, imported a Whittle engine and the drawings into the United States. With Arnold's encouragement, the General Electric Company of Lynn, Massachusetts, under license by the British, built the first Whittle jet engines in the United States. The first engine developed 1,200 pounds of thrust at 20,000 rpm. The life expectancy of the engine was a mere five hours because no metals were available that could resist such high temperatures.

Also with Arnold's encouragement, Larry Bell, founder of Bell Aircraft, negotiated a contract with the Army Air Corps at Wright Field to design, construct, and flight test the first jet-propelled aircraft in the United States. The resulting XP-59A Airacomet was first flown by chief pilot Robert Stanley on October 1, 1942. Bud Kelly, also a Bell test pilot, and Jack Woolams flew numerous early demonstration flights and preliminary low-altitude tests. Now it was time to determine the speed, range, and altitude capability of the airplane.

The airplane was a twin-engine design with tricycle landing gear and a straight wing mounted midway between the upper and lower surfaces of the fuselage. The engines were wrapped in nacelles under the inboard section of the wings at the body juncture. Cockpit access was from the top via an aft-moving hatch. The XP-59A incorporated a pressurized cockpit, which was necessary for proper crew environment at high altitude. Pressurization and cabin heat were supplied via bleed air from one engine compressor, another asset of the turbine engine. Engine tachometers were nonexistent for the high engine rpm (20,000) of the turbine. Consequently, early testing was accomplished using a modified drive system for existing engine tachometers. The pilot had to calculate the actual engine rpm from the observed tachometer reading. The airplane also incorporated the first pressure-breathing oxygen system. Oxygen under pressure was fed through a flexible tube to a regulator suspended from a cord around the pilot's neck and thence through another tube to his face mask.

Crew chief Jack Russell and his troops briefed me on the details and operation of all airplane systems. Don Buttons provided indoctrination on the recording instrumentation, radio equipment, and electrical systems. Ben Hamlin was chief test engineer, Pop Fisher was inspection and quality-control chief, and Mac McKecrin was the G.E. resident representative. Russell and McKecrin indoctrinated me in the precise I-16 engine starting, operating, and shut-down procedures. The engine was extremely vulnerable to destruction if tail-pipe temperature exceeded 700 degrees Fahrenheit. A too-rapid increase in throttle, for example, would result in overtemperature and consequent disintegration of turbine wheel blades and burner liners. Today's high-temperature-resistant metals had not yet been developed.

The purpose of my first flight was strictly familiarization. Visibility during ground maneuvering was good. Initial acceleration following brake release was slow but increased with speed. Landing gear and flap retraction rates were slightly slow. The noise level and complete absence of vibration were impressive, a vast and welcome improvement. The recommended best-climb speed was gratifying, approximately 100 mph faster than a propeller airplane, and resulted in a good rate of climb. Lateral maneuvering revealed rates of roll slightly slower than those of the P-63 and P-51. The 12,000-foot cabin altitude when I leveled out at 25,000 feet was a welcome technical contribution.

I executed numerous engine decelerations and accelerations from idle to full power to familiarize myself with the maximum throttle-advance rates that would not raise tail-pipe temperature above the 700-degree limit. In the process, I observed that engine idle rpm at 25,000 feet was higher than at low altitudes and on the ground, a condition I was soon to learn was unacceptable.

The airplane was stable in trimmed hands-off flight, but with gear and flaps down at slow speed, the airplane exhibited minor directional instability, a right and left oscillation called snaking. The condition, although easily controlled by rudder action, was definitely an undesirable flight characteristic, particularly on landing approach. I experimented with the engine-acceleration rate at low approach speed and made a mental note: "Never get low and slow on final approach. The slow engine-power and airspeed response to increased throttle could result in undershooting the runway." Final approach and landing characteristics were good. The dry lake bed was excellent. What a runway: twenty miles long and ten miles wide.

There were three test airplanes. Two were in commission most of the time, all three occasionally. Performance flights were scheduled at 5 a.m. for low-level, 100-feet-off-the-deck speed runs when ambient temperatures were stable and wind velocity zero, followed by stability and control investigations and performance testing at 5,000-foot increments to 35,000 feet.

The base was closed Saturday and Sunday. Consequently an exodus occurred each Friday at 5 p.m. (with the exception of employees designated to remain at the base for security). The Hollywood Roosevelt was the Bell test crew's home away from home. Another favorite spot was Red Mountain, California. An issue of *Life* magazine featuring "Red Mountain, California: Where the Old West Still Lives" was in the reading-materials rack in the barracks when I checked in.

The town of Red Mountain consisted of two saloons, one on each side of the street. A combination grocery, miner's clothing and equipment store, and post office was 200 feet east of one saloon. That saloon also had numerous cottages a few steps from the back door inhabited by twelve to fifteen down-on-their-luck Hollywood starlets. The balance of the townspeople were goldminers still looking for the mother lode.

The saloon sported an upright piano attended by a good jazz piano player who, if not playing, was available by a request to the bartender. A large papier-mâché kitty with convenient open mouth was in place beside the piano for donations from appreciative customers. Our electronics wizard, Buttons, always brought his voluminous platter recording equipment (tape recording was nonexistent at the time). Today, those old recordings evoke fond memories.

The subject saloon was also a Greyhound bus stop. When the bus arrived, the ladies, who were normally in the saloon at all hours, disappeared through the rear door, to return when the bus departed.

I first met Howard Hughes in that saloon. He was testing his experimental twin-boom, twin-reciprocating-engine airplane at Harper Dry Lake some distance east of Muroc. Red Mountain was also a favorite spot for his crew.

I was logging many flight-test hours. Ben Hamlin and his test engineers were up to their ears in data. During this time, I lost an engine on two consecutive flights while obtaining maximum engine acceleration data for G.E. Rapid throttle application had caused tail-pipe temperature to increase extremely fast and inadvertently exceed 700 degrees. Turbine blades burned off and fuel burner liners disintegrated. Two other engines were replaced because of hot starts. Consequently, my test reports requested improvement in the engine fuel-metering system.

I aborted one takeoff when the pressurized cabin-seal tube exploded; the resulting compression shock gave my eardrums a severe blow. An inspection revealed that one seal tube section had a flaw in the tube wall.

There was a constant flow of security-cleared visitors to witness XP-59A flights and an obvious requirement for passenger flights. So an open cockpit complete with windshield was installed in the nose section immediately forward of the cockpit of one test airplane. The open cockpit limited passenger flights to 10,000 feet and required the use of a warm flight suit and helmet and goggles. Stanley, Woolams, and Johnston became the first jet barnstormers in history. Passengers included prominent government, industry, and military personnel who wanted to experience jet flight firsthand.

The effect of speed is best demonstrated during flight 50 to 100 feet off the deck at full power. The Mojave-to-Barstow highway lay absolutely straight for 30 miles across the desert, the only obstruction a telephone line along one side. After one such demonstration flight, my enthusiastic passenger exclaimed, "When we flew down the Barstow Highway the telephone poles looked like a picket fence."

Without exception, after-flight comments were positive, complimentary, and enthusiastic. The XP-59A today sits proudly in the Smithsonian Institution's National Air and Space Museum in Washington, D.C.

Soon after my arrival at the base, the crew escorted me to Juanita's, an adobe building in Rosamond containing a combination bar, dining room, dance floor, and bowling alley. Juanita, an attractive Caucasian-Spanish lady with enticing hair and eyes, a friendly smile, and beautiful white teeth, was tending bar when we were introduced. Hanging above the back bar mirror was a collection of cutoff neckties. Jack Russell had told me that early in the program, Woolams, ever the prankster, returned from Hollywood with an assortment of English derby hats. Each crew member selected a derby and received a cigar. Woolams didn't smoke but held the cigar clenched between his teeth when wearing the derby. The group was dubbed the Bell Bowlers. In the initiation ritual of a new Bowler, two members seized the "victim" and held him while another member carefully cut his tie just below the knot—thus the tie collection behind the bar. I became the most recent member and received a derby and a cigar.

Early in World War II the military constructed a full-scale battleship replica of heavy timbers on the southwest end of Muroc Dry Lake as a target for aerial gunnery practice. P-38 fighters periodically appeared for air-to-ground gunnery practice. I stowed my derby and cigar in the cockpit on test flights, awaiting a P-38. Descending from high altitude one day, I observed a lone P-38 below. Removing my helmet and oxygen mask, I donned my derby, clenched the cigar between my teeth, and, overtaking the P-38, eased into tight formation with my left wing tucked in behind his right wing. I was so close I could see his instrument panel. He was looking left in preparation for a gunnery run, then turned his head to clear the area on his right and picked up the XP-59A in his peripheral vision. His head swiveled around; he saw an airplane without a propeller and then saw me. I tipped my derby, applied full power, executed a steep chandelle, and disappeared from his view with both engines emitting a trail of black smoke. I've always wondered what the P-38 pilot told his buddies, or if he, unsure of what he had witnessed, retained his secret.

Structural Failure

One day, as I completed performance and engine investigation tests at 35,000 feet, I descended to 10,000 feet to obtain structural data at high accelerations. Being low on fuel, I stayed near the lake in case of engine flameout.

In a slight dive at 450 mph I executed a medium-rate pullout to 7 G on the accelerometer. Simultaneously, I heard a thud in the structure. The ship yawed violently to the right, requiring almost full left rudder to maintain heading. The right main gear warning light came on. Suddenly, the right yaw ceased; I released rudder pressure and pressed the transmit button.

"Tex to Ground. I'm at eight thousand feet over the lake, red light on right gear, suspect it pulled out in seven-G pullup. Visually check area for falling object. During the

Lockheed P-38

seven-G pullup I experienced a severe right yaw as the right landing gear red light came on. Oh-oh, there goes the left engine, out of fuel. I believe the right landing gear extended slightly during the pullup, allowing the wheel fairing to catch the high-velocity air. Damn. There goes the right engine— no sweat. I suspect the high G loads plus the drag load failed the right landing gear torque tube drive system, allowing the right gear to free-fall to the extended position with no down lock capability. The severe yaw ceased when the wheel fairing blew off. Stand by.

"Okay, I'm extending left main and nose gear. Okay, they're in the green."

"Tex from Ground. We see an object falling and reflecting sunlight. Are you bailing out?"

"Hell, no. The airplane is okay. I'm going to land this mother. Get the firetruck onto the lake bed a half city block southeast of the hangar. I'll land as close as possible." I still had 4,000 feet altitude. I saw the firetruck moving into position as I flew a power-off landing approach to place me near the truck at landing rollout.

The touchdown was normal—for a moment—then the right wing started down. I applied slight left brake. The wing dropped faster. Quickly, I applied right brake. The wing came up. The remainder of the landing roll was a continual right, left, right, left braking to prevent the strut from folding. At an estimated 35 mph, the right gear strut finally folded outboard and the right wing went down. I held the left brake as the right engine nacelle and wingtip touched the ground. The airplane slid 25 feet to a stop, turning right approximately 15 degrees. The firetruck was there as I climbed out of the cockpit and immediately extinguished a slight fire in the right engine nacelle.

Jack Russell obtained a chalkline and tape measure from the hangar. The ground crew measured the right gear track and determined it had traveled seven inches right and left of the normal extended position throughout the landing roll. A precarious balance had been maintained by the alternate braking.

Many aircraft with retractable landing gear use up-locks to secure the gear in the full retracted position when power is terminated by the up-limit switch. Bell Aircraft, for mechanical simplicity, used wind-up (twist) in the electrically driven torque tube retraction system to secure the gear in the up position. Structural analysis concluded that the combined weight of the landing gear strut, brake, wheel, and tire, multiplied by the 7-G down load plus the wheel fairing drag load, had failed the landing gear torque tube, allowing the right gear to free-fall. Increasing the wall thickness of the torque tubes solved the problem.

Pancho Barnes

During early flights in the XP-59A, I observed a small desert-sand airport with a corrugated metal hangar a mile or two west of the southwest edge of the dry lake. Adjacent to the airport was a single-level rambling ranchhouse with patio, pool, a horse barn, corrals, and eight cottages. "That's Pancho's place," said Snuffy Stewart, one of the shop crew, when I raised the question at dinner.

"Who's Pancho?"

"Pancho Barnes, the aviatrix." I knew the name. Pancho

had flown in the 1929 Women's Air Derby, the first National Air Races cross-country competition for women, and in 1930 had set a speed record of 196 mph in her Travel Air racer. "A bunch of Hollywood people hang out over there," Snuffy said. "They fly in and land at her airport. She has a bar and dining room. The food's great."

The next weekend I fired up one of the base Jeeps and took off for Pancho's. Opening the screen door, I walked past the tables on the screened porch, through a dining area, to the bar adjacent to a small dance floor surrounded by tables. Two locals in worn blue jeans and boots with run-down heels leaned on the bar tended by a short, scraggly-haired woman. "Howdy," I said, eyeing the two customers' beers. "That draft beer looks good." As she drew the beer, I said, "Nice place you have here. I noticed it the other day when I flew over."

"Where're you from?" she asked.

"Buffalo," I said. I had noticed people on the West Coast didn't seem to know where Niagara Falls was, so it saved time to say Buffalo. "My name's Tex Johnston."

"I'm Pancho," she said as she shook my hand. "How did you get that name in Buffalo?" The two locals turned and grinned at me.

"When I arrived from Fort Worth," I replied.

"I'll buy that," she said, and everybody laughed.

"You got a horse I can use? I want to ride out and see a little of this country."

"Yeah, the barn out there is full of 'em. Take your pick. The gear's hanging on the wall."

Setting the empty schooner on the bar with fifteen cents, I departed for the barn. The horses were in their stalls with halters on, finishing their morning hay. They rolled their eyes at me as I looked them over. I selected a bay mare and threw a saddle blanket and western saddle on her while she remained tied to the manger. She humped up a bit when I adjusted the cinch; a good jolt with my knee to the belly and she let the air out. Easing the halter off, I slipped the bit in her mouth and the bridle over her ears, fastening the throat strap before she knew what happened.

Rent string horses are all the same; they learn early to bluff green riders and develop poor manners. A favorite trick is to run back into the barn when a green rider mounts. It can ruin your whole day, as you get wiped out of the saddle by the door header. I knew my audience of three was expecting a greenhorn show, so I led her out the barn door into the corral. With a good grip on a short left rein, I pulled her head around so we were nearly eyeball to eyeball, grabbed a handful of mane, and stepped up into the saddle as I hauled her head left almost to my knee. She couldn't buck in that position, and I slowly released the left rein pressure as I nudged her with my boot heels, and she walked right up to the corral gate and stopped. Dismounting and holding the reins, I opened the gate, led her through, and closed the gate while continually talking to her. Short reining her again, I swung aboard, kicked her in the flank, and said, "Come on you S.O.B., let's see you run." And she did.

Shortly she began to slow down. A little more influence in the flanks and she was running full bore. "I wish I had my spurs, honey," I yelled. "I'd teach you some manners." We saw a lot of the Mojave Desert and were back at Pancho's for lunch. I watered the mare at the tank, stripped off the gear, and slapped her on the rump. "Remember me, babe. I'll be back."

There were six or eight people at the bar when I returned. From their looks, I suspected that I had been a subject for discussion. "How about a beer, Pancho. It's hot on that damn desert."

She looked at me, nodded, and winked. "Comin' up, Pardner." As she placed it on the bar she said, "It's on the house."

That Saturday was the beginning of a long friendship with Pancho Barnes. Her place was a popular location for Hollywood fly-in festivities. It was there I first met stunt pilot Paul Mantz of aviation-movie fame and renewed my friendship with Milo Burcham, Lockheed's chief test pilot, whom I had met during barnstorming days when he made front-page headlines by flying a Boeing P-12 open-cockpit fighter inverted from San Diego to Los Angeles.

Woolams telephoned from Niagara Falls and announced he wanted to fly the XP-59A with the new fuel regulator and that I could return home to see the family. That airline DC-4 ride was the pits after living in the jet for the past several months. The morning after a family reunion and a celebratory lob-

ster dinner with DeLores at the 81 Club in Buffalo, I arrived
at the plant at about 10:30. Stanley had hired four new pilots,
Slick Goodlin, Red Constants, Bud Milligan, and Willard
Jones. All were Americans who had been in the Eagle Squadron in England and were now assigned to P-39 production
testing.

The Bell XP-83, a twin-engine jet fighter powered with
the new G.E. increased-thrust J33-GE-5 engines, was approaching its factory rollout date. General Hap Arnold had
convinced Washington that considering the shortage of
strategic metals, the Army Air Force could use a substantial
quantity of primarily wood-construction, small, single-
engine fighter planes. Bell had responded to the bid request
and was awarded the contract to build and test the XP-77
plywood fighter plane. The plane would be powered by an
inverted in-line, air-cooled engine. Bell subcontracted the
wood construction to a furniture manufacturing company. I
also learned that Woolams had been traveling much of the
time. Was there another secret program coming up?

During dinner at home with DeLores and the children, I
told her that the testing at Muroc would soon be completed
and that the future was looking bright at the plant because
of ongoing and new contracts.

I returned to Muroc and completed the testing of the XP-
59A. The aircraft was now being prepared for delivery
to the Air Force. The security classification was reduced to
confidential.

Milo Burcham called to request an XP-59A briefing and a
familiarization flight. He had authorization from Colonel
Boyd. The initial flight of the Lockheed XP-80 was coming
up, and Milo had never flown a jet. I briefed him on operation of the jet engine, the aircraft systems, flight characteristics, and performance. He made three familiarization flights.
"That's the way to go," he said.

Lockheed trucked in the XP-80, a sleek single-engine jet
fighter powered by Halford's H.1B turbojet, a significant improvement over the I-16. Lockheed and Northrop had both
recently constructed experimental test hangars slightly south
of the Bell facility. The pioneer days of the jet airplane at
beautiful remote Muroc Dry Lake were rapidly drawing to a
close.

Early on the morning of the scheduled first flight of the XP-80, busload after busload of political dignitaries and almost every general in the Army Air Force arrived at the northwest end of the lake a short distance from our hangar. Scheduled takeoff time passed. I was afraid Milo was having difficulties. Then I heard the H.1B fire up, and he taxied by on the lake bed in front of our ramp. What a beautiful bird—another product from Kelly Johnson, Lockheed's famed chief design engineer—tricycle gear, very thin wings, and a clearview bubble canopy. Milo gave me the okay sign.

This was the initial flight of America's second jet fighter, and what a flight it was. Milo taxied along in front of the generals and politicians, turned south, and applied full power. I could see the spectators' fingers going in their ears. The smoke and sand were flying as the engine reached full power, and the XP-80 roared down the lake. Milo pulled her off, retracted the gear and flaps, and held her on the deck. Accelerating, he pulled up in a climbing right turn, rolled into a left turn to a north heading, and from an altitude I estimated to be 4,000 feet entered a full-bore dive headed for the buses. He started the pull-up in front of our hangar and was in a 60-degree climb when he passed over the buses doing consecutive aileron rolls at 360 degrees per second up to 10,000 feet. He then rolled over and came screaming back. He shot the place up north and south, east and west, landed, and coasted up in front of the spectators, engine off and winding down. I had never seen a crowd so excited since my barnstorming days. I returned to the office and dictated a wire to Stanley: "Witnessed Lockheed XP-80 initial flight STOP Very impressive STOP Back to the drawing board STOP Signed, Tex." I knew he would understand.

The development of the XP-59A, America's first jet aircraft, was complete, and the test aircraft were delivered to the Army Air Force. I closed our facilities. Numerous employees in love with the desert sought work with West Coast aircraft companies. The others returned to Niagara Falls. I spent my last night on the desert between Pancho's and Juanita's. I had fallen in love with the desert, Antelope Valley, Willow Springs (an old pony Express station), and Red Mountain. I felt I would return.

6

Swept Wings and Rocket Power

En route to Niagara Falls, I stopped in Emporia to see Mother and Dad and DeLores's parents. I had pictures of the XP-59A, but it was difficult for them to comprehend the jet. DeLores's father, a conductor on the Santa Fe, considered the railroad train the ultimate in transportation. But DeLores's mother, Marie, and my mother were airplane enthusiasts, and Dad was almost ready to join them.

Arriving in Kansas City the following afternoon, I located a telephone booth and looked up Dinty Moore, my ticket hawker during barnstorming days, now a captain on Mid Continent Airline. "Tex," Dinty said, "you timed it just right. There's a QB meeting tonight at TWA headquarters on the airport at five p.m." (The Ancient Order of Quiet Birdmen, or QB, is the oldest pilot organization in the world.)

I knew many of the guys at the meeting: Art Goebel from the Inman days; Joe Jacobson from CPT and college days; Otto Inderton, my Department of Commerce friend; Jack Frye, president of TWA (I had given him a briefing at Muroc); and Dr. Brock, world-record holder for flying the most consecutive days and owner of a taper-wing Waco, my favorite open-cockpit biplane. Jack Frye insisted I bring them up to date on the jet airplane. I concluded with "Get ready, boys. The propeller is on its way out."

It was a typical QB wingding, complete with entertainment. Frye cornered me and said, "Come to work for TWA.

We are already planning toward jets. We'll check you out as captain, and you can help us get ready.'' I declined, but after much persuasion and booze I agreed to take a physical at eight the next morning, which I breezed through in spite of the party. I stopped at Jack's office and told him I would let him know when I would be available. I almost told him I wasn't interested but decided to think about it on the way to Niagara Falls.

By the time I was a hundred miles from Kansas City I realized I could never leave engineering test flying; I was sure I couldn't tolerate the airline routine. However, I decided to get a feel for Stanley's attitude. His secretary scheduled me for a 1 p.m. appointment the day following my return. I briefed him concerning the final close-down of the base and the flight of the XP-80.

"Familiarize yourself with the XP-83," he said. "I want you to fly it and present your comments."

"Thanks," I said. "I'm anxious after witnessing Milo's XP-80 flight." Continuing, I said, "I went to QB in Kansas City on the return trip, and Jack Frye wants me to come to TWA. They're already planning for jets."

"Tex, don't you know there's a war going on? We've spent money training you. I'm sorry, I can't release you."

"Bob, I didn't intend to accept. He's a friend, and I was looking for a legitimate reason to decline and retain good relations."

"Why didn't you say so? I have enough problems. Get going on the XP-83. There are necessary changes, and we need data. Also, there's another program we need to discuss. I'll call you."

The XP-83 and I got together three days later. Its configuration was similar to the XP-59A, with a larger airframe, significantly increased power, two J35-GE-5's, and a bubble canopy providing 360-degree pilot visibility. The takeoff and climb performance were significant improvements over the XP-59A, and the 360-degree visibility was excellent. However, there were system and component problems to be solved prior to stability and control and performance testing.

Tragedy

Bell had experienced three fatal accidents over the previous three years, each the result of pilot error. One of the replacements Stanley hired during my tour at Muroc was Bob Borchard, a pilot with minimum previous test experience.

An instrumented P-63 was scheduled for high-altitude, increased-power engine testing. Because of my engine-development work for Allison, when I was on loan from Bell, I was assigned as project pilot. Completing an XP-83 flight in late afternoon, I informed the hangar foreman that because of the late hour and the critical nature of the test, I would fly the P-63 the first flight the next morning.

The accident investigation revealed that after my departure, Borchard informed the hangar foreman that he would fly the P-63 test. He came straight in from 30,000 feet. The excavators found the remains of the twelve-cylinder engine at a depth of 22 feet. When they hoisted those remains from the hole, the only identifiable personal object found was a battered fragment of wristwatch. That devastating accident was the result of poor judgment by two pilots: Stanley, for assigning Borchard, whose professional qualifications were marginal, to an experimental flight test; and Borchard, for attempting a test for which he was not qualified.

Afterward, the Bell Aircraft insurance underwriters insisted that all Bell pilots take a flight physical at the Mayo Clinic in Rochester, Minnesota, every six months instead of on the twelve-month schedule, an unjustified and expensive demand that had no bearing on the cause of the accident.

A study of the engine revealed that detonation had burned holes in the dome of two pistons, resulting in an engine fire that spread to the cockpit. Detonation is the major enemy of highly supercharged reciprocating engines. The phenomenon is the result of pre-ignition (early burning of the fuel mixture during the compression stroke of the piston), caused by the extreme heat of supercharging plus the heat of compression. The extreme heat ignites the fuel mixture before the piston reaches top-dead-center on the compression stroke. The energy of the early explosion therefore works to reverse the direction of rotation of the engine, turning at 3,000 rpm. The intense heat burns through the top of the piston, allowing the high-temperature flame and pressure into the crankcase. The piston connecting rod can also fail, which greatly adds to an already catastrophic condition. The result is a severe engine fire that progresses to the low-pressure area, the cockpit.

High-performance testing of this type should not be attempted without complete technical knowledge of the subject and experience in the operation of highly supercharged engines. Test pilots with experience in high-power engine testing develop a feel, sensing a change in the vibration and sound of the engine at the approach of detonation. An instantaneous power reduction can prevent the catastrophic result.

The Technical Horizon

Stanley and Woolams were seated at the conference table when I arrived the following morning. Stanley said, "The purpose of this meeting is threefold. First, today Larry Bell will announce my escalation to chief engineer, Woolams becomes chief test pilot, and Tex becomes senior experimental test pilot."

Then Stanley went on to number two: "N.A.C.A. has verified by high-speed wind-tunnel testing that captured German data is true: that significantly increased speeds can be achieved prior to wing airflow problems—like you encountered at forty-six thousand feet, Tex—by sweeping the wing thirty-five degrees. Tunnel data also reveal poor low-speed characteristics, namely unsatisfactory stall characteristics. Bell Aircraft has negotiated a contract with N.A.C.A. to modify a P-63 to a thirty-five-degree swept-wing configuration for low-speed flight and stall investigation. To maintain longitudinal balance, an extension of the aft fuselage will be required. The realigned landing gear will be fixed [nonretractable]. Full-span, leading-edge slats developed by N.A.C.A. in three removable sections for each wing will be mounted slightly forward of the wing leading edge to permit flight testing of three spanwise configurations."

Finally, he turned to the subject of a rocket engine discovered by Bob Woods (chief of preliminary design), financed by Wright Field, and developed by Aerojet Corporation. "This is a significant propulsion breakthrough. Woods has sketched a composite airplane design using this new engine. Aerodynamicist Paul Emonds is looking at the aerodynamic considerations, and Ben Hamlin is studying design considerations. The turbojet engine, the swept wing, and the rocket engine will usher in the most significant performance advancement period in the history of aviation. Gentlemen, Bell Aircraft is in an enviable position. Our future depends upon our ingenuity, performance, and integrity."

Two elated airplane drivers departed Stanley's office following our congratulations to the new chief engineer.

Design Decisions

Woolams and I participated in the decision-making process concerning the X-1 cockpit interior configuration, aerodynamic controls, escape system, and design load factor. Given the mission objectives and propulsion system configuration, the airplane was a pilot's dream, the only compromise being the escape system. However, at the altitudes and velocities predicted for the mission, a pilot's odds were probably better inside the cockpit than outside, except in cases of explosion or fire.

Stanley, Woolams, and I endorsed the structural load factor of 18 G, a 100-percent increase over the conventional fighter airplane factor of 9 G. Severe aerodynamic loads were predicted in transonic flight, but their precise nature was unknown, as were loads resulting from uncontrolled return to lower altitudes and increased air density in the event of loss of control due to divergent instability at extreme altitudes.

A Boeing B-29 was selected as the X-1 transport and launch vehicle. Modification of the bomb bay was required to accept the X-1, along with onboard top-off capability of the rocket engine's onboard fuels. Liquid-oxygen, water-alcohol, and high-pressure nitrogen facilities adjacent to the rocket plane's loading pit were planned, scheduled, and constructed at the fledgling Army Air Force Muroc Flight Test Base.

B-29

Another Voice: Benson Hamlin

Tex requested that I provide this previously unpublished story of the design conception of the Bell X-1, a project first secretly considered while I was still senior flight research engineer under Bob Stanley. (It was originally called the XS-1, but the "S" for "supersonic" was later dropped.)

In December 1944, while Bell was still supplying P-63 Kingcobras to Russia via the Ferry Command through Alaska to Siberia, Bob Woods (the short, roly-poly chief of preliminary design at Bell) went fishing for new business at Wright Field. Woods was chitchatting from office to office when he walked into Major Ezra Kotcher's office and learned that Aerojet had a contract to develop a liquid rocket engine with 6,000 pounds of thrust, turbopump-fed using acid-aniline propellants. The problem was its imminent success. "What are we going to do with it?" Kotcher asked.

As the two men talked, they quickly perceived that an airplane powered with this new propulsion system should be able to attain supersonic speeds. Woods agreed that Bell would accept a preliminary design contract for an experimental airplane to "be stable and controllable and capable of at least 800 mph." That guaranteed outrunning the speed of sound, which varies from 762 mph at sea level to 660 mph at 35,000 feet in an N.A.C.A. "standard atmosphere."

As 1945 began, Bob Stanley, the new chief engineer, called on me to become the project engineer for the preliminary design of the supersonic airplane, under Woods. I was given a design that Woods had sketched on the back of an envelope while riding back to Buffalo on the train. It was a conventional midwing arrangement, with a body of revolution without protuberances—no windshield or canopy. The fuselage space below the wing center section was to house the main wheels of a tricycle landing gear. A 1,500-pound thrust turbojet engine (contemporary turbojets exceed 60,000 pounds of thrust) with kerosene fuel for thirty minutes of power was to be used for takeoff and climb to 35,000 feet. Four rocket combustion chambers, clustered around the turbojet tail pipe, would then provide 6,000 pounds of thrust for three minutes to blast the airplane through the sound barrier.

My immediate reaction was that this underpowered turbojet just couldn't hack it. Furthermore, encumbering a rocket airplane with the volume and weight of an air-breathing engine would negate the advantages of rocket propulsion. Nevertheless, I was told to start with that design. So I set in motion a small effort to produce a three-view drawing, a weight-and-balance statement, and the engines' characteristics to provide Paul Emonds, chief of aerodynamics, the basis for performance estimates. The design effort was dead on arrival.

Meanwhile, I had camped in an empty office sixteen hours a day for about five days with my ten-inch log-log decitrig slide rule to find out what kind of performance this rocket engine could produce. Writing a book on the determination of performance by flight testing had given me quite a bit of experience in estimating "paper airplane" performance, so I felt comfortable with the task. Actually, the constant thrust of rocket power, no matter what, was a simplification I'd never before enjoyed. Using step-by-step calculations of half-second intervals from a standing start on the runway to 35,000 feet, I analyzed five "superplane" designs. The calculated performance of my choice of the five designs nearly knocked me out of my chair—60,000 feet per minute rate of climb at altitude.

The calculations convinced me of the feasibility of the X-1. However, the low supply of rocket propellant remaining after climb to altitude would severely limit supersonic research capabilities. From that I concluded that the X-1 should be 100 percent rocket-propelled, launched from a B-29 at 35,000 feet, and have a skid gear for landing to save weight and space useful for tanks and plumbing. Woods responded, "Well, if we're going to design an all-rocket airplane, we should design an all-turbojet to see how they compare."

Although I couldn't understand his bias for turbojets when the contract called for rocket propulsion, I went through a design exercise using G.E.'s TG-180, a turbojet engine then in design stage. The maximum velocity of that configuration was calculated to be 725 mph at sea level, 75 mph shy of the desired 800 mph. We met with G.E.'s designers to ask if they could deliver 50 percent more thrust to attain 800 mph. No dice.

To accumulate information on aerodynamic shock waves and their effect upon aircraft stability and airloads, Paul Emonds and I visited Dr. Clark B. Milliken, professor of aerodynamics at the California Institute of Technology, site of Dr. Theodore Von Karman's advanced research in fluid dynamics. His general guidance was to use sharp shapes in confronting the air and thin following bodies to reduce disturbed airflow.

Another quest took us to the Wright Field armament lab to find out how those designers selected the shape of a .50-caliber bullet, a projectile that had reached 2,491 mph. When we queried them regarding the aerodynamics of bullet shapes, we got blank stares. So I changed the approach and asked if they had experimented with different bullet nose shapes.

"Oh, yes."

"What did you select?"

"An ogive." (Ogive elements are arcs of circles, whereas cone elements are straight lines, we learned.)

"Interesting. How did you conclude that an ogive was the best shape?"

"We fired a variety of bullet shapes from a machine gun held in a vise. The ogive produced the minimum dispersion at the target.'' Paul and I didn't know if that was really the answer we sought, but it was good enough for me.

I'm reminded of the question, Where does a gorilla sleep? The answer is, Anywhere he chooses. Like the gorilla, we returned with a pact to design the X-1 any way we pleased without fear of criticism. We would use an ogive nose—and no windscreen.

On January 24, 1945, the triumvirate of Air Forces, National Advisory Committee for Aeronautics, and Bell Aircraft met at Langley Field in Virginia to review the X-1 project. N.A.C.A. requested provisions for 500 pounds of instrumentation on any given flight, a 10-percent thick wing on one airplane and 8 percent on another (the thinnest wings in those days were 15 percent or 16 percent), an N.A.C.A. laminar-flow 65-110 cambered airfoil section, and a few other items, all fine.

However, my suggestion to go to a landing skid and eliminate the tricycle landing gear to save weight and space provoked a hot tongue and cold shoulder from Bob Woods. After the conference, during a wait at the Old Point Comfort ferry pier to cross Chesapeake Bay to Cape Charles and the train north, Woods told me, "This airplane is going to have a landing gear on it, and one more word from you about it and you will be removed." After that, we didn't talk much during the long trip home. The next day I told Stanley about the disagreement. Stanley agreed with me, and for the next two days we didn't see Larry Bell, Stanley, or Woods as they hashed out the problem in the Ivory Tower, Larry's office. Finally, Stanley came in to tell me that Woods had been moved up to corporate staff and that I henceforth would report directly to him, Stanley. However, the X-1 would have a landing gear. I had lost another battle, or had I? The grand finale was to be the X-2, another Bell supersonic rocket airplane, this time with a swept wing, a nose wheel, and two landing skids.

Years later I learned that Woods had had an ulterior motive. He envisioned converting the X-1 into a supersonic interceptor. That was why he had stubbornly insisted on that landing gear, which was in the wrong place at the wrong time. That must have been the reason for his insistence on the turbojet too. But the X-1 was a research airplane, not a military operational machine.

On to red fuming nitric acid and aniline, which are hypergolic. If the two liquids mix, there is instant combustion. We demonstrated it by taping two small bottles (one containing acid, the other aniline) together and hurling them against the concrete structure of the machine gun butt. Furthermore, Aerojet's development of the turbopump system was lagging. We agonized over a better way to go.

Following a tip from Wright Field, I learned from the Navy that Reaction Motors was developing a rocket engine using liquid oxygen and an alcohol-water mixture. A visit to Pompton Plains, New Jersey, revealed that the Reaction Motors system had no turbopump unit, so propellant tanks had to be pressurized with nitrogen to deliver fuel and oxidizer to the rocket motor thrust chambers at 300 psi. Because of heavier propellant tanks to withstand the pressure, and the additional weight of the high-pressure nitrogen system to pressurize those tanks, the system would be considerably heavier than the Aerojet system. Furthermore, to produce 6,000 pounds of thrust for the same length of time, the alcohol-water rocket engine requires more fuel and oxidizer than the acid-aniline engine does. Despite the weight penalties, we decided to switch engines.

We finally sized and located the nitrogen gas bottles without using the fuselage center section housing the landing gear and instrumentation. There were twelve bottles, including seven small spheres behind the pilot's seat in a ring around the tank head. At 4,500 psi, each was a potential bomb.

Less than three months after the first mention of the study contract, Bell Aircraft submitted a preliminary design proposal to the Air Forces. On March 16, 1945, a contract for the detail design, manufacture, demonstration, and delivery of three airplanes was signed. Airplane number 46-062 was rolled out December 27, 1945, with ballast in place of rocket motors; it was dropped from a B-29 at Pinecastle Field, Florida, on January 25, 1946, for its first glide flight.

The Russians

I was aware that the plant had resident Russian representatives, including a pilot I had not met. Stanley's secretary called and said Mr. Bell was hosting a party for the Russian representatives. I was to represent Flight Test. "Things are looking up," I thought.

I had met Larry Bell one time and recognized him conversing with the Russians when the public relations person escorted me to meet them. During the introductions and handshakes I noted that Colonel Kerchetkoff was about five feet ten inches tall and Major Suprune roughly six feet, and that they both spoke English. Looking the colonel in the eye, I said, "How do you like the P-39?"

Maintaining eye contact, he replied, "It is a good airplane. The armament is strong."

As the cocktail period proceeded, the colonel and major toasted various Bell executives with straight vodka, concluding each drink by holding their empty glasses upside down above their heads. "This could get rough," I thought. However, I could see that Larry Bell was well aware of the situation as he directed the public relations people to announce dinner. When everyone was seated, Colonel Kerchetkoff arose and proposed a toast to Mr. Bell, again bottoms up, with the empty-glass-over-the-head routine. At that moment, I knew how I was going to handle those boys.

Several weeks later, I invited the colonel and the major and production pilot Bob Pierce, a good party man, to cocktails and dinner. I escorted them to McVan's, the oldest dinner club in Buffalo and by far the most famous, its history spanning the violent prohibition era. On arrival I suggested we visit the stand-up bar, a rectangular layout, two sides thirty feet long and two sides twenty feet long, with ten bartenders. Observing the Russians, I was sure they had never seen a bar of this magnitude. "You may order anything you wish. However, I suggest you try my drink."

"Da," they said, "that is good."

I motioned to a bartender I knew and said, "Give us four of your best tequila." He looked at me and, smiling, provided four 3-ounce shot glasses, filling each to the rim. While the Russians were observing the procedure, I licked the area between thumb and index finger of my left hand and deposited a sprinkle of salt on the moist area. As the last jigger was filled, I picked mine up with my right hand and said, "Here's to your annihilation of the Germans." I emptied my jigger, passed the side of my left hand past my lips, and licked off a bit of salt as I held the empty jigger upside down over my head.

The colonel emptied the glass, held it above his head, swallowed a couple of times, and said, "Vhat vas the name of that drink?"

"This is our most popular drink in Texas," I replied, "tequila." I motioned for another round.

After the third round, I was afraid Pierce was going to bust a gut holding a belly laugh, so I suggested we proceed to the table. Our table location was ideal for viewing the floor show. The star was my longtime friend dating back to Ferry Command days, famed fan dancer Sally Rand.

Per my prior arrangement with the maitre d', our tequila glasses were never empty. The steaks and wine were impeccable. Brandy and coffee had just arrived when the floor show began. Kerchetkoff and Suprune, displaying the effects of the tequila, were impressed by the preliminary acts and overwhelmed by the superstar and her backup troupe. It was a professional and talented performance with no hint of vulgarity. I was afraid Kerchetkoff and Suprune would turn the table over in surprise when, as I had prearranged, a waiter placed a chair between them and Sally appeared at our table. I proceeded around the table, received a peck on the cheek from Sally, and introduced her to my guests. That evening cemented a friendship between Kerchetkoff, Suprune, and myself that continued through their tour at Bell.

When dignitaries visited—such as General Arnold, Harry Truman (when he was leading the much-publicized Truman investigating committee), senators, congressmen, and heroes from the war in Europe (for example, the heroes of Bastogne)—I flew flight demonstrations with low-level aerobatics, concluding with a landing out of a loop originating from a low-level pass and gear extension while inverted at the top of the loop.

Kerchetkoff, having witnessed my demonstrations, attempted the upside-down gear extension in a P-39, fortunately at 10,000 feet. He stalled out on top of the loop and ended up in an inverted spin. Not recognizing the inverted spin, he applied normal spin recovery control action, which maintained the condition. He bailed out successfully, landing in a snow-covered field. His Oxford-type shoes had abandoned his feet when the chute opened, and he was forced to walk barefoot in the snow carrying his rolled-up parachute to the nearest road. Hitching a ride, he arrived at the factory with frostbitten feet and wounded pride.

An Air Force Wonder

The spin characteristics of the P-39 were confusing for unobservant pilots. The conventional spin is oscillatory, meaning the nose of the airplane passes through the horizon two times per 360-degree rotation. Conventional spin entry is accomplished at stall speed with full back stick (up elevator) and full rudder in the direction of spin rotation desired. Recovery is achieved by application of full opposite rudder followed by full forward stick. The inverted spin requires full forward stick for spin entry and back stick for recovery. The inverted spin is also oscillatory.

Air Force pilots asserted that the P-39 tumbled, which, of course, was an illusion caused by the aforementioned spin characteristics. After several crashes were attributed to tumbling, Wright Field decided to send a pilot from a P-39 group who would tumble the P-39. We were to equip an airplane with tail and wingtip miniature parachutes, referred to as spin chutes. Bell had used them successfully during spin tests for extreme aft center of gravity.

The tumbling lieutenant arrived in Niagara Falls complaining of a bad head cold and spent ten days at the Niagara Hotel. Wright Field supplied a Lockheed Lodestar photo ship to obtain motion pictures of the tumbling demonstration. The photo airplane flies in the vicinity of the airplane to be photographed, and photographers aboard the photo ship shoot movies from side hatches.

Flying a production airplane, I observed the demonstration, conducted in the vicinity of 10,000 feet. The lieutenant executed an aileron roll, two chandelles, and then pulled up in an attempted Immelmann (half loop concluded with a half roll on top). His speed was too slow to complete the maneuver, and he spun out at the top in an inverted spin, from which he obviously did not know the recovery technique. I followed him down, expecting deployment of the spin chute. I couldn't contact him. The production airplane radio did not have the test frequency. He bailed out at approximately 2,500 feet, and the airplane dug a hole in the New York state real estate. The photo plane cameras recorded the entire incident, including spin entry, pilot bailout, and aircraft impact. The airplane had simply spun in. The photo plane and lieutenant departed for Wright Field.

I briefed Stanley, and he called Wright Field, explaining the inverted spin and probable confusion of the pilot. The project office was skeptical. The following day the project office called and ordered another airplane prepared for test. The office would provide a squadron pilot who would demonstrate both nose-over-tail and wingtip-over-tail tumbling. I suggested we install instrumentation to record the real-time history of elevator and rudder position during the maneuvers. The situation was deteriorating; it was in the best interest of Bell Aircraft and the customer to provide conclusive data.

The precision-tumbling lieutenant and the photo plane arrived. I briefed the lieutenant regarding the spin chutes and the data switches and told him that I would fly a chase plane and, via the test frequency, coordinate the maneuver entries and data on-and-off periods. I also explained the inverted spin entry and recovery techniques, emphasizing that unless he was thoroughly familiar with the oscillatory spinning characteristics of the P-39 it was easy to become confused.

We flew a total of three planned tumbling flights in two days. The airplane was never on its back or in a spin. Some uncoordinated erratic flight maneuvers of no consequence were performed and photographed. The pilot reported that the subject airplane handled differently from the squadron machines and that he couldn't perform the so-called tumbling maneuvers in this airplane. That was probably true, as the Bell service representatives at the squadrons continually reported that squadron maintenance failed to ballast operational P-39's adequately when flown without ammunition load.

Wright Field returned the photo plane to Niagara Falls. I flew the tests, recording real-time data of stalled inverted maneuvers resulting in inverted spins and recoveries. The coordinated photographs and real-time data put the P-39 tumble hoax to bed for good.

Tail Heavy

The L-39 was ready to fly, with extended aft fuselage, nonretractable landing gear, and full-span three-section wing leading edge ''slats'' installed on the 35-degree swept wings.

Woolams conducted the first flight. Immediately following takeoff he experienced a severe longitudinal control problem. When the airplane became airborne, it was extremely tail heavy. With full forward stick (nose-down control), the airplane continued to climb. At 3,000-feet altitude, by reducing power, he was able to achieve level flight, with the stick remaining full forward. However, the airspeed at the reduced power setting was reduced to near stall speed.

With a slight power reduction and full forward stick, he could attain a nose-down attitude and slowly decrease altitude while retaining flying speed. A slight extension of the flaps slightly increased the rate of descent, and he succeeded in landing the airplane. Woolams claimed he was the only pilot in history to take off, climb, fly level, let down, and land with the control stick full forward the entire flight. He was fortunate. Had the center of gravity been farther aft he could not have controlled the airplane in flight.

An error in the aft body extension calculation was the cause of that serious in-flight control problem. The airplane was returned to lay up for additional modification of the aft fuselage.

7

Cobra I and II: The Thompson Trophy

In early 1945, Hitler's forces, seriously depleted by the Battle of the Bulge on the western front, were retreating under the devastating Russian onslaught in the east and the relentless and savage allied offensive in the west. With Germany's surrender on V.E. Day, May 8, 1945, followed by the capitulation of the Japanese empire on September 2, 1945, World World II became history.

The renowned National Air Races, held annually on the Labor Day holiday and discontinued during World War II, were reinitiated. The Thompson Trophy race (sponsored by the Thompson Products Company, the manufacturer of sodium-cooled valves for aircraft engines) was the major closed-course racing event. At the Free-for-All event in 1929, Douglas Davis won in his Travel Air "mystery ship" with a speed of 194.9 mph, a new record, and for the first time in the history of aviation a civilian aircraft had been faster than a military ship in speed competition.

Woolams and I had our eyes on the Thompson Trophy. We knew that below 12,000 feet, the P-39, at 4,000 pounds gross weight and 398 mph, could outperform both the Messerschmitt Bf 109 and the British Spitfire. Our in-depth analysis with Stanley indicated that a modified P-39 could win the Thompson.

In the postwar reduction of the U.S. military aircraft inventory, hundreds of aircraft were declared surplus. Two surplus

P-39's with fewer than fifty flight hours each were purchased for $3,000 and available at Ponca City, Oklahoma. Stanley discussed the matter with Larry Bell, who agreed that Bell Aircraft would cooperate in preparing the two P-39 Airacobras for the race.

Coincidentally, this was an extremely busy period for the Bell flight test organization. Jack Woolams was spending most of his time preparing for the X-1 flight test program at the new and expanding Air Force flight test facility at Muroc Dry Lake. I was monitoring modification of the L-39 configuration, conducting engineering test flights of the XP-83, and participating in flight tests of the Navy remote-controlled F7F twin-engine fighter. Now with the go-ahead to prepare two race airplanes, Jack and I were also involved with engineer Lefty McEuen in the modification of the two surplus P-39's.

Bell provided the hangar space for the preparation plus one engineer and five mechanics for the duration of the program. Woolams and I would participate in financing the operation. Our hangar space was two single-plane production preflight hangars adjacent to the X-1 rocket-engine test facility. Our select airplane race crew consisted of engineer McEuen, Cobra II crew chief Frank "Chick" LaJudice, Cobra I crew chief Art Kregee, six flight-line mechanics, Bell Aircraft structures and systems specialists, and Allison's Bill Wise, engine specialist. Our objectives were maximum weight reduction and maximum power increase.

I contacted my friends at Allison Engine Corporation, briefed them concerning our project, and requested their recommendations for a major increase of engine power. Jack contacted Goodyear Rubber Company regarding minimum-weight fuel cells. McEuen initiated studies on ways to reduce landing gear retraction time and to reduce gross weight.

In the meantime, the delivery date for the X-1 rocket engine slipped. Political pressure for an early flight was intense. A high-level decision to conduct a series of glide flights to investigate flight characteristics and counter the adverse effects of engine delays was announced. The location for the flights was Pinecastle Field in Orlando, Florida, where a 10,000-foot runway was available. Woolams would make flights 1 and 2, and Johnston number 3. With all glide flight plans and support arranged, the X-1 was delivered to Pinecastle in its launch position in the belly of the B-29 launch aircraft.

We had to coordinate the pickup of our surplus P-39's with X-1 activity. A service department representative was dispatched to Ponca City to ground-check the two P-39's. I would pick up one P-39 and fly it to Florida for my X-1 glide flight. A Bell Aircraft service mechanic had selected two excellent airplanes. One was serviced and the preflight inspection complete when I arrived. I loved the P-39. A pilot could slip it on like a glove. "Get ready, babe," I said as I fastened the safety harness. "We're goin' to have a long romance." Envy was apparent at every fuel stop. Everyone was visualizing his own fighter plane.

I arrived at Pinecastle shortly after Jack's second X-1 glide flight and parked the P-39 near the B-29. Jack watched me taxi in and greeted me as I stepped out of the cockpit. "Wait till you fly the X," he said. "She's a fighter pilot's dream." Then, looking at the P-39, he said, "Is the other airplane this nice?"

"They're twins," I replied.

"Hey," he said, "that's it. Let's name them Cobra One and Two."

"I like that," I said. "You're Cobra One."

Cobra I and II Modifications

My X-1 glide flight was postponed indefinitely when Wright Field ordered the X-1 to Dayton for high-level inspection and review. The next day, I fired up Cobra II and departed Pinecastle for Mustin Field in Philadelphia to confer with Commander Herbst, director of the Navy F7F remote-control program.

Herbst said the Navy high command had requested a flight demonstration of the remote-controlled F7F without a safety pilot aboard. I agreed to coordinate a flight demonstration date with the Bell F7F program engineers upon my return to Niagara Falls. That Navy program was one of several activities that proceeded concurrently with our preparations for the Thompson Trophy race.

Following a late evening with Navy friends at Mustin Field Officers' Club, I arrived at home base with Cobra II ready for the modification destined to put her in the history books. Lefty McEuen reported that Allison and Goodyear engineers were arriving in two days to discuss their recommendations for the modifications. Woolams, involved with the X-1 conference in Dayton, agreed by telephone that we should proceed with the conference.

The meeting convened with the entire Bell race-airplane organization present except Woolams. Allison engineer Bill Wise presented the Allison Company recommendations: install an increased-diameter supercharger impeller, install undersized pistons, increase the maximum engine speed from 3,000 to 3,200 rpm, and increase the inlet area of the engine carburetor air scoop. Those changes would increase the engine manifold pressure from 75 inches to 86 inches of mercury, increasing the power rating to 2,000 horsepower. The power increase required replacing the P-39 three-blade propeller with the increased-diameter, four-blade King Cobra (P-63) propeller. To suppress detonation at that high power, a continuous water-alcohol solution would have to be supplied commencing at 57 inches of mercury. Assuming the entire 300-mile race would be flown at full throttle, we needed 85 gallons of water-alcohol solution.

"With two thousand horsepower and a four-thousand-pound airplane, we calculate a speed of four hundred twenty-five miles per hour," commented Lefty McEuen. "These numbers significantly exceed the P-51 numbers we recorded during the stability and performance tests."

"Any other changes we can make to increase engine power?" I asked.

"Yeah," Wise said, "we can increase the blower speed and reach one hundred six inches of mercury; however, the resulting temperatures are severe and affect reliability to some degree."

The Goodyear representative produced a sample of material from his briefcase and said, "This is our new ultralight fuel-cell material, trade name Ply-A-Cell. It's tough, very flexible as you can see, and is impervious to high-octane fuel and oil."

"Will high G loads present any problems?" I asked.

P-51

"We plan a lightweight insulation protection against protrusions and abrasions. You will also realize a ten-percent fuel-capacity increase."

"Thank you, gentlemen," I said. "You will hear from us soon."

After the departure of the Allison and Goodyear representatives, Lefty presented suggested weight reductions and system modifications, saying, "A structural study reveals we can reduce the landing gear retraction time from twenty-two seconds to four seconds." The suggested modifications were: (1) Increase the strength of the landing gear retraction torque tubes and increase the electrical power to the drive motor. (2) Install manually operated landing gear up-locks to assure the wheel fairings will not protrude in high air and G loads. The landing gear will require manual extension due to severe gear chatter during powered extension. (3) Remove the pilot-operated aileron and rudder trim tabs and install fixed-position trim tabs. (4) Remove all armament and structural attachments. (5) Remove all armor plating, cabin-door retractable windows and mechanisms, and install fixed-position Plexiglas windows. (6) Remove all gyro instruments. (7) Install accelerometer. (8) Install quick-detachable radio and external antenna. (9) Remove wing Pitot tube and install in propeller hub, giving a position error of zero for indicated airspeed and helping to keep the center of gravity forward. (10) Construct and install an 85-gallon water-alcohol tank in nose section. (11) Add one P-40 coolant radiator in a streamlined fairing on the belly of the aircraft to augment the engine cooling system.

Stanley and I approved the recommendations, Woolams agreed by telephone, and Cobra II entered modification. Woolams picked up Cobra I at Ponca City, and both airplanes were in rework. Allison was modifying four engines, and Goodyear was manufacturing the lightweight fuel cells.

Two of a Kind

Modification of Cobras I and II was nearing completion. The reworked super Allison engines and four-blade propellers were installed. Stops were installed on the nose gear shock struts to restrict shock strut travel, preventing the increased-diameter four-blade propellers from striking the ground during maximum engine power ground operation. With the ship on jacks, the four-second landing gear retraction time was gratifying. Every available pound of airframe weight had been eliminated. The Pitot tube (airspeed pressure sensor) extending four feet in front of the hollow propeller hub provided true airspeed information and a streamlined appearance. The 85-gallon alcohol-water tank was in place in the nose section.

The first flight was a revelation. It was a different airplane. Full right rudder was required the first 100 feet of the takeoff roll to combat the pronounced left-propeller torque, the result of the increased power. The four-second landing-gear retraction shook the airplane when it hit the up stops and the airplane was climbing at a 60-degree angle. The engine power increase was gratifying. I noted the slightly low engine-coolant temperature; the added coolant radiator was doing its job. The engine was smooth at the increased maximum of 3,200 rpm. The water injection cut in at 57 inches of mercury, and at full throttle I was looking at 86 inches of engine intake manifold pressure, the highest manifold pressure yet achieved in a reciprocating engine. I passed over the airport at 415 mph and climbed straight up to 10,000 feet. The performance was awesome.

I was delighted with Cobra II as I taxied toward the hangar and noted that the ramp was crowded with spectators. I had forgotten it was lunch hour. The ground crew said they could hear the never-before-heard roar of the super engine before the airplane was visible. During preparation testing of Cobras I and II, the population of Niagara Falls and the surrounding area came to recognize the impressive sound of those two 2,000-horsepower Allisons. The local press continually reported our race preparations, speculating on the performance. The Cobras' high-speed performance, however, was a total secret until I qualified for pole position at Cleveland.

Considerable oil was being discharged from the engine oil tank breather vent, streaking the aft fuselage. Art Kregee and the Allison representative determined that at the high engine powers the blow-by due to the undersized pistons was resulting in severe aeration (foaming) of the engine lubrication oil. Flight tests resulted in the installation of two oil-air separators in the engine-to-oiltank return line. Cobra I and II were both nearing race configuration.

Conditions were perfect: It was 8:30 a.m., zero wind, no turbulance, temperature 76 degrees Fahrenheit. I was 100 yards off the south shore of Lake Ontario, 30 miles east of old Fort Niagara, 100 feet above the water, heading west, 3,200 rpm, 86 inches of mercury. The airspeed needle was approaching 420 mph, all conditions normal.

As the needle reached 422 mph the stick instantly jerked forward out of my relaxed hand. Instinctively, I grabbed for the stick, just as I felt the pressure of the seat belt from the pitch-over. I caught the stick in the curve of my wrist and hand and hauled back, simultaneously snapping the throttle closed. I was in a steep climb. Glancing at the recording accelerometer, I saw the needle recording a 9.2-G load during the pullup. The stick was vibrating slightly, and the elevator control response was significantly reduced. I was in level flight at 7,000 feet. It was obvious there was a problem with the elevators (the longitudinal control). Calling the tower, I reported my location and altitude. Extending the gear and flaps and reducing speed, I determined I could not control the airplane longitudinally below 140 mph, 35 mph above normal touchdown speed. No problem. I would fly her on the deck at 140 and retract the flaps to get more weight on the wheels for braking. No sweat.

The crew couldn't believe their eyes. The left elevator was missing. There were a few small pieces of fabric clinging to the elevator hinge line and the frazzled end of the broken trim tab cable. It was a classic case of trim tab flutter. Similar to an explosion, it had instantaneously disintegrated the left elevator. Fortunately, there was only one elevator trim tab, left elevator only.

All the P-39 control surfaces—ailerons, rudder, and elevators—were fabric covered. The airplane had always been criticized for the significant longitudinal trim changes with speed. This incident solved the problem. The postflight conference with Lefty, Stanley, Paul Emonds, Woolams, and myself concluded with the decision to remove the elevator trim systems (the rudder and aileron systems had been removed for weight savings); use metal skin for the ailerons, rudder, and elevators; and install fixed trim tabs, manually adjustable on the ground. One flight, and permanent aileron, rudder, and elevator trim was established. The total longitudinal control stick pressure change from 120 mph to 425 mph was now only five pounds. The cause of the excessive elevator trim had been increased ballooning of the fabric-covered elevators with speed increases.

Cleveland

Cobra I and II were ready for Cleveland. Woolams made a deal with Mobil Oil to provide 140-grade aviation fuel and water-alcohol solution for the time trials and Thompson Trophy race in exchange for advertising. Woolams and I arranged for ramp space and access to shop and hangar space, if required. The crew drove to Cleveland and were set up when I arrived with Cobra II.

Tony LeVier, Lockheed chief test pilot, was there in his specially equipped P-38; George Welch, North American chief test pilot, in his company-prepared P-51; Forest Tucker, Northrop test pilot, in his clipped-wing P-63. Art Chester, Steve Whitman and Cook Cleland, Howard Lilly, Howard Pemberton, Earl Ortman, Bruce Raymond, Woody Edmondson, William Newhall, Bill Ong, and Dale Fulton were flying their respective P-63's, P-51's, and Corsairs. As I anticipated, my buddies, now competitors, glanced at Cobra II, shook their heads, and walked away. I don't believe any of the competition had significant flight time, if any, in a P-39, but they considered themselves well informed by military hearsay. The punchline occurred when DeLores arrived the following day.

Corsair F4U

Woolams and Cobra I appeared the same afternoon. Jack and I arrived at the hotel and agreed to meet in my room after he freshened up. Opening the door, I saw DeLores sitting in a chair with a dejected look on her face. "What happened to you?" I said.

"While awaiting my key at the desk," she said, "a group

of men, some pilots I recognized, were discussing the race airplanes." She paused.

"Go ahead," I said. "What did they say?"

"One of them said, 'Did you see that clipped-wing P-63 of Tucker's? He's a cinch to win.' Another said, 'What does Tex think he can do in that P-39?' 'Yeah, Woolams also,' another one agreed. What are you going to do?" she asked.

"Win the damn race," I said, laughing. "They don't know what they're talking about. That clipped-wing 63 is slower now than it was, the drag of those hacked-off wings is awful, and I wouldn't taxi it, let alone fly it. He removed the self-sealing fuel cells and tried to make an integral fuel tank of the wing by sloshing sealer inside the wing. Fuel drips out of it twenty-four hours a day. But the important thing is, not a one of them knows anything about a P-39. Forget about those guys. The only competition is that North American P-51, but we will beat the hell out of Welch also."

"You sure?"

"Damn right I'm sure. I've flown every type airplane out there. I know what the score is. You know we laid out an exact duplicate of this race course at the Falls. I've flown that course at full throttle ten laps, three hundred miles. The only way we can lose is by engine failure, and that Allison loves it. Why don't you hunt those jokers up and bet them. They'd give you two- or three-to-one odds."

While I was building a drink, DeLores answered the door. It was Woolams. As he entered the room, she said, "Jack, take those pants off."

"Damn, DeLores." He was laughing so he could hardly speak. "This is awful sudden."

"Jack Woolams, I'm not going out to dinner with you in those wrinkled pants. Why didn't you keep the parachute on; they wouldn't look so bad." Jack and I had a Scotch while she, on the floor with her travel iron and a bath-towel pad, pressed his trousers.

The racecourse was a parallelogram, with two 5-mile legs, two 10-mile legs, two 75-degree turns, and two 105-degree turns. A tethered barrage balloon marked each of three pylons. The start and finish pylon by the observation bleachers was a tall slender triangle displaying the Bendix logo on each side. On our course at the Falls, I had flown timed laps pulling 2-G, 4-G, and 6-G turns. The 4-G laps were the quickest. The larger diameter 2-G turns increased the mileage and proportionally decreased lap speed. The speed decay during the 6-G turns also resulted in lower average speed.

Chick LaJudice, my crew chief, was with me during an increased-power engine-testing program I had flown for Allison and was a wizard at mixing the water, ethyl, and methyl alcohol injection fluid. The extremely high engine power we were employing required precise measurement of the water-alcohol mixture. Mobil had furnished its commercial water-alcohol product, but I refused to use it and was present when Chick mixed Cobra II's antidetonation mixture. We also had an antifoam fluid that Chick added with an eye dropper to the fresh oil before each high-power flight. When cowling, inspection doors, carburetor air and coolant radiator duct plugs were removed and reinstalled, nonremovable seals were applied, the result of my conversations with Paul Mantz, Roscoe Turner, Joe Jacobson, and Pancho Barnes regarding sabotage over the years in both the Bendix and Thompson races.

Qualifying

I was number one, Woolams number two, for the two-lap qualifying runs the following morning to determine our position in the fifteen-abreast race-horse starting lineup. I spoke to Roger Kann, official air-race timer, and agreed to fly one warm-up lap and two qualifying laps. The race finish line was directly in front of the timer's station in a small area of the first and second rows of bleacher seats.

The airspeed indicated 420 mph, altitude 60 feet, as I crossed the start line for the first qualifying lap, simultaneously triggering my stopwatch, 425 mph at the start of the second lap, and 425 mph when I crossed the finish line and stopped the watch. I throttled back to 90-percent power and leisurely flew another lap and landed. Using the stopwatch time and the two-lap mileage of 60 miles, I came up with an average 408.5 mph. Cobra II was functioning perfectly.

Completing the two qualifying laps, Woolams landed and

taxied to Cobra II. With Cobra I's engine at idle, he opened the door and motioned me up on the wing and shouted in my ear, "I had severe detonation. I'm returning to the Falls to change engines tonight. Tell Kann I had detonation, to scratch those runs. I'll qualify tomorrow p.m. with a new engine. See you at noon tomorrow." We shook hands, and as I climbed off the wing, he slammed the cockpit door and taxied away. The timing crew had departed. I would catch Kann in the morning.

Before going to dinner, I was scanning the Cleveland evening paper, the *Plain Dealer*. Suddenly I jumped out of the chair. Startled, DeLores cried, "What's the matter?"

"That sorry S.O.B. Roger Kann screwed up my qualifying time. Three hundred eighty-two miles per hour this paper says." I called the hotel desk. "Get me Roger Kann. He's registered here. This is an emergency."

Following a delay, "Sorry, sir, there is no answer in Mr. Kann's room."

"Page him in the lobby, bar, and dining room," I replied.

"That will require some time, Mr. Johnston. I'll call you." Ten minutes later the phone rang. "I'm sorry, Sir, Mr. Kann does not answer the page."

I was on the phone at 6:30 the next morning. Kann was still in bed. Following my statements, he said, "Meet me at the timer station. We will check yesterday's data." I'm sure he didn't go back to sleep.

I was waiting when he and his crew arrived. He scanned the timer data, and it was obvious they had used the times of the last two laps of the four laps flown. They calculated the average speed for the second and third designated qualifying laps and came up with 409 mph, only half a mile per hour different from my stopwatch time, which gave me pole position, placing Welch and his P-51 in the number two position. Woolams was number three, which I thought was good, considering that he had been running at significantly reduced power. I thanked Kann and apologized for my early-morning comments. He said, "I don't blame you. I'd be pissed off too."

I explained Woolams's problem, and he said, "Okay, if that's what he wants, but third ain't too bad."

Roger Kann informed the newspaper of the timing error, and

the evening paper carried the story, including the qualifying-position correction: Cobra II and Johnston number one position, P-51 and Welch number two.

Catastrophe

It was midday. I was helping the crew wax Cobra II. An airport guard arrived by official car looking for Tex Johnston. I identified myself. "There is a long-distance call. I'll drive you to the office."

I recognized the voice that answered my hello. It was Larry Bell. "Tex," he said, "we lost Jack this morning."

We were both silent for a moment, and I said, "How? What happened?"

Silence, then, "He crashed in Lake Ontario. Divers haven't located the airplane yet. Tex, we don't want you to fly the race."

I was silent for a moment, my mind racing. "Larry," I said.

"Yes," he replied.

"I'm devastated. Jack was my dear friend, but I must say, I know this airplane. There is nothing wrong with it. I'm going to fly the race. In fact, that's what Jack would do if it was the other way around."

Silence, then, "Tex, I must order you not to fly."

With no hesitation, I replied, "I don't want to, but you leave no alternative. I herewith resign from Bell Aircraft, and I'm going to win this race," and hung up.

Two hours later it was Larry on the phone again. "Tex," he said, "we don't want you to resign. Stanley suspects a structural failure in the aft fuselage. He is bringing material, tools, and personnel and will add reinforcement to the aft fuselage. They will arrive in the Beechcraft."

The Thompson Trophy

It was a renowned crew: chief engineer Stanley, vice president and director of the helicopter division Dave Foreman, a structure man, and two mechanics. They worked all night and scabbed on four aft fuselage reinforcements and spray-painted them to match; they were almost undetectable.

The whole crew was depressed. I called them together and laid it on the line. "We have suffered a great loss, but draggin' ass ain't going to do a bit of good, and someone is apt to make a mistake. There's no room for mistakes in this game. If anyone screws up, I'm going to be the roughest S.O.B. you've ever seen. I want the fuel tanks full and caps secured when I start the engine to taxi out and a man on each wing with a five-gallon can of fuel to top the tanks off when I shut her down on the starting line and check and double-check the tank filler caps. Chick, is she full of new oil?"

"Yes, sir, and I measured it as I filled the tank. It took the full twenty gallons, and the antifoam drops are in and the coolant system is full."

"How about the battery?"

"It's at full charge. So is the spare, and it will be at the start line with a jumper cable."

"Chick, carefully check the tires for slashes, tacks, smallhead nails. We can't tolerate a flat. And check the engine air scoop and coolant ducts for any foreign objects. What about the water-alcohol? Detonation is our vital enemy."

"Eighty-five gallons, full to the cap. I mixed it this morning."

"I want two men, awake, with the airplane all night tonight."

Chick said, "Kregee and I will be here; we'll alternate."

It was one hour till race time when I convened the next race-crew meeting beside Cobra II. "Kregee," I said, "how's the engine?"

"I checked all control linkage, fuel, oil, and coolant lines and clamps; no leaks and every item safety wired."

"Okay, boys, you're half of this team. You give me a perfect airplane, and I'll give you that Thompson Trophy. Let's get set. It's almost race time. And don't allow one S.O.B. near Cobra II. She's going in the history books today."

When we taxied to the starting line, Chick and Kregee were perched on each wing leading edge, each with five gallons of 140-octane fuel in his lap. They were dedicated men, the best in their business.

Welch was parked in a number two position on the race-horse start line, headed straight for the number one pylon. I taxied into number one position and parked at a 45-degree angle headed toward Welch's takeoff path and shut the engine down. He jumped out of the cockpit, ran over, jumped up on the wing of Cobra II. My cockpit door was open. He was hot. "What the hell you doin'? Don't you know where the damn pylon is?"

"Don't worry, Wheaties," I said. (Wheaties was his nickname.) "I'll be flyin' with the gear up while you're still trying to get off the deck." With a big smile, I added, "I don't want to wear my right brake out; the torque from this two-thousand-horsepower engine will pull her around right on course." Losing my smile, I said, "You fly your airplane, I'll fly mine."

"Go to hell," he said, and stomped back to his bird.

Fourteen modified World War II fighters were lined up, wingtip to wingtip, awaiting the start-engine flag. The flagman was on location ahead and to the left, visible to all the pilots, the start-engine flag held high. The flag dropped and fifteen engines roared to life (LeVier's P-38 was twin-engine). Following three minutes of warm-up time, the flagman held the start flag high, the signal for takeoff power.

With the throttle full forward, brakes full on, I glanced at the manifold pressure, 83 inches of mercury. When the start flag started down, I released both brakes, Cobra II leaped forward, the nose swung left. I could feel the rudder become effective as the speed increased. A glance at the airspeed, 90 mph, slight back pressure on the stick, the nose came up, and as I felt the wheels leave the ground, I actuated the gear up switch, simultaneously increasing the climb angle to maintain 105 mph. Four seconds after I tripped the gear up switch, I felt the gear hit the up stops and pushed the nose down.

The altimeter indicated 300 feet as I entered a shallow dive and flashed by the first pylon at 100 feet altitude, indicating 340 mph, and picked up the heading for the number two pylon. Taking a quick look behind, I saw Welch was 200 yards behind and to the right, LeVier behind Welch.

Before race time, I cut ten narrow strips of adhesive tape and adhered them one-half inch apart on the lower edge of the instrument panel. Each pass in front of the timing officials, I removed one strip of tape to count the laps.

On my second look aft, I could see LeVier's P-38 but not the P-51. After the race, I learned the P-51 engine had overheated and blew the expansion tank. Welch fortunately was able to return to the airport.

That ol' Allison was smooth as silk, intake manifold pressure 86 inches of mercury, rpm 3,200. During the second lap the cockpit temperature began to increase as the entire engine reached best operating temperature, 180 degrees Fahrenheit. The air from the engine compartment traveled forward to the cockpit. Aware of the high-temperature condition, I was wearing no shirt, only my leather flight jacket (initial protection in case of fire). By the fourth lap it was well soaked with sweat.

Checking the back course following pylon turns, I could see LeVier in number two position but a bit farther behind on each lap. Cobra II's super engine operated at 86 inches of mercury and 3,200 rpm the entire race, and we took each pylon turn at 4 G. It was beautiful. Cobra II lapped competitors on the ninth and tenth lap. We were overtaking the third one, a P-63, as we approached the fourth pylon on the tenth and final lap.

The air race rules state that when lapping a competitor the overtaking airplane must pass on the right, unless the overtaken airplane is off course. The P-63 was flying a significantly looser course (farther from the pylons) than Cobra II. As the fickle finger of fate determined, I overtook him on the final pylon turn onto the homestretch. It had to be a snap decision. If I passed him on the right (outside) at 425 mph, I would be a quarter of a mile wide on the homestretch course to the finish line. There was only one answer, he was off course. I held my course heading at 100 feet altitude, laid her in a vertical 4.5-G, 90-degree turn between the P-63 and the pylon, rolled back to level flight, and flashed over the finish line and checkered flag at 430 mph at 50 feet altitude.

As I rounded the number one pylon and entered the victory lap I peeled the final strip of tape from the instrument panel. I concluded the full-power victory lap with a 50-feet-off-the-deck, 430-mph pass in front of the stands and a 60-degree climbing slow roll. The final event and feature of the 1946 National Air Races, the 1946 Thompson Trophy race, became history.

Cobra II and Tex Johnston had established a new world speed record for closed-course air racing: 373.908 mph, an increase of 90 mph over the previous record, established by my good friend Roscoe Turner, one of the first to greet me at the postrace festivities.

Fred Crawford, president and chief executive of the Thompson Products Company, presented me with the coveted Thompson Trophy. Another company representative presented the Allegheny Luddlum Cup for establishing a new world speed record. Roscoe Turner and industry, city, and state dignitaries graced the award ceremonies.

The Thompson Trophy victory was the culmination of the expertise and dedication of individuals and organizations. Unfortunately, it was overshadowed by the tragic and untimely death of Jack Woolams. Cobra I and II were identical twins, and my race-speed numbers indicated we would have achieved our goal of winning first and second. Jack and I were close friends but also competitors in the cockpit. It would have been a great race.

Cobra I was recovered from Lake Ontario. The examination of the destroyed airplane suggested the windshield may have blown in, decapitating the pilot.

DeLores and I received a message to call Larry Bell at his suite. In spite of his deep sorrow, he was proud and elated over the success of his P-39 and invited us to a victory dinner. During cocktails, I briefed Larry concerning our prerace activities and details of the race. The dining room was overflowing with pilots and crews, with the festivities in full swing. There was a constant flow of industry and personal friends expressing condolences for Jack and congratulations to Larry and myself. That evening was my first experience with the varying degrees of sorrow that frequently accompany success.

8

Remote Control and Swept-wing Tests

Bell Aircraft had successfully developed electronic-control equipment for remotely controlling aircraft in flight from a ground station and by a mother airplane flying in formation with the drone (remotely controlled airplane). Together with my other activities, I was program coordinator and remote-control pilot on a Navy remote-control Grumman F7F twin-engine shipboard fighter program. The mother airplane was a Grumman F6F single-engine shipboard fighter.

The ground equipment consisted of a military utility trailer with two remote-control stations, each equipped with electronic controls to fly the drone, one station on the roof for visual control and one inside the trailer, where an F7F on-board instrument panel was displayed on a television screen, allowing the remote-control pilot to fly the drone by observing the flight instruments.

A date was established for the remote-controlled demonstration. Slick Goodlin and Joe Cannon flew the F6F and F7F to the Cherry Point Navy-Marine air base. Our ground crew's transportation was a surplus Cadillac funeral hearse. When we arrived at Cherry Point with the remote-controlled aircraft and the hearse, the military personnel (for some unknown reason) dubbed our operation the Bell Flying Circus.

F6F

Successful Failure

The electronic equipment was stabilized at operating temperatures. The remote-control truck was in position thirty feet to the side of the approach end of the live runway, and Cherry Point Base was closed to all aircraft. The array of Navy brass, political and technical representatives, and press were assembled in the designated area. Goodlin in the F6F mother ship was in flight, prepared to accept control of the F7F after takeoff. I was in the remote controller's chair atop the control truck. Cannon was in the cockpit of the F7F in takeoff position on the runway adjacent to the control truck. I proceeded to coordinate an F7F airplane and electronic control checkout. "Remote brakes on. Clear the cockpit and secure canopy."

"Brakes on, clearing cockpit," Cannon replied, and climbed out of the cockpit. Astride the fuselage, he actuated the close-canopy switch. (The turning propellers on each side of the cockpit prevented standard deplaning over the left side.) A stepladder secured by a mechanic at the intersection of the wing trailing edge and the body provided a departure route.

F6F from Control: "Ready for takeoff."

Control from F6F: "In position for pickup."

I slowly advanced both throttles to full throttle. The TV-screen observers on interphone said, "Temperature and pressure's okay. Clear for takeoff."

I pressed the brake-release switch, and the airplane sped down the runway. I maintained accurate takeoff heading by alternate left and right braking until the speed increased and the flight controls became effective. Utilizing the miniature control stick mounted on the swivel-control chair arm, I applied up elevator, and the F7F was airborne. I actuated the landing gear up switch, and the gear retracted as the mother ship moved into formation position. "Control transfer on the count of three. One, two, three."

"I have control," Goodlin said from the F6F.

Flying formation with the F7F, the mother ship proceeded to climb to 12,000 feet while circling the base to remain in view of the spectators. I descended to the control position inside the trailer. The F7F instruments displayed on the TV screen showed all temperatures and pressures in the green.

F6F: "Twelve thousand feet, airspeed two hundred sixty-five knots, southeast of base, ready for dive, three hundred sixty–degree heading."

Control: "I have control. All systems go. Full throttle, entering dive."

The dive angle and airspeed were increasing. I stabilized the dive angle at 65 degrees. The altimeter was unwinding through 9,000 feet, airspeed 340 knots, and I beeped in a slight roll correction, airspeed 390 knots, altitude 6,500 feet, airspeed 450 knots. Back on the miniature stick, the accelerometer began increasing—2 G, 3 G—heading 360 degrees, airspeed 460 knots (target speed)—4 G, 5 G, 6 G—airspeed 410 knots—7 G, 8 G, 9 G—airspeed 400 knots, and forward on the stick, altitude 6,000 feet, climb angle 45 degrees, heading 360 degrees, cruise power, airspeed 240 knots, level flight altitude 9,000 feet.

Control to F6F: "In position?"

F6F: "Affirmative."

Control: "You have control."

F6F: "Control normal. Beautiful dive."

Control: "Going topside. Set her up for the fly-by."

F6F: "Roger."

As I appeared from the trailer, the crew was jubilant. "It was beautiful. Just east of the base you could see the entire dive and the wingtip streamers on the pullout," they said.

In position atop the trailer, I took control of the F7F southeast of the base. The F6F was to orbit west of the base. Applying full throttle, I flew the airplane on a 360-degree heading slightly east of the runway in a shallow dive to 200 feet, established a 40-degree climb, and executed three consecutive left aileron rolls, reestablished level flight, reduced power, and returned control to the F6F for the landing approach.

On the downwind leg the F6F called, "Gear coming down," then added, "No gear extension."

I had the airplane in sight. No landing gear had appeared. I called the F6F. "Give me control. I will try my gear control on the count of three. One, two, three." Nothing happened.

Control to F6F: "Climb the F7F to six thousand feet and do several pushovers. Maybe that nine-G pullout jammed something up."

F6F: "I have control."

I called the observation area and informed them of our problem and told them to stand by. If necessary, we would execute a belly landing. I also notified the control tower to have the crash truck and fire crew stand by.

The negative G maneuvers failed to correct the problem. After notifying the control tower and observation area, I called the F6F: "Put the F7F on final approach."

It was tough flying that beautiful airplane down final approach with the gear up. Flaps down, I eased her onto the center of the runway. The props struck the runway simultaneously, and the airplane slid straight ahead, then turned ten degrees right and stopped on the runway. No fire. Then the tragedy occurred. The fire truck, traveling at high speed, turned from the taxi strip onto the runway and rolled, killing two firemen.

When the crew opened the F7F canopy they immediately identified the cause of the gear-extension failure. The cockpit floor was covered with an inch of hydraulic fluid. A high-pressure landing-gear hydraulic line routed across the cockpit floor under the pilot's seat had ruptured, depleting the hydraulic-system fluid.

The statement released by the Navy officials was: "The remote control of an unmanned operational F7F fighter was impressive and successful, demonstrating a military potential. The mechanical failure of the hydraulic system was unfortunate but not associated with the purpose of the flight demonstration."

The 35-Degree Answer

The Thompson win was sweet, the loss of my dear friend bitter and sad.

The L-39 rework was complete. Jack and I had concluded from the captured German data that the 35-degree swept wing was the next aerodynamic step to increase the airplane's high-speed performance. The combination of jet power and the swept wing would affect the industry more than anything else in the history of flight. I climbed in the L-39 cockpit and fastened the safety belt and shoulder harness as I said, "I'm sure you'll be aboard, Big J (my name for Jack Woolams). Let's see what she'll do."

The first flight objectives after the modification were twofold, to investigate the longitudinal control and stability and, second, to obtain low-speed and stall data with full-span wing slats. A check of the elevator position as the airplane became airborne showed that the problem with center of gravity and longitudinal control was corrected. Climbing to 10,000 feet, I conducted a stall investigation, including stall during turns. The stall and recovery characteristics were identical to the straight-wing P-63.

Flight number two, with the inboard section of the slats removed, was also satisfactory.

The third flight, with outboard slats only, exhibited a slight deterioration in stall warning characteristics and a slight roll tendency at the stall, though that was easily controlled.

Flight four, with all slats removed, was a challenge. During takeoff I held the airplane on the ground until the airspeed exceeded the stall speed by 20 mph and applied slight back pressure on the control stick; the aircraft rotated and became airborne. All control was normal throughout the climb to 10,000 feet. In a 25-degree angle climb I slowly closed the throttle, increasing up elevator (pulling control stick aft) to keep the nose 25 degrees above the horizon. The airspeed decreased as the power moved to idle. I felt a slight tremor (stall warning), and instantaneously the plane rolled to an almost inverted position.

On the next stall I watched the flow pattern of the tufts. As the airspeed decreased, the outboard tufts pointed more spanwise and a fraction of a second before the slight stall warning, the wingtip tufts on the outboard three feet of the wing stood almost vertically and were fluttering. This condition is referred to as tip stall and results in violent rolling movements, the direction of the roll being a function of a slight right or left yaw. I repeated the condition several times, recording altitude, stall warning and stall speeds, altitude change, and altitude loss during stall and recovery. I also obtained motion pictures of the tuft action during deceleration, stall approach, complete stall, and stall recovery. The camera operated by actuating the cannon trigger on the control stick. The studies were a real challenge. I attempted unsuccessfully on several flights to anticipate the direction of roll and prevent the near or complete inverted condition.

Those tests provided the solution to the undesirable stall characteristics of the 35-degree swept wing: leading-edge slats on the outboard third of the wing. N.A.C.A. at Langley Field distributed the data throughout the industry, clearing the way for incorporation of the 35-degree swept wing on future aircraft.

9

The X-1

"Go in. They're waiting," Larry Bell's secretary Irene Jacobs said as she opened the office door.

"Come in," Larry Bell said, gesturing me to a chair beside Stanley. "Tex," he said, "your work at Bell has been very satisfactory. Bob and I believe you can handle the chief test pilot job."

"Thank you," I replied. I had wondered why I had been called to Larry's office. Now I had the feeling there was a problem.

"Your salary is increased to twelve thousand dollars per year."

"Thank you," I replied.

"Tex, the loss of Woolams reduces our experimental test pilot experience. You are the best qualified, however. As chief test pilot you are responsible for all Bell Aircraft fixed-wing test activity. We believe we should assign another pilot for the X-1. Stanley suggests Goodlin."

Stanley, before he became Chief Engineer, had moved Goodlin to Experimental on a trial basis. Goodlin had been a satisfactory production pilot but was handicapped, in my opinion, by insufficient technical education for Experimental Test.

"Goodlin is a good stick-and-rudder pilot," I said, "but limited by his minimal technical knowledge."

Woolams and I were both prepared to fly the X-1. I suggested that under the circumstances, with my technical background, piloting experience, longevity with the company, plus the significance of the program to the company, I should test the airplane.

The final decision was: The program was under my supervision. If I questioned program progress or test data, I would fly the airplane. It was a bad decision that Larry would regret.

Reaction Motor's rocket-engine development was complete. The four-combustion-chamber rocket motor cluster was installed in the X-1 and test-fired at the Bell rocket engine test facility. I flew a company P-63 to the Air Corps's expanding Muroc test base to check final preparations for the arrival of the X-1. The X-1 would be ferried to Muroc in the B-29 launch airplane.

X-1

There were now two high-bay steel and concrete hangars, concrete ramp areas, and a 15,000-foot runway joining the southwestern edge of the lake bed. The X-1 fueling and loading facilities were complete and in final checkout. The railroad spur for delivery of rocket fuel was complete and functional. Adobe-constructed family housing was available at Willow Springs. Also, a minimum number of rentals were available at Rosamond. An evening at Pancho's, and it was evident the military had discovered the place. Nothing had changed except the number of customers.

In Niagara Falls, Goodlin had completed his briefing by engineering and learned the rocket engine operation technique at the rocket test facility with the X-1 on tiedown. Flight-test equipment, shop crews, inspectors, and support personnel were on location at the military's new test base at Edwards and were prepared for the arrival of the X-1. Goodlin and I flew in the B-29 with the X-1 hanging in its launch shackle to the Mojave Desert test base.

The many words written regarding the hardships of working and living at the isolated Muroc Flight Test Base are basically erroneous. Bell was aviation's pioneer at Muroc, and of all the personnel Bell sent to Muroc, I do not know of one who didn't love it. In fact, many of the initial group on the XP-59A program resigned at the completion of the program and obtained jobs with other contractors and the government, preferring to remain on the desert. That was before paved roads, government housing, B.O.Q.s, and swimming pools.

Likewise much has been made of the purported pilot bonus (hazard pay) committed by Bell Aircraft for the Phase I testing of the X-1 aircraft and the amount demanded by Goodlin. I was never privy to those two numbers; however, my personal intention before the Goodlin decision was to accept whatever compensation the company might offer. If no hazard compensation was offered I was prepared to conduct the Phase I program for my regular salary. I had been involved with the X-1 design and construction. The airplane was indestructible in flight, and I could sure as hell fly it.

I was also convinced that the hazards predicted in conducting the Phase I flight-test program were overstated. The contract with the Air Corps defined the tests conducted by Bell as onboard systems verification, handling characteristics evaluation, stability and control, and performance testing to Mach 0.99 (99 percent of the speed of sound), thereby reserving the privilege of being the first to fly supersonic for the military.

Bell Aircraft aerodynamicists working with N.A.C.A. laboratories at Langley Field and at Ames Laboratory, Moffett Naval Air Station, California, predicted significant longitudinal trim change during transonic flight (Mach 0.99 to 1.2) but no severe stability problems. They did, however, predict the loss of stability on any or all axes in the event of over-burning (operating the rocket engine too long), resulting in overshooting mission altitude and encountering extremely low-density air. Later, in the X-1A test program, that condition occurred during a flight by Chuck Yeager. The airplane became divergently unstable on all three axes simultaneously (out of control), Yeager was knocked unconscious, and the airplane fell during unknown gyrations to lower altitude and denser air, where its inherent stability restored it to normal flight. Fortunately, Yeager came to and landed safely at Edwards. The 18-G design-load factor of the aircraft structure was justified.

All X-1 preflight activity at the base was progressing on schedule, and I returned to Niagara Falls. The flight-test schedule there required my attention.

X-1 First Flight

Goodlin made the first powered X-1 flight December 9, 1946. Bell experimental pilot Dick Frost flew chase in a Lockheed P-80. The operation of the rocket engines was satisfactory, singly and in groups of two. Each burn time was limited to avoid excessive speeds. Goodlin reported satisfactory handling characteristics and sensational speed-acceleration rates, with no comment concerning aerodynamic control or longitudinal trim characteristics.

After numerous power flights, I received a call from the X-1 contracting officer at Wright Field in Dayton, Ohio. "Tex, what's going on at Muroc?"

"What do you mean?" I replied.

"Our technical people are complaining. They say Goodlin is uncooperative. I think they have gone to Colonel Boyd."

"I'll depart for Muroc today," I said. "Tell your people to hold still. I'll get things straightened out, and thanks for the information." I was between a rock and a hard place. When the contracting officer calls, there is a problem, and if Colonel Boyd is involved, it's worse. Larry needed to be informed, but Stanley had to make that call and Stanley was out of town. I decided the contracting officer would keep things under control and give me a chance to work the problem.

The Bitter Solution

The X-1 test engineers were surprised when I arrived unannounced the next day. Attempting to maintain an informal and congenial atmosphere, I asked to see data from the most recent flights. Following a detailed look, I tossed the papers on the desk and said, "You're not making much progress." They glanced at each other as their chairs seemed to become uncomfortable. "Let's go see the airplane. What's going on today?"

"B-29 maintenance" was the reply.

I surveyed the X-1 fueling and loading area and spoke with crew members. It was obvious there was no esprit de corps. En route to the office, I asked, "Where's Goodlin?"

"In Hollywood. That's where he spends most of his time when we're not flying."

I closed the office door and said, "Sit down, fellas. We're going to have an honest-to-God talk. I want to know what in hell is going on out here. We have the hottest program in the world, and everyone is flat on their ass." The answer was that Goodlin had engaged a Hollywood agent to handle his affairs. The Wright Field X-1 program people had been asked to schedule meetings with Goodlin through the Hollywood agent. Hollywood types, including would-be starlets, frequently appeared to observe X-1 flights.

The X-1 flight the following morning was routine, basically a repetition of previous flights. Following an uninformative conversation with Goodlin and a review of the flight data, I scheduled a flight for the next morning, May 22, 1947, with myself as pilot.

The X-1 pilot occupies the B-29 cockpit during ground taxi, takeoff, and initial climb, a safety precaution in case of a ground accident or early climb emergency. Access to the X-1 from the B-29 is by ladder, extending from the bomb bay to the X-1 cockpit entrance. The ladder is shielded from the windstream by a metal housing on the upwind and outboard side of the ladder. My parachute was stowed in the X-1 cockpit before the flight. The descent to the X is relatively routine. I slipped into the cockpit and chute harness; fastened the harness, shoulder straps, and seat belt; and donned crash helmet and oxygen mask. The cockpit door arrived via detachable cable controlled by a crewman at the top of the ladder. Freeing the cable, I installed the door and locked it. With the oxygen system, radio, and interphone to the B-29 on, the onboard prelaunch checklist complete, and chase pilot Dick Frost in drop position, the condition was go. We were at launch altitude of 20,000 feet.

"Stand by for launch," Captain Dow said from the B-29. "Count down from ten. Launch on the count of one." On the count of one, there was a mild negative G as the X fell free of the mother ship. I glanced up to locate the B-29. It had disappeared. I was gliding at 225 mph, descending through 18,000 feet. Figure 1 is a reproduction of my detailed pilot report of the flight.

Concluding the postflight conference, I said, "The X-1 aircraft are grounded until the safety of flight items listed in the pilot report are corrected."

Hard Facts

My in-flight affair with the X-1 was relatively short but sufficient to make astute observations and provide factual evidence confirming my convictions.

First, the airplane was a professional test pilot's and fighter pilot's dream. It was capable of undreamed-of speed and altitude performance combined with light control forces that provided instant and precise response, and an 18-G load factor that made it indestructible in flight. What else could a pilot ask for?

Second, the airplane had only one unacceptable system, extremely rare in a technical advancement of such magnitude.

Third, it was inconceivable that a pilot could fly this airplane for two months and never mention the severe and dangerous deficiency in the longitudinal trim system. It was equally inconceivable that a pilot would adversely affect his employer by failing to comply with established procedures for contractor-customer program interface.

Friends invited me to dinner that evening at their home in Willow Springs. After dinner, we adjourned to the saloon next to the old Pony Express corral. A honky-tonk piano player provided the atmosphere. I was conversing with friends from the XP-59A period when Goodlin and entourage arrived. My plan was to deal with Goodlin the following morning, but that plan unfortunately was doomed. I was standing at the bar with friends when Goodlin joined us and said, "What did you think of the X?"

"Beautiful," I said, "all but the longitudinal trim."

"Oh, what's the matter with the trim?"

"Let's talk about it tomorrow, okay?"

I was returning from using the outdoor plumbing when Goodlin showed up again and said, "What's your problem with the trim?"

The place was all right, but the time was wrong. "Slick, I don't have a problem with the trim, but you sure as hell do."

"What does that mean?" he said.

"I told you we would talk tomorrow, but this suits me if that's what you want. The X-1 airplanes are grounded until the longitudinal trim system is modified."

It was 9:15 a.m. EST when Stanley came on the phone. I gave him a complete briefing commencing with the call from the Wright Field NS-1 contracting office. Silence. The seconds seemed like minutes.

"There's more, Tex. Larry received a call from Boyd. Wright Field is taking over the X-1 program." Now it was my turn to be silent.

"Bob," I said, "I saw .72 Mach on my flight. We fix the longitudinal trim system and that airplane is ready to fly supersonic. I know I can satisfy our contractual commitments in three flights, assuming the trim fix is right, four at the outside."

"I suspect you're right, but it's too late. Another subject, and this is confidential. I have resigned. I am organizing my own company."

I was speechless for a moment. "Bob, what's going on?"

"The war is over, Tex. Things are changing."

BY b. Johnston DATE 6/22/47	**BELL** *Aircraft* CORPORATION	MODEL XS-1 #2 PAGE 2-17A
CHECKED DATE 5-28 47		SHIP 6063 REPORT

PILOT'S REPORT

Place: Muroc Army Air Field, Muroc, Calif.   Flight #17

Pilot: A. M. Johnston

Weather: Wind WSW 25 MPH - Gusts to 35 MPH   CONFIDENTIAL

Purpose: Check Flight and Pilot Familiarization (Power Flight #13)

Changes Since Last Flight:

CONFIDENTIAL

C.G. 25.0 %M.A.C.   Gross Weight 12,102 Pounds   Time Take-Off

1. This flight was conducted as a familiarization flight to enable this pilot to investigate the "power on" and "power off" handling characteristics of the XS-1 aircraft.

2. The entrance to the cockpit of the XS-1 was executed during the climb at a pressure altitude of 8,000 feet. The XS-1 door was secured and the entrance ladder was retracted at a pressure altitude of 10,000 feet, at which time the routine cockpit check was conducted.

3. During the climb it was possible for the pilot of the XS-1 to see a small portion of the horizon both to the left and right. When the B-29 makes a turn, the XS-1 pilot can see the ground over the side. While checking the controls of the XS-1 during the climb in the B-29, the ailerons are quite effective and cause the XS-1 to roll slightly in its shackle. The elevator and rudder are ineffective.

4. At a pressure altitude of 20,000 feet the first and second stages were loaded in preparation for the starting of the engine immediately after the drop.

5. The B-29 started its drop run at a pressure altitude of 21,000 feet and dropped the XS-1 at an observed 270 mph at a pressure altitude of 20,000 feet.

6. The drop was very satisfactory with the XS-1 falling away from the B-29 quite rapidly. The sensation received during the drop can be compared to a "push-over" of level flight in a conventional aircraft at a rate of approximately negative 1.5 g.

7. As the XS-1 dropped away from the B-29 the radio switch was placed in the "on" position, and the No. 4 cylinder switch turned on. The igniters failed to operate, and consequently the No. 4 cylinder switch was turned off. The second attempt to start No. 4 cylinder was successful, and the aircraft was flown through a series of turns, climbs, and shallow dives involving Mach numbers ranging from 0.55 to 0.72.

Form C1-7

FLIGHT #17

8. The ratio of forces between the elevator, aileron, and rudder controls is considered excellent. The control forces are very light and very effective, and the control force increase with speed increase is negligible. The ailerons, when displaced and released, failed to center, which condition is no doubt due to friction within the system, which is quite noticeable on the ground. It is well to note, however, that the ailerons are very light in flight and very effective. During this rapid investigation it is estimated that the rate of roll of this aircraft is approximately that of the P-80 aircraft; however, the absence of the "hunting" characteristics, prevalent with boost control systems, makes these ailerons very desirable.

9. The directional stability of this aircraft is very positive; however, some fuel sloshing is prevalent after a portion of the fuel has been consumed, which results in "Dutch roll".

10. The time interval necessitated a very rough longitudinal stability check; however, it is believed to be slightly positive.

11. The absence of aileron centering prevented a qualitative lateral stability investigation; however, the aircraft flys straight and level without excessive pilot effort; therefore, the lateral stability is considered satisfactory. The present longitudinal stabilizer control is considered very unsatisfactory. Rapid, precise, longitudinal trim changes are impossible with the present control system. This condition is believed to be the result of lost motion within the linkage, which results in over-travel. The rate of actuation of the horizontal stabilizer is considered satisfactory. A more rapid rate of longitudinal trim change applied during extremely high velocity flight might result in more damage to the pilot or aircraft structure than the theoretical pitching moments anticipated in the transonic range. The present horizontal stabilizer control requires excessive movement to obtain stabilizer travel, and is also an awkward control to operate. A spring-loaded toggle switch utilizing the "beep" method of adjustment, or a wheel control of considerable radius are recommended to replace the present lever type control. During this flight, while applying nose-down trim, over-travel resulted, which was accompanied by a negative 2.5 g acceleration. This nose-over was followed immediately by failure of the engine. The panel ignition switch was immediately turned to the "off" position. This engine failure is due to the location of the outlet in the loxygen tank. This outlet is located in the bottom of the spherical loxygen tank, and is obviously inoperative during application of negative accelerations. It is assumed that normal engine operation will resume when the negative acceleration is removed; however, this will be checked during the next flight. At this point, Mr. Frost, who was flying the observing P-80 aircraft, reported trailing smoke or vapor from the XS-1. The fire warning light was observed to be off, and there was no indication of fire within the aircraft. Mr. Frost then reported that the smoke or vapor had ceased. At this point No. 4 cylinder was again ignited, followed by No. 2 cylinder and a climb executed to maintain a Mach number in the vicinity of 0.7. The fuel liquidometer remained in the "full" position throughout the flight; consequently, when the loxygen liquidometer indicated approximately 1/4, No. 4 and No. 3 cylinders were turned off, and the fuel and lox jettisoning switches moved to the "jettison" position.

A. M. Johnston	6/22/47		XS-1 #2	2-145
BY_____DATE_____	**BELL** _Aircraft_ CORPORATION	MODEL__6053		PAGE_____
CHECKED_____DATE_____		AIRPLANE_____		REPORT_____

FLIGHT #17

12. During the blow-down operation the fuel line pressure failed to decrease during the first attempt. At this time the jettison switches were again placed in the "jettison" position, which resulted in satisfactory dissipation of the fuel line pressure.

13. At this time the landing gear and flaps were extended. This operation is quite rapid, and results in considerable airflow noises within the cockpit. It is well to note that very slight trim change is caused by the landing gear and flap extension. Obviously, however, the glide angle is increased. The landing gear and flaps were extended at an observed 210 mph at a pressure altitude of 14,000 feet. This pilot had assured that the visibility from the XS-1 was very marginal. For this flight a parachute of the seat pack type was worn, which placed the pilot's head approximately 1/4" from the windshield when wearing a crash helmet and sitting in a slightly stooped posture. From this position it is possible for the pilot to see the horizon forward and to either side during level power flight. It is necessary to bank the aircraft, however, to see the ground in the immediate vicinity. During glide flight, with landing gear and flaps extended, the forward visibility is very good.

14. The downwind leg and base leg of the traffic pattern were flown at an observed 200 mph. The approach leg was flown at an observed 180 mph, and the touchdown executed at an observed 140 mph. The entire approach, landing, and landing roll were executed looking over the nose of the aircraft. The visibility from this aircraft is considered to be of no hazard when operating under normal conditions. The landing referred to was made on Muroc Dry Lake on the marked extension of the East-West Runway. The landing was made on a west heading, with the touchdown occurring at approximately the center of the Lake, and the landing roll terminating about 200 yards from the east end of the surfaced East-West Runway. The wind direction at the time of landing was west-southwest at a velocity of 25 mph, with gusts to 35 mph. Due to the slight crosswind, slight left aileron and right rudder was utilized during the landing roll to maintain a constant heading. Very slight braking was necessary. The "power off" ground handling characteristics of this aircraft are considered very satisfactory. The shock strut action is very desirable, inasmuch as they do not present any of the lying down characteristics such as are encountered on some narrow tread landing gear fighter aircraft. A statement regarding brakes employed in this aircraft cannot be made at this time, due to the fact that they were not used enough to base an opinion.

15. In summary, this aircraft is considered a pilot's aircraft, i.e., that it presents ideal handling characteristics and satisfactory visibility for this type aircraft. The operation of the rocket engine is considered quite simple, providing the pilot has thoroughly familiarized himself with the fuel, loxygen, and pressure system of the aircraft, and with the operation procedure of the engine itself. The performance of this aircraft, utilizing only two cylinders of the engine, is remarkable, and it is with keen interest that another flight is awaited to further investigate the characteristics of this aircraft utilizing more power.

16. Post-flight investigation revealed that the fire screen between the aft end of the combustion chambers of the engine was completely burned away. The burning of this screen is believed to be the origin of the smoke trail reported by Mr. Frost (refer to paragraph 11). It is recommended that this screen be replaced with a screen made of material which will withstand higher temperatures, or be replaced by an asbestos curtain of the type used satisfactorily on XS-1 #1).

A. M. Johnston 6/22/47		2S-1 #2	2 17D
DATE	**BELL** *Aircraft* CORPORATION	MODEL 2S-1 6063	PAGE
CHECKED DATE		AIRPLANE	REPORT

FLIGHT #17

17. Data were recorded by means of the cockpit camera and the NACA recording equipment.

TOTAL FLIGHT TIME TO DATE: 4 hours and 7 minutes.

AMJ:emh

The X-1, with a modified longitudinal trim system and Yeager in the cockpit, flew into aviation history, the first supersonic airplane in the world.

After Goodlin arrived at Niagara Falls, Stanley informed him that Bell Aircraft would not honor his X-1 contract. June 10, 1947, was an eventful day at Bell. Stanley accepted Goodlin's written resignation and immediately submitted his own formal resignation to Larry Bell.

Rotary Wings

Upon my return to Niagara Falls, I went to Larry's office for a meeting I had requested. Larry's greeting was unusually formal. "You want to discuss the X-1."

"Yes, Sir, the test program at Muroc."

"What about it?"

"Larry, I flew that airplane at .72 Mach. It's a test pilot's dream. With the longitudinal trim fix, I can meet our contractual agreement of .99 Mach in three flights."

"I believe you could, Tex, but it's gone too far. Colonel Boyd has made up his mind, and he has adequate support. Now let's change the subject. World War Two is history. The future is commercial products. You are aware of our technical and financial effort in rotary-wing aircraft. Today, we have the first certificated helicopter in the United States. It has a unique and usable capability. We must develop a market. I want you to take that job."

"Larry, I'm a fixed-wing pilot. High-speed and altitude airplanes are coming soon. That's my business, and I want to play a part in it."

"I want you to check out in the helicopter. I'll have salespeople brief you. Go to engineering and familiarize yourself with what you need to know and inform me when you're ready."

"I'll consider it," I said, and departed.

10

Bell Helicopters

Back at Flight Test, I instructed my secretary to hold my calls, closed the door, and started counting the marbles and looking at the options. Production at the airframe manufacturers had stopped or soon would. They all had a pilot staff. Lockheed was in great shape with P-80 production. My buddies Tony LeVier and Herman Salmon and their staff had that wired. Why not call my friends at TWA? No, that wasn't my type of flying. Would it be worthwhile to call Colonel Boyd? No, colonels don't change their minds, and I didn't want to burn any bridges.

So, helicopters didn't look so bad after all. What about my bride of eleven years? We had already moved seven times. I knew what her response would be: Where and when? And that's exactly what occurred. I called Irene and asked her to inform Larry that I was arranging helicopter training.

Two days later I was checked out in the Bell helicopter and taking notes from the salespeople and engineers. In ten working days I was back in Larry's office, total helicopter time twenty hours, with reasonable knowledge of the engine, rotor, transmission, tail rotor system, and the flight control systems and informed on the marketing experience to date. "What's your plan?" Larry asked me.

"With your permission, I plan to take the company-owned P-63 and make a round-robin trip: Gulf Coast, Midwest, and western states, including California."

"What about the East Coast area?"

P-80

"Larry, this machine carries one passenger, has a very limited payload, and judging from my briefing from the salespeople, they have worked that area with negligible results."

"What particular locations are you planning on investigating?"

"Because of the payload and range problem, I believe our best bet is first the oil business, second agriculture. For your information, I did some crop dusting in Louisiana and Texas back in the biplane days. This copter is short on payload, but the downwash from the rotor will do a better dust job than the fixed wing and it can land practically on the job. I plan to investigate Tulsa, Dallas, Houston, and New Orleans for the oil business; Harlingen, Texas, Phoenix, Fresno and Salinas, California, for agriculture. The northern states are too short-seasoned temperature- and weatherwise and too high altitude for this machine."

"Tex, you've done your homework. Keep me posted. And take the P-63. I believe it's worth it."

Believe me, I was well aware how important this effort was to Larry Bell. He had a large percentage of the marbles in the helicopter effort, and the board of directors and stockholders were breathing down his neck. It was serious business.

The photo department supplied me with ample helicopter photos; the engineering department provided performance information. So with fighter-pilot luggage (shave kit, two pairs of drawers, and two shirts), I launched the first helicopter assault by way of a P-63, by far the best part of my assignment. I had pilot friends in almost every city, guys I had flown with in the Army Air Corps training schools and the Ferry Command. I contacted them en route, and after they drooled over my peashooter (P-63) and quit laughing when I told them I was in the helicopter business, they introduced me to contacts in both oil and agriculture. I made a number of new friends and was confident I could see the light at the end of the tunnel.

Yes, there was a market in both areas, but it became increasingly clear that each required a technical and functional education regarding the capability of the machine. That meant demonstrations on location. Meetings in Tucson, Phoenix, the Sacramento Valley, Los Angeles, and Salinas indicated future agriculture potential. That is, when the payload of the helicopter increased, the market potential was there.

Helicopters in Texas

The meeting convened in Larry Bell's office at 8 a.m., including department heads of the helicopter division, engineering, sales, marketing, public relations, contract administration, finance, and legal. Larry opened the meeting. "You have all been briefed on the purpose of Tex's trip, namely, the first step in selecting a satellite base for developing a market for the Bell helicopter. I can't overemphasize the importance of this effort. Tex will brief us on his trip and recommendations. Delay your questions until the conclusion of his comments."

The helicopter market potential indicated by my survey resulted in my assignment as director of Bell helicopter field operations, based in Houston, Texas.

The post–World War II boom was in full swing in Houston.

I purchased a home in a new residential area in southwest Houston, and DeLores, daughter Judy, and son Gary arrived in our new Oldsmobile 98 convertible (the third one off the postwar production line) and settled into our new home. I opened a small office in uptown Houston and started working both sides of the street, exploration companies as well as the major oil companies.

The arrival of our first helicopter received appreciable publicity, but less than I had anticipated, considering it was the first helicopter in the area. I changed that. Foley's, a significant department store chain in the area, was constructing a new building, outstanding in its architecture and size. I contacted the manager and arranged to land on the roof of the new building on opening day, pick up the store's first bank deposit, and deliver it to the roof of the bank. The operation went off well, and between Foley's and the bank the helicopter made the headlines with photos. Simultaneously, I was making pitches to the Shell and Texaco exploration departments.

Nearby Galveston was an entertainment center and enjoyed exceptionally large crowds during the winter season. The most popular restaurant and ballroom was constructed on a pier extending over the water. Sam Maceo was owner and manager of the club. For the grand opening of the winter season I contracted to carry a lady acrobat on a trapeze suspended under the helicopter over the bathers on the beach while she performed. Then over the water she was to drop into the surf and swim to shore.

The day before the show, as arranged, I drove to Galveston to Maceo's office to collect our fee for the helicopter activity. They kept me cooling my heels for an hour, and when I was called into the office I was pretty teed off. Maceo opened the conversation with the statement, "There is some kind of foul-up. The check didn't get issued, and the bookkeeper isn't in."

"Maceo, our agreement was cash—no check—a day before the show." I had cut my teeth in show biz, where the philosophy is, "Don't pay till you have to," so I simply turned around and started for the office door.

"Where're you going?" he asked.

"No cash, no copter," I replied with my hand on the door knob. I left with the cash and a pass to the joint; it's a game everyone plays in that business, and the beginners come out hungry.

Show day was lousy: a strong onshore wind, blowing sand, and rough water. Everything went well until the trapeze girl dropped into the water. She swam toward the beach but drifted to sea. Pilot Stansbury, recognizing the situation, hovered the helicopter low enough to place the trapeze in the water. She grabbed on, and he slowly dragged her to shallow water. Good publicity.

One morning I received a call from my contact in Shell Oil. Could we conduct a gravity demonstration in the marshlands south of New Orleans? My reply was, "What date are we looking at?"

"Ten days from today, and make all your arrangements with our exploration office in New Orleans. They are waiting for your call."

I notified the pilot, Stansbury, and maintenance crew foreman, Nickerson, of our mission and that I would meet with them at 1 p.m. to firm up our logistics.

We arrived in New Orleans three days before demonstration day. Fuel and support equipment was cached at the survey location in the marsh in the vicinity of Golden Meadow, Louisiana. Our quarters were in a house barge secured on a bayou near the survey area. The structure contained a so-called kitchen, a mess hall, and sleeping quarters filled with two-decker bunks. The temperature was 100 degrees to 105 degrees Fahrenheit, 95-percent humidity, with no wind and unbelievable swarms of mosquitoes, particularly after sundown, and no air conditioning. The water in the survey area was twelve to sixteen inches deep. The sawgrass was two to five feet tall with occasional water moccasins and alligators.

The helicopter was equipped with air-inflated floats. The gravity meter was mounted on a rigid tripod, which when released from its up lock could be lowered through a large hole in the cockpit floor and allowed to sink to firm footing in the marsh base completely detached from the helicopter structure. After landing on the designated point determined by triangulation, we stopped the engine and brought the rotor to a stationary position. The gravity meter, an extremely sensitive instrument, cannot record reliable data with any vibration in the area. After recording the data, we retracted the tripod and meter, started the engine, and flew the helicopter to the next survey point.

The demonstration was a complete success in that we covered such a large number of data points in an incredibly short period of time in comparison with the airboat method. Our major problem was environmental. The 100-degree temperatures significantly reduced the performance of the engine. We had anticipated the problem and were flying with partial fuel load, which necessitated more refueling stops, but at that temperature and humidity it was mandatory. The demonstration continued for two full days, with prospective customers making actual flights to data points. The enthusiasm for the program was obvious.

Back in Houston I moved the office to a small turf airport south of Houston to improve our operating efficiency.

Anticipating exploration work for the oil companies, I contacted Dave Foreman, director of the helicopter division of Bell at Niagara Falls, and made three requests: a tractor-trailer unit equipped with shop facilities, machine tools, gasoline-powered AC power unit, and anticipated spare parts to support two helicopters on a ten-hour-per-day schedule of exploration work in the Louisiana coastal marsh area; a second helicopter with appropriate modification to accommodate a tripod and gravity meter; and one additional pilot and two additional mechanics. Two days later Foreman informed me that my request had been approved and equipment and personnel would arrive within thirty days. I now had new ammunition to fire at Mobil and Texaco, pictures of actual gravity exploration in the marsh conducted by helicopter, and it attracted their attention.

The following week I received a request from Shell Oil for a bid to conduct a gravity survey near Golden Meadow, Louisiana. It was a sizable area, and after studying Shell's maps to determine the number of data points, the fuel logistics, and all operation functions required, we were confident we could conduct the mission in ninety days.

My secretary, Vivian Herzog, was a former oil company employee, and she and I spent several long days hammering out a contract in concert with the bid request, defining customer and contractor responsibilities and liabilities, operational procedures, contract period, and cost, including backup detail. My strategy was to let the customer try the contract on for size before taking it to Bell headquarters. I was worried that a contract written at Bell's main office would suffer from a lack of knowledge of the petroleum exploration business and from complete ignorance of the environment in which this operation was to occur. The last thing I wanted was contract delays that could cost us the program and set back the potential helicopter market.

Three days after I hand-carried the bid response to the customer, I received a call. "Come in. We want to talk." By this time I knew the head of the exploration department, and when I arrived I was ushered to his office without delay. He was in a good mood. "Come on, we have to go to the legal department," he said.

After introductions, we sat at the conference table with the two company lawyers at one end. The one who seemed to be in charge waved at the contract on the table in front of him. "Who prepared this?" he asked.

I felt a momentary misgiving. "I did," I replied, looking him straight in the eye.

"By yourself?" he questioned.

"Just my secretary and myself."

He studied me, then smiled and said, "It's a good job, straight to the point," and picking up the papers, he handed them to me. "They are all signed except for you."

"Sir," I said, "I don't have signature authority, but I plan to fly the contract to Niagara Falls and get a signature."

"Okay," he said, "send me our copy and get this show on the road."

I called Stansbury and told him I had to go to Niagara Falls. "Stay by the phone and have the copter ready to go; I'll be back in three or four days." I climbed in that old P-63, making fuel stops only, and was in Dave Foreman's office at eight o'clock the next morning.

"What are you doing here?" he asked.

I opened my briefcase and placed the contract on his desk. "Here," I said, "is our first contract with the petroleum industry. I came to get a signature. Get us an appointment with Larry, and then I'll brief you."

The next morning, with the signed contract in my briefcase, I was sitting at 25,000 feet and that old Allison was purring like a kitten. We were in business.

During the following two and a half years, Bell helicopters successfully demonstrated their operational and financial advantages in actual contract petroleum exploration in the hostile environments of the Louisiana coastal marsh and the Canadian bush country north of Athabasca, Alberta.

In addition, we demonstrated the helicopter's capabilities as a crop duster during contract work and demonstrations in the Texas Rio Grande Valley. I knew that business. In the thirties I had dusted cotton in Louisiana and Texas before insecticides had replaced sulfur. Occasionally, you'd look over your shoulder to check the sulfur cloud and see instead a ball of fire ignited by static electricity generated as the sulfur slid from the hopper exit chute. Fortunately, flight speed was faster than the flame propagation rate, so closing the chute stopped the fire. Dusting and spraying are best done when zero wind allows the poison to settle and not drift away. Helicopters have a slight edge in this regard because rotor downwash helps deposit the dust. Additionally, helicopters are better for small fields, where tree and high-line borders make fixed-wing dusting difficult and dangerous.

Also during that period, in Missouri and Arizona, our first successful helicopter airborne uranium explorations ushered in a heretofore unavailable service.

At the same time, as an economy measure, I had returned the P-63 to Niagara Falls and leased a Beechcraft Bonanza. During multihour flights at 145 mph between operations, my mind continually returned to my profession, high-performance airplanes. Returning to Houston one day from a trip to Athabasca, I refueled at Omaha, Nebraska. During the climb out I said, "Old girl, to hell with Houston, we're going to Vandalia, Ohio." Civilian aircraft were not permitted to land at Wright Field.

11

The Move to Boeing

The familiar roar of F-80's and F-84's at Wright Field made me feel I'd finally returned home. On a second-floor office door beneath the control tower I found the nameplate of Colonel A. Boyd. He'd been promoted to full colonel since my Muroc days. The secretary announced my arrival, and I heard him say, "Who? . . . Well, what do you know. Send him in."

"Where you been?" he said as he leaned across his desk and shook hands.

"I just completed a job for Larry Bell involving helicopters, and I want to get back to my profession. Do you know anyone who needs an engineering test pilot?"

"I sure do. Do you know anything about the XB-47?"

"Only that there is one," I said.

He thought a moment and said, "I believe Boeing has a really great airplane, but they need a professional test pilot. They hired a pilot named Osler, who might have done something, but the canopy blew off and took his head with it. Why don't you contact them?"

"May I use you as a reference?"

"You bet. Tell them to call me if they wish."

Taking leave of Colonel Boyd, I immediately called the Boeing Airplane Company in Seattle. A Mr. Showalter came on the line. "Our chief of flight test, John Fornasero, is in

Chicago," he said. "Yes, we are looking for a pilot for the XB-47. Could you meet Fornasero in Chicago tomorrow?"

The next morning I landed at Chicago's Midway Airport, parked the Bonanza at 10 a.m. on the transit aircraft ramp, and took a cab to the terminal to meet John Fornasero. He turned out to be personable and dapper, five-foot-nine with a thin black mustache and an easy manner. He spoke enthusiastically of the XB-47, saying that although it had been underpowered when first flown with the GE J35 turbojet engines, it was being reequipped with General Electric J47's. Simultaneously, the cockpit canopy fix was being incorporated. Fornasero was aware I was interested in the XB-47 test job and had already contacted Colonel Boyd, so we quickly settled on the following Monday as my arrival date in Seattle, where I would take the required physical and get to know the Boeing organization.

Boeing, Seattle

As the Boeing Stratocruiser passed over the Cascade Mountains to begin descent to Seattle's Boeing Field, I saw for the first time snow-covered Glacier peak and Mount Baker on the right and Mounts Jefferson, Rainier and St. Helens in Washington and Mount Hood in Oregon on the left, their snowy crests sparkling in the afternoon sun. Seattle occupies the hilly ground between Lake Washington on the east and the deep blue waters of Puget Sound on the west. As we approached for landing, I became aware of the predominant green beauty of field and forest on all sides. This was my kind of country. As it turned out, the Pacific Northwest became my favorite area of the world and, thanks to the Invisible Hand, our home.

As I deplaned and looked across the one-runway airport toward Boeing's headquarters, I saw numerous B-50's (upgraded from the B-29) and KC-97's (the military version of the Stratocruiser) but nothing resembling an XB-47. The hack driver seemed happy to answer my tourist-type questions. In his opinion Seattle was a Boeing town, the weather ideal, no violent temperature variations, a boaters' paradise, excellent fishing and hunting, and, of course, the University of Wash-

Boeing Stratocruiser

ington. While paying the fare I said, "I'm going to recommend you to the chamber of commerce." He squinted his eye, and as he pulled away called, "Thanks, I'm happy on the street."

The next day started with a beautiful morning as a taxi took me to the guard gate at the flight-test facility. The environment reminded me of Bell—airplanes and airplane support equipment—but the World War II wood-frame flight-test quarters were less impressive. The secretary who arrived at the guard desk to escort me to my second meeting with Fornasero was trim and all business. "My name is Lola Beck. Follow me, please." That wasn't difficult. Only three steps, around a corner, and there we were in a large room with a glassed-in office in the southwest corner. Through the glass I recognized John Fornasero at his desk. The unwalled section of the room contained row upon row of desks occupied by flight-test engineers—as I categorized them, judging from the paperwork, slide rules, and documentation on their desks. "What would you like to see first?" Fornasero asked.

"John, I'm in your hands. I'm here to learn."

"Good, we'll take a quick look at Flight Test. I expect you will feel at home. Then we'll have lunch in the executive dining room at headquarters. I have a small Cruiser. This evening we have a few people coming aboard. We'll have cocktails, a nautical snack, and take a cruise on Lake Washington."

"John, that fits me. I observed the lake during our landing approach."

"I have scheduled you for a company physical in the morning and could arrange a little tour of the city if you wish."

"That sounds excellent. I'll skip the tour. Plenty of time to see the town. How about the XB-47?"

"At present the airplane is in lay-up. The work is taking place at Moses Lake, east of the mountains. We could fly over to Moses Lake if you wish."

"No, John, that's not necessary. It's just that as a result of Colonel Boyd's description I'm anxious to see the airplane. Let's get first things first."

During my plant tour and introductions I met Mr. Showalter, my first telephone contact at Boeing.

At quitting time John said, "Take a cab and tell the driver to take you to the Leschi boat dock on Lake Washington. We'll be tied up there. You can't miss us. My boat is a double-ender." It was a memorable evening. The views from the water were magical. I had heard stories of Seattle, its lakes and natural beauty, but now the stories seemed inadequate in their praise.

John did well to schedule my physical exam at 9:30 a.m. The heavy Boeing employee traffic was over. I know a little bit about physicals, having taken them since I was a seventeen-year-old student pilot. The Boeing physical was complete and professional.

I recalled a discussion during the boat cruise about new state legislation legalizing the dispensing of alcoholic beverages at bars and restaurants, the result of a hard-fought political battle. At my hotel I asked the doorman to recommend a good restaurant. His answer: the Ben Franklin Hotel's Outrigger Restaurant. The food and beverages were excellent, and while I savored the evening I considered the events of the past two days. They had all been positive, except why the next day's appointment with a psychoanalyst? I was to find out later that a few guys in management, including my new acquaintance Showalter, were promoting the session with an analyst prior to employment.

At 9 a.m. I arrived at an immaculate, three-story, early-1900's residence much like others I had admired en route. Early Seattleites lived well. The receptionist ushered me into a delightfully furnished office. Waiting at the door was an attractive young woman, quite tall, probably five feet nine or ten inches, with an extra-full masculine-style hairdo and a magnificently tailored pantsuit and accessories. Her brown eyes complemented her dark brunette hair and her full and enticing mouth. It was impossible to ignore the long mani-cured nails, iridescent green. I must be in the wrong joint, I thought.

"Good morning. I'm Dr. Weidmyer."

"Tex Johnston, Dr. Weidmyer, my pleasure," I said, star-ing into those liquid brown eyes.

As she strolled gracefully across the room to a chess-type table she said, "Would you be seated, please," and seated herself directly across the table. From the cabinet to her right (a coordinate for the chess table), she removed an object I recognized at a glance, and the thought flashed through my brain: What am I doing alone with this very attractive woman with an adolescents' game of "put the round pegs in the round holes and the square pegs in the square holes"? The ridiculous has always been amusing. I answered my own question: Have some fun.

"Mr. Johnston, place the pegs in their respective posi-tions." So, looking her in the eyes, I picked up the pegs with my right hand while feeling for the holes with my left and rapidly satisfied the objective. "Very good," she said. The remainder of the interview, with the exception of the last part, was equally juvenile. Finally, she asked, "Why do you want to be a test pilot?"

"Just a moment. I am a test pilot, have been for six years."

"Sorry. Why are you a test pilot?"

"Because I possess the skills and the technical education, and I love it."

"Do you fly for the money?"

"Damn right; everyone has to eat. But I took a two-thousand-a-year cut to go to work for Boeing."

"Why did you choose Boeing?"

"Because I believe their new airplane will be the best in the world, and I want to help make it happen."

"What do you like better than anything in the world?"

"Copulation." I had another word in mind but now wasn't a time to be crude.

It was very quiet as she stared back at me. As she rose, she murmured, "Excuse me," and left the room. In only a few moments she returned to say in a routine manner, "The interview is complete."

I hesitated a moment, then said, "I'm new in Seattle, but I understand the Ben Franklin has a delightful restaurant, the Outrigger. Would you have dinner with me tonight?"

She hesitated a moment and replied in a drawn out "No-o-o, I believe not."

As I turned to depart, I looked again into her eyes and said, "It was indeed a pleasure." And that's how I was declared psychologically qualified to test fly for Boeing.

The next morning I arrived at Flight Test at ten. John was in his office. "What did the medics say?"

"Just talked to them," he said. "Everything is clear. You're all set."

"Great," I replied.

"Okay, I have a one p.m. appointment for you with personnel for a photo and employee badge. Welcome aboard."

I had accepted a salary of $10,000 per year, $2,000 less than at Bell, but that didn't bother me. I was headed for the best airplane in the world. "The future is here and now," I thought. "It's time to get the show on the road." My return flight departed Seattle late in the evening, and I was in Houston next morning. I told DeLores and the kids about Seattle. Everyone was hot to trot. We called the real estate agent and the movers.

Approaching Seattle by car on July 3, 1948, we made our first trip over Snoqualmie Pass, the main east-west pass over the Cascades fifty miles east of Seattle. Two days later we located a lovely unfurnished rental property in north Seattle. When the moving truck arrived the movers could install the furniture precisely as DeLores directed. The location was a mistake, however. Highway 99 was the only north-south thoroughfare in Seattle, and travel time to and from Boeing was 60 to 75 minutes each way during rush hours.

My first day at work, Lola told me that the pilots were in the revetment and Fornasero was waiting for me there. The revetment was a large building on the east side of the airport with dirt banked up to the roof, the special protection required for this high-loft building during World War II. Entrance to the flight crew quarters was through a tunnel. The room was large, with rows of desks, file cabinets, and lockers. John introduced me to everyone present: pilots, copilots, flight engineers, instrumentation engineers, data transcribers, and flight-test engineers, people I was to have the privilege of working with for nineteen years.

The next few days were spent getting acquainted with people and facilities. I made two flights as observer in a B-50. The pilot was Cranston "Boo" Paschall, the stepson of William Boeing himself. Boo and I were destined to become close friends, as did our families.

12

The XB-47

I met Jim Frazier, copilot on the tragic XB-47 flight, who had successfully landed the airplane. Jim had elected to discontinue flying because of pressure from his family, but he was cooperative and agreed to accompany me to the Moses Lake facility, introduce me to the personnel, and brief me regarding his experience in the airplane.

John informed me that the new J47 engine installation was complete and ground runs were to commence, so Jim and I drove to Moses Lake. There he introduced me to the test crew engineers Ben Werner, T. Johnson, and Smith; instrumentation engineer Mel Blount; and shop foreman Don Whitford and his crew. All Boeing personnel at Moses Lake lived in the barracks on the base and relied on the restaurants of Moses Lake for their meals.

The XB-47 was parked adjacent to the hangar. The gleaming fuselage, tapering aft, terminated with swept-back horizontal and vertical tail surfaces. The 35-degree swept and tapered wing intersected the top of the fuselage. The airplane appeared poised to spring into the air. Under each wing were two engine pods suspended on streamlined struts. The two inboard nacelles contained two engines each and the two outboard nacelles one engine each for a total of six engines.

Another unusual feature of the airplane was the bicycle landing gear, one set of trucks (wheels) forward and one set aft, thus the term "bicycle" gear. The narrow configuration of the bicycle gear required outrigger struts and wheels to prevent the ship from heeling over in crosswinds or in turns during ground maneuvering. The outriggers attached to and retracted into the respective inboard engine nacelles.

The bombardier position in the nose was traditional, but the seating configuration for the pilots was not. They sat in tandem on a raised deck, the pilot forward, the copilot aft. A plastic clear-view canopy covered both positions and mated with the bullet-shaped windshield just forward of the pilot's head. That configuration resulted in excellent 360-degree external visibility, but it complicated pilot-copilot communications by making an intercom necessary.

General Electric engineers briefed me in detail on the J47 multistage compressor turbine engine, a significant configuration change from the centrifugal compressor design of the I-16 on the XP-59A. The B-47 project engineers for Wright Field, Boeing, and General Electric were eager for flight-test data, so as soon as the pretest conference for the first J47 engine runs adjourned, we headed for the aircraft.

The wheels were chocked; the air duct line from the ground air machine, which supplied high-velocity air to the engine turbine starters, was connected. All test personnel were in position. I occupied the pilot seat, Frazier the copilot seat, while the General Electric engineer stood in the cockpit aisle. All personnel were equipped with microphones and earphones or crash helmets. I turned the number six engine fuel valve to the tank-to-engine position and began the start procedure. "Stand by for the number six engine start. Instrumentation on."

Ground: "Ready for start."

Instrumentation: "Instrumentation on."

With all throttles closed, I actuated the number six starter switch, the engine rpm began increasing, and I turned on number six ignition. When the rpm reached 10 percent, I opened the engine fuel valve and simultaneously observed the fuel pressure increase. I heard the slight rumble of engine ignition and watched as the tail-pipe temperature increased. "Start on number six."

The tail-pipe temperature was increasing through 550 degrees; as it reached 650 degrees, the rpm reached 20 percent (idle), the fuel pressure stabilized, and the tail-pipe temperature decreased to 500 degrees. I was impressed with the smoothness of this multistage compressor turbine engine. What an achievement in power source. The reciprocating engine in large high-performance airplanes would soon be history.

After that initial engine run, Frazier returned to Seattle. I remained at the test facility and, with the excellent and enthusiastic cooperation of engineering, shop, flight-test, and quality-control personnel, became an integrated member of the group destined for a long, invigorating, and productive program.

For the engine ground tests, the landing flaps were extended in the takeoff position. During a subsequent run with all six engines at takeoff power, I saw the ground crew motioning to cut the power (the noise level was so intense a ground microphone was useless). I immediately cut the power to i_le, then shut off the fuel. The ground crew reported that a section of the flaps had failed and blown away. I climbed down the ladder and walked under the right wing. Sure enough, only the flap track remained. The crew transported the pieces back to the hangar. One look, and it was obvious the flap had structurally disintegrated. The engineering members of our team called project engineer Bob Plath in Seattle and informed him of the failure, then sent the failed flap to Seattle immediately by truck. The failed flap was of conventional design—spars and ribs with metal skin. The structures engineers concluded that the failure resulted from the high-intensity sonic vibration combined with the buffeting of the flaps in the exhaust wake of the engine. That incident during preflight testing was my introduction to the in-depth engineering capability of the Boeing Airplane Company. It resulted in an engineering study that led to honeycomb construction.

By the time the redesigned cockpit canopy was installed, redesigned flaps had arrived. By then, I had concluded an intense study of the XB-47 handbook, system schematics, description, and operation information of all systems aboard the airplane and was ready to become airborne.

During the new flap installation I returned to Seattle to meet a new-hire pilot, graduate engineer Doug Heinburger. He was eager to see the XB, and I filled him in on the activity at Moses Lake. I was surprised to learn that his flying time was limited and in light airplanes. Doug's wife, Harriet, was a charming lady, and DeLores and she became friends. Doug and Harriet were house hunting, and when we told them the house next door was for rent, they rented it. That solved our transportation problem. Doug and I alternated driving to work.

After my ground transportation problem had been solved, John called me in the office and said, "It has been decided to transfer the B-47 developmental test program to Wichita, Kansas, where the B-47 production line is being set up." (Now it's twelve moves in fourteen years, I thought.) "We will take the XB to Wichita as soon as the flaps are installed."

I was disappointed about having to move to Wichita, but the family was really upset. They had fallen in love with Seattle, as had I. But for me, the XB-47 was worth moving anywhere for. "Come on," I said, "we'll be close to our families. You kids can see your grandparents, find new school chums, and I believe we will eventually return to Seattle."

DeLores took care of the moving while I continued work at the revetment. I checked out flight gear and got to know pilots Dix Loesch, Boo Paschall, Dick Taylor, and Tom Lane. All of them had good personalities and good educational backgrounds, but not one had experience in developmental flight testing or high-performance airplanes. Chief production pilot Clayton Scott, formerly a seaplane pilot, was originally employed by William Boeing, Sr., founder of the company, to fly his Douglas Dolphin seaplane. I also learned that two pilots, Harts and Knutson, whom I had known while instructing for the Army Air Corps, were production pilots working in Scott's organization.

As a result of many hours with the B-47 project and flight-test engineers, I was well briefed regarding the flight-test program. We were facing an intensive test schedule. The XB had flown only a few flights, mainly for familiarization and demonstration. Bob Robins, a design engineer in the B-47 project and a pilot with minimum multi-engine time, had flown the initial flight. Major Guy Townsend, one of Colonel Boyd's well-qualified pilots from Wright Field, had flown a number of demonstration flights. Scott Osler had entered the program and died in the tragic canopy accident. The airplane had less than fifteen hours total flight time when it entered lay-up for the J-47 production engine installation and the canopy modification. It was time to count the marbles and come up with the game plan.

Dix Loesch had the best qualifications for a copilot. His big-airplane time was limited, but a Navy fighter pilot who had made it off and on a carrier at sea during World War II had to have something on the ball; plus, he had an M.I.T. degree. In my opinion he had a leg up at the start; how it turned out was dependent on his piloting skill and attitude. I debated with myself the wisdom of opening the copilot subject with John Fornasero and decided to sit tight and see what happened. Two days later, Saturday evening, John called and said the XB was ready to fly. He wanted to fly the airplane and asked if I would object to flying copilot. "I'll be happy to, John," I replied. I was surprised by his request. He had zero flight time in high-performance airplanes and had never operated a turbine engine. This would be the first flight with the new engines, the reworked cockpit canopy, and the redesigned flaps. "When do you plan to go to Moses Lake?" I asked.

"Let's go over Monday, check everything out, conduct two checkout flights, and proceed to Wichita Friday," he said.

"That's great. DeLores is ready to leave. I'll ride to Ellensburg with her and meet you at the truck-stop restaurant. What time shall we meet?"

"Eleven o'clock," he replied. "We can have lunch at Moses Lake."

DeLores, the children, and I were at the Ellensburg truck stop when John arrived. Our good-byes were a bit reserved. DeLores was apprehensive about the long drive to Wichita, and the children were downhearted about leaving Seattle.

By the time we arrived at the base the ground crew had everything shipshape. The airplane was fueled and ready for flight. The swept wings and tail gave the impression of speed, truly a beautiful aircraft.

With John in the forward seat, I stood in the side aisle and gave him a cockpit check. John had been an F.A.A. inspector before joining Boeing and had been assigned to fly with Boeing crews during certification of the Stratocruiser. With that expertise and his study of the XB pilot's manual, he had no difficulty understanding the fuel, electrical, hydraulic, and mechanical systems and controls of the airplane. He had never operated a jet engine, so we practiced dry (no fuel) runs, including the starting, emergency, and regular shutdown procedures.

Via interphone I directed the ground crew to prepare for engine runs. Remaining in the aisle position, I observed John as he started number four engine. As the engine started, he slowly advanced the throttle, continually monitoring the percentage of power and tail-pipe temperature. I was certain he was impressed by the absence of vibration. His baseline was the vibration associated with a Pratt and Whitney 4360 with a four-blade prop turning 2,000 rpm. With the engine at idle, I asked for medium and fast acceleration to 100-percent power, and cautioned, "Monitor the tail-pipe temperature to familiarize yourself with heat rise rate with the more rapid acceleration rates."

With the engine checkout complete, I gave him the cut-engine sign. He shut off the fuel and observed the rpm and tail-pipe temperature decrease. "That engine puts out power with no vibration," he exclaimed.

"Wait until you fire up all six," I said.

That evening at dinner I briefed him on my XP-59A experience. "It was a big step ahead of reciprocating power plants," I said, "but the XP-80 and XP-83 made the P-59 look sick. Now, looking at the projected performance data for this airplane, I'm sure the B-47 will become the number one airplane in the military inventory."

I gave him some pointers. "John, because of the significant gross-weight change in large-jet aircraft as fuel is consumed, it is mandatory to determine the gross weight for both takeoff and landing by adding the fuel onboard and payload weight to the aircraft weight and then to calculate the respective takeoff and landing speed. Also, as you observed today, the turbine-engine acceleration and deceleration rate is significantly slower than for reciprocating engines, and there is no propeller drag to assist deceleration when power is reduced. Therefore, it is mandatory on landing approach to accurately maintain the calculated approach speed. Power changes must be anticipated to avoid undershooting or overshooting. In the event of an overshoot, make an early go-around decision to overcome the slower power response. In the event of a go-around, I'll handle the gear and flaps. Okay, John, I'm ready when you are."

"Nine tomorrow morning," he replied.

Flight

We were in the conference room at 8 a.m. for the final review of the test plan for the first flight with the new General Electric J47 engines. Engineering was eager for performance data, so the plan included stabilized speed runs at numerous power settings at altitudes of 10,000, 20,000, and 30,000 feet.

With the preflight conference completed, the action shifted to the airplane. The ground crew was in position, auxiliary power cart connected, ground fire extinguishers manned and in position, and a foam-equipped fire truck standing by. In the cockpit, we had seat belts and shoulder harnesses adjusted, oxygen system connected, and interphone checked. "Stand by for control check," John directed the ground crew on the interphone. With the control check completed, the next order was: "Stand by for engine start. Ignition on, turning number one." When the engine tachometer reached 12 percent, "Fuel on."

"We have a light," reported the ground crew chief as the engine started and flame appeared at the tail pipe. Meanwhile, we monitored tail-pipe temperature and engine rpm.

When the engine reached idle power, John continued: "Ignition off, turning number two." The procedure was repeated until all six engines were at idle power.

Cockpit: "Ship's power on; disconnect external power. Park brakes on; remove wheel chocks and down locks and place them on the ramp visible to the pilot. Disconnect ground interphone." I immediately switched to radio, selected tower frequency, and requested taxi instructions. John released the brakes, added power, and we moved out of the parking area.

The wind was from the southwest. En route to takeoff

position, a distance of approximately one and a quarter miles, John did slight S turns to familiarize himself with the nose-gear steering ratio. We received clearance from the control tower to take position for takeoff. When the before-takeoff checklist was complete—all engines tank-to-engine, hydraulic pressure, canopy secure, flight control freedom check, takeoff flap position—John radioed the tower, "Ready for takeoff."

"Cleared for takeoff."

With all six engines at 100-percent power, he released the brakes. The airplane lurched forward. I was pleased at the rapid acceleration. As the airspeed reached 135 mph the airplane gently raised from the runway with the control wheel remaining in the neutral position, the result of the 6-degree angle of incidence of the wings. John retracted the landing gear. The wheel-well buffet ceased. I retracted the flaps, and John pulled the nose up into a medium climb. As airspeed approached 270, he retarded the throttles to climb power. At 10,000 feet he leveled off, accelerated to cruise speed, and set cruise power. "I'm going to make some turns and power changes in climbs and dives to get the feel of her," John said.

"Great," I replied, "take a look back at the wings. How do you like that slight upward bend with the in-flight loads?"

"Some difference from the stiff straight wings," he replied.

He finished his maneuvers and suggested I take over and feel out the airplane's characteristics. The control forces were excellent, much lighter than those encountered on previous large airplanes. The streamlined airframe of the XB-47 and the absence of propeller drag caused the deceleration rate with power reductions to be much slower than that of conventional airplanes. The roll rate from a 60-degree left bank to 60-degree right bank with full aileron was excellent, exceeding that of other large craft. The longitudinal trim rate was satisfactory throughout the speed envelope. The visibility from the cockpit was excellent. My impression of the airplane at this point was: "Magnificent. Performs like a fighter."

During takeoff and climb and the test runs at 10,000,

20,000, and 30,000 feet, the engines performed flawlessly. As John let down, he was enthusiastic—impressed with the phenomenal performance and the lack of vibration.

Dutch Roll

Aerodynamics personnel had briefed me regarding Dutch roll, an inherent characteristic of swept-wing aircraft. It starts with yaw. A yaw is a left or right deviation from heading without banking. An oscillating yaw in a straight-wing airplane is called snaking. That condition was prevalent in the straight-wing XP-59A.

In a 35-degree swept-wing airplane, a yaw is accompanied by a simultaneous roll in the direction of yaw. The roll is caused by changing lift factors as the airflow path over the wing changes. For example, in a left yaw the left wing slews toward the rear so that airflow is displaced spanwise from its normal front-to-rear path over the airfoil section. That reduces lift. Simultaneously, the advancing right wing gets more chordwise flow, and so its lift is increased. In combination the two conditions create a left roll. Similarly, a yaw to the right results in a roll to the right. An oscillation is set up. The aircraft will continue its undesirable flight behavior until the pilot executes corrective aileron and rudder action. Dutch roll is obviously unacceptable to both the flight crew and passengers and varies in magnitude with gross weight and altitude.

Some swept-wing airplanes under this condition are neutrally stable. That is, if the condition is not corrected by the pilot, the airplane will continue to oscillate right to left, with each yaw and bank identical in degree. Some aircraft, however, have divergent Dutch roll. If the condition is allowed to continue, each oscillation increases in magnitude until the airplane reaches a dangerous attitude.

After letting down from our performance tests, John leveled off at 7,000 feet to familiarize himself with airplane performance in the landing configuration. Slowing down, he extended the landing gear and the flaps and adjusted the power to hold 200 mph in level flight. He made numerous turns simulating traffic-pattern maneuvers. As the airspeed decreased to 180 mph, we witnessed our first Dutch roll. The yaw was 3 to 5 degrees right and left and the bank angle 8 to 10 degrees. I was eyeballing the airspeed and the rudder and aileron control action. John's rudder and aileron corrections were out of phase, being applied too late in the oscillation. The airspeed had been allowed to decrease to 170 mph, and the Dutch roll was increasing slightly. John came on the interphone. "I'm having trouble with this yawing. Have you had any experience with this condition?"

"Yes," I replied.

"See what you can do with it," he said.

In fighter aircraft your heels are on the cockpit floor, the ball of your foot on the rudder pedal. The heel thus acts as a stabilized support, allowing the foot to make small rudder-pedal movements. In large airplanes, the rudder-pedal travel is so great the heel is cradled in a stirrup on the bottom of the rudder pedal. That allows the whole foot to travel with the pedal, making small, precise rudder applications difficult, particularly at lower speeds. I applied corrective opposite rudder and simultaneous lateral control and stabilized the nose on a constant heading.

"How did you do that?"

I explained, and after a bit of practice he was able to control the situation.

John received landing clearance from the tower. We were about thirty miles west, so he retracted the gear and flaps and approached the downwind leg. Following gear extension and half flaps, we were coming in from the northeast on a long final approach leg. The Moses Lake Airport is on a plateau. Approached from the northeast, the airport appears to be on a mesa. Just short of the northeast end of the runway is a cliff face, more than two hundred feet of vertical rock.

We were about two miles out and too low. I was looking at the face of the cliff. We were below the edge, the runway out of sight. I'm thinking, "Spool-up time," to allow for the delay between the advance of throttles and the time the power takes effect. There wasn't time to talk about the situation. I placed my hand on the throttles and was just ready to jam them forward when John did so. We pulled up above the cliff about a city block from the wall.

I anticipated he would go around for another try as he passed over the approach end of the runway, slightly high and 20 mph too fast. I was about to advance power and say, "Let's go around," but we were almost on the deck and had about 6,500 or 7,000 feet remaining. She settled in. The fore and aft trucks touched down simultaneously. As they made contact I pulled the drag chute. It popped out, and we could feel the deceleration. John had considerable big-airplane time, and he was fully aware of the 6-degree wing angle of incidence and was light on the brakes until we decelerated to 90 mph. Employing heavy braking, we executed a 180-degree turn with 200 feet of runway remaining. I pulled the drag-chute release, and we taxied to the ramp area and shut her down.

I followed John down the entrance ladder. The test engineers, ground crew, everyone was there. I grabbed John's hand and said, "Congratulations, you're now a jet jockey."

"Not a very good one," he said.

"Come on," I said, "you did well. This is a big change for you."

The postflight conference convened, and comments concerning the flight were recorded. We congratulated the General Electric people on the performance of their engines. They were as delighted as we were. Another flight was scheduled for the following day, wheels up at 9 a.m. After lunch we convened the preflight test conference and dictated the test conditions and test results. The new honeycomb flaps showed no adverse effects from the severe buffeting of our maximum-power takeoff.

Wichita

The fourth day at Moses Lake we departed for Wichita. John had a direct course plotted and en route radio frequencies identified. It was C.A.V.U. (ceiling and visibility unlimited).

Communications and navigation equipment aboard the XB-47 were minimal, which was standard for experimental aircraft because testing is conducted during good weather and in the vicinity of the test facility. The XB was equipped with only ADF (automatic direction finding) equipment and communication radio. John was having a problem identifying some of the stations, and we were a little north of course. I knew this country like the palm of my hand. That Bonanza and I had worn grooves in the air in this area. This was a short flight, roughly a thousand miles, only 2 hours and 15 minutes. About 1 hour and 45 minutes out, we were almost directly north of Wichita.

On the interphone I said, "We must have picked up a crosswind. We are almost directly north of Wichita." John said he didn't think so. "Let's turn south on that next section line, and I'll bet you can make a slight right or left correction and get a straight-in clearance for Eighteen" I said. (Runway 18 was the north-south runway aligned with a compass heading of 180 degrees.) We followed the section line and hit the Wichita Airport right on the nose but had to circle several times to lose altitude. We had cruised at 31,000 feet and should have started our letdown at least 100 miles out. John made a satisfactory landing. I pulled the drag chute and jettisoned it when we arrived on the taxiway.

We were both astounded at the spectators along the road that bordered the airport. The word was out, and Wichita was proud that the six-jet-engine bomber was to be tested there. Also, the B-47 production program was a major factor in Wichita's financial well-being. The flag truck led us to the parking ramp just across the street from the factory and flight-test hangar. As we climbed down the egress ladder, we were greeted by management and engineering personnel, all strangers to me, and friends of John's. I looked at the guard gate and, sure enough, there were DeLores, Judy, and Gary. I walked over, and the guard allowed them to come on the ramp. "Did you have a good trip?" I asked.

"Yes, up until we arrived here about an hour and a half ago," she said.

"What do you mean?"

"When we arrived I asked the guard if the XB-47 was here. He said, 'Not yet, but should be arriving soon. The crash wagons are getting ready.' "

"That all he said?" I asked.

"Yes, he just went back in his shack."

It struck me sort of funny. Then I realized she thought the airplane was in trouble. I had seen some fire trucks and an ambulance on a taxiway as we taxied to the parking ramp. "Oh, don't worry about it," I said. "That's just a precautionary procedure they follow."

She gave me their motel telephone number and said, "Call. We'll come and pick you up."

John and I were escorted to the flight-test facilities, which included the standard offices, instrumentation section, data-transcription department, and flight-test engineering. The flight crew locker room was far superior to the revetment at Seattle.

I was introduced to Elliot Merrill, senior pilot and head of Wichita Flight Test. Elliot had real longevity at the Boeing Company with a fine track record. He had been test pilot on the B-17, B-29's, B-50's, Stratocruiser, and Stratoliner. We became good friends. Seattle announced that John Fornasero, Boeing chief of flight test, was moving to Wichita to manage the B-47 test program, Elliot Merrill was returning to Seattle to manage flight-test activity there, and I had been appointed project pilot on the XB-47.

To date no engineering flight testing had been accomplished on the XB-47, so the technical staffs and Wright Field were demanding information on takeoff and landing, stability and control, and performance throughout the speed, gross weight, and altitude envelope. In addition, they wanted a flight demonstration to maximum design structural load factor as early as practical so that any necessary structural changes could be incorporated in the production program as early as possible. John called me to his office and said, "I'd like to ride with you in the morning at nine a.m."

"Great," I said. Driving home that evening I thought, "Mr. Fornasero, I know you F.A.A. guys. Give me something I can't handle. I've been waiting for this flight since that day in Colonel Boyd's office." I slept well that night.

After completing the walk-around ground check the next morning and climbing into the pilot seat, I quietly said, "Look alive, old girl. It's time for you and me to get acquainted." With all engines at idle, all preflight checks com-

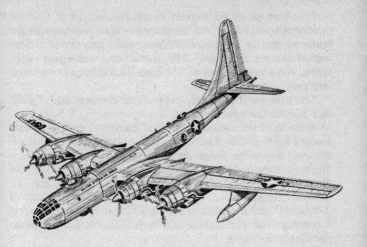

B-50

plete, and external power removed, I pushed the mike button
and announced, "We're ready to go. You ready?"

"All ready," John replied.

I signaled the crew chief to disconnect the interphone. He
pulled the phone jack, coiled the wire, cleared the area, and
gave me the clear sign. I already had taxi clearance, so I
released the brakes, added a little power, and we were under
way.

She handled sweet. The nose-gear steering was just the
right ratio. As we approached the takeoff end of runway 18
I checked all engines tank-to-engine, flaps at takeoff position,
longitudinal trim set, aileron and rudder trim zero, hydraulic
pressure on the money, altimeter set, calling out each checklist item to John on the interphone, and concluded, "I'm
ready. How about you?"

"Okay," he replied.

On tower frequency I called, "XB-47 ready for takeoff."

"Clear for takeoff," came the reply.

Taking the runway, I lined up on center line, held the

brakes, brought all six engines to 100-percent power, and on the interphone said, "All temperatures and pressures okay; brake release on the count of three. One, two, three." She leaped like a scalded dog. The acceleration was sensational, and as the airspeed reached 150 mph takeoff speed, we were airborne.

"All temp and pressure, okay. Gear coming up," I said as I moved the gear handle to the up position. I pulled the nose up to climb attitude, retracted the flaps, and set climb power, holding 260 mph climb speed. Out of the corner of my eye, I saw the power dropping on number six. Holding the mike button, I said, "Losing power on number six, no fire warning." If there was, I would cut number six and hit the fire extinguisher.

"Okay," John replied, "let's go to Salina. That runway is ten thousand feet, and the facility is closed down. We have permission to use it."

"Okay," I said, as I leveled off at 10,000 feet and set cruise power. I could already see Salina, so I closed the throttles and started the letdown. As we approached, I saw the airport wind T indicating a south wind, verified by smoke from a chimney in Salina. "We have a south wind. Do you want a touch and go or full stop?"

"Just a touch and go. We don't want to use the chute here."

I had lowered the gear and flaps and added a bit of power. Approach speed on the money. I eased the power off, and she settled on. I allowed her to roll a few seconds, then eased the throttles to full power. As the airspeed approached takeoff speed, I saw the power start to fade on engine number three. "Number three engine failure," I announced in the interphone. "No evidence of fire."

"Good, let's go to Wichita," John replied.

I raised gear and flaps and set climb power. Gently I lowered the nose to level flight and kept one eye on the airspeed. It was beautiful. That needle just kept winding up as we accelerated. I kept adding nose down trim to maintain zero elevator control pressures. The airspeed needle approached 450 mph. I reduced the power to idle, worked the Wichita tower, and made a left turn into the traffic pattern.

In the locker room John said, "Good flight. You're approved as a B-47 pilot. Dix Loesch is on his way to Wichita as copilot. It's up to you to get him qualified. We're going to need more pilots.''

"Good," I said, "his qualifications look good."

Escape System

Several days later John said, "Because the production airplane has ejection seats, the project office at Wright Field has issued an order that all B-47 pilots must come to Wright Field for ejection-seat indoctrination."

"What the hell for?" I said. "All you do is actuate the eject switch and pray. We don't even have an ejection seat in the XB."

"I know," he replied, "but you know how Wright Field is."

The airplane was in lay-up for installation of additional instrumentation, so I departed for Wright Field for the seat ride and to meet the B-47 project officer, Captain Jack Shaffer. Bell personnel stayed at the Dayton Biltmore. Boeing people stayed at the Van Cleve. The Van Cleve had the best food in Dayton. I had an 8:30 date for the seat ride at the structural test hangar, a huge building originally built to handle the static testing of the consolidated B-36. I was escorted to the ejection-seat trainer and saw another customer already there.

"Meet Herman Salmon," the technician said. "They call him Fish."

That got my attention. I knew Tony LeVier, chief test pilot of Lockheed at Burbank, California, and had heard complimentary pilot talk regarding Fish Salmon. "Fish, I'm glad to meet you. Think we can operate this thing?"

"Let's get on with it," he said. "I had a rough night." He looked a little peaked.

"Go ahead," I said, "you're first."

"Thanks," he muttered as he climbed into the seat.

The technician began his briefing on where to place your feet and where to pull the seat trigger. Fish was attempting to comprehend the instructions and neglected to fasten the shoulder harness and safety belt. He leaned forward slightly to peer under the seat's left arm where the technician was pointing out the location of the ejection switch. Feeling for the switch with the index finger of his left hand, Fish accidentally actuated it. There was a blast. The seat shot toward the ceiling of the high bay area. Fish's neck was stretched about a foot, and he was mashing his fingerprints into the arm rests. The seat latched at its peak, and Fish gazed about with a confused look 75 feet above the hangar floor. It was a close call. The left footrest had flashed by close to the technician's head. The seat and Fish were lowered by the ratchet mechanism. "Would you like to try it again, Mr. Salmon?" the technician asked.

"What the hell for?" Fish said as he left.

Fish and I were close friends until his untimely death, after his retirement from a fabulous career as an experimental test pilot at Lockheed.

At 1 p.m., I kept my appointment with Captain Shaffer, the B-47 project officer. Shaffer, handsome, six feet one or two, and around 210 pounds, had been famed at West Point as a broken field runner in football and was still known as Shifty Hips Shaffer. "I hear you been flying the bird; what do you think of her?" he asked.

I brought him up to date on my experience with the aircraft to date and said, "The B-47 will convert the Air Force to jets."

"We're glad to hear that," he said, "but when are we going to get some conclusive data?"

"As soon as I get off these silly-ass trips, like riding that ejection seat up to the hangar roof," I joked.

"Yeah, I know," he said, "it's top brass." Then he told me he'd just come from a top-level B-47 meeting on weight saving and said, "They made the decision to remove the ejection seats from the production airplane."

I just sat and looked at him. "Did you contest the decision?"

"Nothing I could do."

"Jack, you know LeMay will not accept this airplane without a flight crew escape system." General Curtis E. LeMay was Commander of the Strategic Air Command.

"He may have to."

"I'll bet you right now he will not accept the B-47 without

an escape system. You know as well as I the ejection seat is the only escape from a high-performance airplane.''

I returned to the hotel and called Fornasero. "Someone in management should get on this one, John. LeMay won't accept the airplane without those seats.''

John didn't think anyone would want to muddy the water. "The decision is probably cleared all the way up,'' he said.

Subsequently, numerous B-47 airplanes were built without the escape system, but LeMay would not accept them until they were returned to the production line and modified to the original flight crew ejection seat configuration.

Experience an Asset

Bell and Lockheed were the only U.S. aircraft companies with any jet aircraft experience. The uninformed media doomsday entrepreneurs were predicting damage to and failure of the turbine engine during ground maneuvering and takeoff due to the ingestion of foreign material such as small stones, debris, and birds. Consequently, Boeing power-plant people designed screens of thin-gauge, maximum-strength metal to cover the engine air inlets. With the onboard instrumentation complete, Dix and I had begun the comprehensive flight-test program. Early on, a postflight engine inspection revealed engine-compressor damage from pieces of a failed inlet screen. The engine was changed and the screen replaced. Then we had another screen failure, another engine change.

I discussed the problem with John and project and power-plant personnel. I pointed out that at Muroc, the XP-59 engine air inlets were only one-fourth the distance above the ground of the B-47 inlets, and they had experienced no problem. Lockheed's XP-80 was flying under similar conditions and experiencing no problems with ingestion of foreign objects. The discussion concluded with a decision to remove the inlet screens. After that, the only foreign object that caused a problem was a wrench inadvertently left in an engine-inlet area.

The XB-47 retractable midsection and outboard wing leading edge slats were a weight penalty. Aerodynamics, comparing data on the NASA L-39 swept-wing spanwise airflow with wind tunnel tests of the damming effect of the XB-47 engine pods on spanwise flow, elected to deactivate the midspan slats on the test airplane. I flew the tests with the slats deactivated and the wings tufted to reveal the airflow. The damming effect of the engine pods and struts retarded spanwise flow at low and stall speeds, resulting in satisfactory stall characteristics. In the final test, with mid and outboard sections deactivated, stall characteristics were satisfactory. Consequently, leading edge slats were removed from the production B-47. The weight savings were significant.

Colonel Boyd arrived for a demonstration flight, our first meeting since my visit to Wright Field. After an airplane walk-around briefing, we climbed the entry ladder to the aisle on the port side of the elevated pilot and copilot positions. As he started to move aft toward the copilot seat, I said, "This way, sir. You're flying this bird." I explained the side-hatch emergency exit, he climbed into the pilot's seat, and I gave him a cockpit checkout. With helmets and microphones hooked up, I talked him through the six-engine start procedure and then climbed into the copilot's seat. After I worked the tower, I said on the interphone, "We're cleared; she's all yours."

At the runway, cleared for takeoff, he lined up, applied 100-percent power, released the brakes, and started the takeoff run. When airborne, with gear and flaps retracted, he stabilized at the best climb speed of 260 mph and executed climbing turns to level off at 25,000 feet, where he conducted some high-speed, level-flight maneuvers. Then he continued a climb to 35,000 feet, checked the high-altitude handling characteristics, executed a 180-degree turn south of Tulsa, and at 97-percent power headed for Wichita. His letdown, approach, and landing were well executed. We returned to the locker room, and he said, "Tex, this is the greatest bomber in the world. The performance is phenomenal."

The citizens of Wichita maintained their enthusiasm for the XB-47. Each day a constant flow of observers crowded the public areas surrounding the airport. Several of the Wichita police controlling the crowds were my friends. One day during flight testing of the Sperry autopilot, I used Douglass Avenue, Wichita's main east-west thoroughfare, for a low-level tracking reference. Approximately an hour after landing, one of my police friends, accompanied by two Boeing guards, appeared at my desk. With a stern expression on his face, he gave me a traffic ticket. The charge: running a stop signal on east Douglass Avenue. With concern, I continued to read the citation and noted, "Vehicle: XB-47," and as I rose from my chair, everyone burst into laughter. That story floated around for days. My secretary, Donna, framed the citation and displayed it on the office wall.

Knowledge

The force that pilots were required to apply to operate the controls of large airplanes increased as airplanes increased in size. That led to the development of power-operated controls. The XB-47 employed hydraulic boost in the lateral control system. If the boost system failed or was shut off, it took two hands and maximum pilot effort to make large lateral control movements. That condition was accepted for two reasons. First, the hydraulic system was reliable. Second, the roll-due-to-yaw characteristic of the swept wing allowed the pilot to correct a wing-low attitude by yawing the airplane with the rudder.

To prepare for the arrival of the B-47 bombers, General LeMay established a B-47 crew training base at Wichita. The commanding officer was General Paul Tibbets of Hiroshima atom bomb fame. His two ranking colonels were Pat Fleming, whom I knew on a first-name basis, and Dick Lassiter, a close friend. One Friday afternoon, after the military B-47 flight training school was in operation, I received a call from Colonel Fleming. "Tex, the B-47 lateral control system is unsatisfactory. Boeing must modify the system."

During a landing with the aileron boost off, to simulate the loss of aileron boost in a crosswind, he had dragged a wingtip on the runway. I suggested a meeting at his office, which he rejected. "Who was flying the airplane?" I asked.

"I was," he replied. "I applied full lateral control with no response."

I called Colonel Lassiter. We were friends and I could talk to him. "Dick," I said, "I just talked to Fleming. Pat says they dragged a wingtip. He's really hot. I need to see the airplane.''

"Okay," he said. "Tomorrow is Saturday. Come to my office at nine a.m.''

The airplane was parked on the ramp. A look at the left wingtip revealed little damage. Obviously, it had barely touched the runway. I climbed to the cockpit, released the flight control lock, and returned to the wingtip. Reaching up, I deflected the aileron full down and said, "See where the aileron tip is? It's below the damage area on the wingtip. Pat believes he applied full aileron, but as you can see, he did not. Full control deflection at touchdown speed with boost off would require both hands on the wheel and a hell of a lot of effort. Since Pat was flying, he had his right hand on the throttles. Sure, he was applying full left-hand pressure, but that was not enough. Let's fly this airplane. I'll demonstrate what occurred and how it can be corrected by yawing the airplane.''

During the flight, I demonstrated the roll-due-to-yaw characteristics of a swept wing. Back on the ground, Dick said, "You're correct. That's what occurred. I'll brief Pat.''

"Don't your instructors demonstrate this boost-out technique? It's in the training manual.''

"No, but they will in the future.''

"Okay," I replied, "let me know if I can be of assistance.''

Salute to William Allen White

In response to a request by the chamber of commerce of my hometown, Emporia, Kansas, 75 miles northeast of Wichita, the vice president and general manager of the Boeing Wichita plant, Earl Shaffer, approved an XB-47 fly-by farewell salute to William Allen White, renowned journalist and founder of the *Emporia Gazette*. He was a friend to my father and the author of my first letter of recommendation upon graduation from the Spartan School of Aeronautics.

Arriving over Emporia at the scheduled time, I gave the citizens of Emporia a close view of the six-engine XB-47 at 500 mph, two hundred feet above the buildings. An article in the evening *Gazette* quoted a chamber of commerce member who had observed the aerial salute to Mr. White from the roof of the Broadway Hotel: "We could feel the heat from the jet engines as the airplane flashed over our heads."

Devastation and Recovery

Vice President Shaffer informed me of the scheduled arrival of Secretary of the Air Force Finletter and Under Secretary McComb for a B-47 briefing and a possible demonstration ride in the XB. The day of arrival was spent in conference. A demonstration flight was scheduled for the following morning, but the ceiling was below minimums. By 10 a.m. the weather had lifted enough to permit their Lockheed Constellation to depart for Fort Worth, Texas.

At noon, plant director Shaffer called and said the Air Force had reported excellent weather for a demonstration at Fort Worth. Approaching the 10,000-foot runway at Fort Worth's Carswell Air Force Base, I elected not to use the drag parachute on the landing roll to save the time required to install another for the demonstration flight. Touching down on the first 200 feet of the approach end of the runway, I retracted the flaps to get additional weight on the wheels and allowed the airplane to decelerate for approximately 3,000 feet. I applied the brakes carefully to avoid any tire skidding and resulting tire blowouts. I felt the slight deceleration. Everything was perfect, with 6,000 feet of runway remaining, when instantaneously all wheels locked. I could hear the tires blow and felt the airplane shuddering as they disintegrated, littering the runway with hunks of rubber. The airplane came to a stop heeled to one side; one tire of the eight was still inflated. "It must look like a ruptured duck," I thought.

What an ordeal. Not only Finletter and McComb but also many high-ranking Air Force officers had witnessed it. I knew what they were thinking. "That dumb S.O.B. locked the brakes." With the flat areas on the wheel rims and the remains of the tires, it required almost full power to taxi from the runway onto a taxi strip. I shut down the engines and climbed down the ladder. I didn't know what our problem was, but I knew I hadn't locked those brakes. It had to be a malfunction.

The first to arrive was General "Wild Bill" Irvine, an extremely capable officer and rougher than a cob. If there was anyone in the Air Force who would understand the problem, it was General Irvine. "Damn, Tex, what happened?" he said, which proved my opinion of him. Many officers would have said, "What do you think you're doing?"

"I don't know, General. Everything was in the green when suddenly all the brakes locked."

"What's your plan?"

"I'll call the factory and have them fly in eight new tires, wheels, and brakes via our C-46. I'll have the XB on the line for flight at nine a.m. tomorrow."

"You sure you can make it?"

"We'll be ready."

We had a crew chief with us. I instructed him to get the airplane up on jacks and wheels off. "Check out the brake hydraulic system. There has to be a problem in the system. I'll call the factory for personnel and parts. We're going to be on that flight line at eight a.m. tomorrow. I'll get someone to help you arrange for jacks from the Consolidated B-36 factory across the airport. Don't allow anyone around this bird. I'll keep you informed."

The Wichita factory responded. The C-46 arrived with equipment and personnel, including hydraulic and brake engineers. I remember more pleasant nights. However, the airplane, with new brakes, tires, and wheels, was refueled and ready to taxi to the ramp area at 7 a.m. The hydraulic engineers discovered a faulty sensing valve in the hydraulic brake system, which solved the problem. At 7:50 we taxied into position adjacent to the secretaries' Lockheed Constellation.

The entourage arrived. As Secretary Finletter and McComb approached the XB, I stepped forward, introduced myself, shook hands, and stated my regrets for yesterday's mishap. I briefly explained the problem. They strolled around the XB, surveying the exterior, and told me, "It's an interesting airplane, a significant configuration change."

As Finletter strolled toward the Lockheed I said, "Mr. Secretary, the XB-47 is a significant advancement in bomber aircraft. I believe you will be impressed with its performance.

Please don't be concerned regarding yesterday's problem. The airplane is in perfect commission."

The secretary checked his watch, turned slightly, and said, "We have a tight schedule."

McComb said, "Mr. Secretary, perhaps we should take the time. This airplane is being well received."

The secretary turned and said, "Is everything ready?"

"Yes, sir," I replied, and motioned for the flight suits and crash helmets. With their flight gear on, I ushered them up the entrance ladder. I seated Secretary Finletter in the copilot's seat and McComb in the bombardier seat in the nose. I plugged in their radio and interphone. Dix remained in the side aisle during flight. I finished the cockpit check as General Irvine climbed up the ladder, winked, and handed me a note. As the general departed, the crew chief closed the entrance hatch. The note said, "Buzz the field."

Executing a steep climbing left turn after takeoff, I headed for Dallas. On interphone I kept our guests informed of speed and altitude. The public relations people had informed me that the secretary had a private pilot license, so, when I leveled off at 30,000 feet, I said on the interphone, "She's all yours, Mr. Secretary. Fly it just like you do a Cessna." I held my hands above my head so he could see them.

He made two very shallow turns and said, "Thank you."

"Stay on the controls, Mr. Secretary, and follow me through a couple of turns." I laid her over in a 30-degree right then left turn and said, "It's all yours." He continued the turn and became more aggressive and executed a medium climb and dive. McComb commented frequently regarding the absence of vibration and the quietness. I said, "Make a one-hundred-eighty-degree turn. We are one hundred miles east of Dallas." When he had achieved a westerly heading, I said, "We are at twenty-five thousand, Mr. Secretary. Pull all six throttles back to the idle stop and start the letdown."

We were approaching Carswell when I observed a B-36 equipped with jet pods on the outboard wings preparing for takeoff. Calling it to their attention on interphone, I said, "That B-36 will be in the climbout soon. Would you like a fly-by to see it?" The answer was affirmative. "Okay," I said. "I have control." The B-36, with gear and flaps up, was in the climb. Approaching the B-36 from the rear and slightly below and to the right at 100-percent power, indicating 500 mph, we flashed past slightly below and to the right. I pulled up in a loop and was on our back at 12,000 feet. "Look through the top of the canopy," I said. "There's your B-36."

As the nose came down in a vertical dive, power off, McComb said, "Mr. Secretary, did you ever imagine anything like this?"

His laugh came over the interphone. "No, and I don't think many people have."

In the letdown for landing, I said, "Mr. Secretary, I received a request to buzz the tower prior to landing. Do you have any objection?"

"None," was the reply.

We came east to west about 200 feet off the deck, 500 mph on the clock. If you looked real quick, you could see the tower operators through their windows. Pulling up in a near vertical climb, we were on our back again at the top of a loop at 16,000 feet, looking straight down through the canopy at Fort Worth and Carswell Air Force Base. I executed the approach and landing, and Dix pulled the drag-chute control after touchdown. I turned off the runway at the number two taxiway, Dix released the chute, and I taxied up and parked by the Lockheed.

It was a completely different crowd that greeted us as we deplaned. It was a relief to see smiles instead of grim faces. They spent an hour discussing the airplane and the flight. Everyone was climbing in and out of the cockpit. Later, I heard from a friend who worked in the Consolidated factory, "Everyone thought the factory blew up when you buzzed the tower."

The B-47 was a terrific airplane, loved by every pilot who was fortunate enough to fly it. I received a letter ten days later from Secretary Finletter complimenting the XB-47 and expressing his appreciation for the forever-memorable flight aboard the XB-47.

Wing Windup

The XB-47 contained many new, state-of-the-art configuration and structural design concepts. One of significance was the flexible-stress wing design, which provided a strong, flexible structure, allowing the wing to flex during gust and maneuvering loads, thus relieving high-stress areas and providing a smoother ride.

During a low-level flight demonstration at Wichita for observing dignitaries, I increased the air speed to approximately 435 mph and applied right aileron and up elevator for a right climbing turn. The airplane rolled left. I snapped the throttles closed and the lateral control to neutral, simultaneously increasing the climb angle. As the speed decreased to 425, the lateral control became normal. Analysis of the problem determined that at the high air loads at speeds above 425 mph, when the ailerons were deflected, the flexible wing began to twist, changing the angle of attack of the outboard wing sections, resulting in control reversal. This twist was called wing windup. "It sure gets your attention," I said.

That event led to the development of lateral control spoilers to eliminate the wing-twist problem on all Boeing airplanes. A lateral control spoiler is a rectangular door, hinged on its forward edge, which fits flush with the upper surface of the wing. During a turn in flight the doors are raised on the wing at the inside of the turn, decreasing the lift of that wing so that the airplane rolls in that direction. When the spoilers are raised on both wings simultaneously, they serve as air brakes while retaining their lateral control function, an extremely valuable control for dissipating excessive airspeed.

F.A.A. Air Traffic Control

To verify long-range fuel-consumption data, a nonstop flight was scheduled from Wichita to Los Angeles and back, to be conducted on a profile of altitude versus gross weight. T. Johnson, our chief flight-test engineer, was aboard to monitor the continuous-recording instrumentation. The weather was C.A.V.U.—ceiling and visibility unlimited. Conversing with F.A.A. stations along the route, we responded to questions: "What type of aircraft? Is the time hack right? That's almost six hundred miles an hour and thirty-five thousand feet. Are you serious?" Those were the days of DC-3's, 4's, and 6's, Lockheed Constellations, and Boeing Stratocruisers, and a preview of things to come for the F.A.A. As we made a U-turn at 35,000 feet over Santa Monica, California, the control-tower operators were observing our progress with binoculars.

T. Johnson was complaining about the low temperature in the bombardier's area when he presented us a hot cup of coffee. Dix and I were comfortable, receiving sun radiation through the bubble canopy. My comment was, "T., you should have worn your longjohns." Just then, I spilled some of my hot coffee on the metal floor of the cockpit. It froze solid on impact, a blob with several short splashes around the circumference. The outside air temperature was holding at –55 degrees F, and the metal of the airframe was cold-soaked to approximately that temperature.

13

The B-52 Program

John Fornasero had returned to Seattle. I was senior experimental test pilot and representative in charge of WIBAC (Wichita Boeing Airplane Company) production and experimental flight testing. The XB-47 contractual compliance testing was nearing completion, and production airplane deliveries were on schedule.

Rumors in Wichita indicated a new airplane was in the preliminary design stage in Seattle. I was delighted when Fornasero requested my presence at a mockup meeting in Seattle. The technical staff described an airplane with a B-47 configuration in the gross-weight category of 300,000 pounds. The design included eight turbojet engines, integral wing fuel cells, in-flight refueling, crosswind landing gear, lateral control spoilers, and a crew of five, with increased operational altitude, speed, and range capability.

Proceeding to the full-scale mockup of the cockpit of the proposed model XB-52, I was disappointed to find that the pilot and copilot stations were tandem, as in the B-47. The arrangement of the three crew members on the lower deck was satisfactory. All crew members had ejection seats, the lower deck downward. Early in the B-47 program, following a demonstration flight with General LeMay, I had concluded that he was delighted with the airplane but considered mandatory use of the interphone for crew coordination undesirable. I agreed. Seating the pilot and copilot side by side allows simplified and more efficient flight crew coordination. During the cockpit review session I recommended a side-by-side cockpit for improved pilot-copilot coordination. Aerodynamics disagreed, predicting a negative effect on high-speed and range performance.

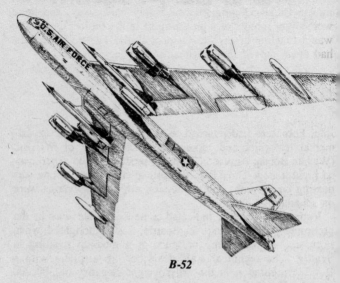

B-52

Arriving at the design-engineering department, I was introduced to a child's four-wheel coaster wagon modified to allow the track of the four wheels to be adjusted right or left 1 to 15 degrees with reference to the wagon bed, demonstrating that an aircraft under crosswind conditions could be landed in the crab angle required to prevent drifting. The wheels adjusted to the required crab angle would roll directly down the runway, eliminating the complicated piloting technique for crosswind landings.

Douglas had modified a DC-4 with a crosswind landing gear for Wright Field. Colonel Wethe, B-52 project officer at Wright Field, arranged for me to fly the crosswind DC-4. The flight was interesting. The crosswind gear removed the sweat from crosswind landings. The only difference from a direct-wind landing was that the pilot was viewing the runway from one side of the windshield. The crosswind gear was standard on B-52 aircraft.

Early in 1951 I was appointed XB-52 project pilot and scheduled to return to Seattle—thirteen moves in sixteen years. DeLores and I were confident this would be our last move. The B-52 program was barely under way, and there were slight rumors of a jet transport in the future. Our future was a function of my professional skills. The invisible hand had again moved the chessmen in my game of life.

Daughter Barbara Jean

Daughter number two, Barbara Jean, made an unobstructed approach and landing on May 2, 1951, in Wichita and arrived in Seattle two months later via United Airlines DC-7. She was escorted by a proud father, delighted mother, and eager sister and brother. The rental waterfront home I had procured on Evergreen Point in Bellevue prior to escorting the family to Seattle was enthusiastically received.

One afternoon, Seattle was notified of a tragic in-flight collision of two production B-47's at Wichita. There were no survivors. On board were Boeing pilots Heinburger and Steve Gatty, and Culltharp and Oppenhimer. I returned to Wichita to participate in the accident investigation. It concluded that in the airplane flown by Culltharp and Oppenhimer a red light had indicated unsafe landing gear after extension and they requested another B-47, piloted by Heinburger, to fly in formation and verify, if possible, the gear position. The observing airplane approached the problem plane from the rear and to one side and proceeded to fly slowly forward slightly below the problem plane to visually check all the landing gear trucks. Through an error in judging vertical distance separating the two aircraft, the vertical tail of the observing airplane contacted the outrigger landing gear of the other aircraft, causing loss of control of both planes.

XB and YB-52

The XB and YB-52's under construction in plant 1 were nearing completion. Because the X required some rework, the YB was completed first. To accommodate some difficult-to-comprehend security precautions, rollout of the YB was scheduled at 1 a.m., with the airplane completely draped in hundreds of square yards of white muslin cloth. Colonel Guy Townsend and I observed the operation, the rain-soaked muslin clinging to the upper surface of the airplane glistening in the floodlights. East Marginal Way, the highway separating the Boeing factory from Boeing Field, was closed to traffic. The YB was towed across the highway to the airport ramp area for preflight check, engine runs, and preflight inspection. The tests, of course, required removal of the muslin.

The daily schedule was a challenge, consisting of test planning, coordinating flight-test instrumentation design and checkout, attending conferences with the B-52 project engineers. There was also much coordinating with the Air Force plant representative General Austin Davis and his staff: Colonel Townsend, Colonel Wayne, and Colonel Arnold, all friends from the B-47 Wichita days. Townsend was the assigned military observer on the B-52 program. In that position, his detailed knowledge of the airplane was excellent. We had flown together throughout the B-47 program, and I was delighted with his assignment as copilot on the initial flight of the YB-52.

Preflight checkout of a new airplane the size and complexity of the YB-52 is a detailed and time-consuming operation. The special-design blast fences behind the airplane parking and engine test areas had originated with the B-47 and were expanded to accommodate the B-52. The engine noise level was so high that nighttime engine operation was forbidden.

YB-52 Initial Flight

During manufacture of the X and YB-52, the engineers involved in the design of the cockpit display for the crosswind landing-gear position indicator requested a meeting to discuss the subject. I explained that a pilot executing a crosswind takeoff or landing thinks in terms of the heading of the airplane in reference to the runway. I also described a cockpit display consisting of a rotatable miniature airplane in a circular housing, mounted over a background runway aligned with the longitudinal axis of the airplane.

The display mounted between the pilot and copilot seats and equipped with a glasstop lens would allow the flight crew to check the crosswind crab angle of the miniature airplane visually in reference to the runway. A right and left rotatable control adjacent to the display would allow either crew member to select the required crosswind crab angle, computed by using wind direction and velocity information received from the airport control tower. As the required crab angle (in degrees) is dialed in by turning the control, the aircraft landing gear rotates to the required angle. At the same time, the miniature display airplane also rotates to the required crab angle above the runway display. That gives the pilot a clear visual reference to verify the correct crab angle and heading during completion of the cockpit takeoff and landing checklists.

The initial taxi testing was conducted at slow and moderate speeds to investigate ground handling. Nose-gear steering with the rudder pedals was simple and effective, but the 185-foot wingspan and far-outboard location of the outrigger gear required great care in taxiing in the vicinity of other aircraft and in negotiating turns to and from taxiways. After practice, use of the crosswind gear during taxiing became routine. People stared in wonder at the mammoth XB-52 taxiing partially sideways on ramps and runways.

At 95 mph, the maximum speed achieved during high-speed taxi tests, the lateral control spoilers provided adequate control. But before the first flight, the aerodynamics engineers elected to change the control-tab setting of the small feel aileron to eliminate any chance of overbalance in the lateral control system. The feel aileron is a small conventional aileron that provides the minimal lateral control needed up to the spoiler pickup point, where the spoilers become active.

On April 15, 1952, a date publicized by the Boeing public relations and news bureau, spectators jammed Boeing Field's perimeter streets and the hillside east of the airport. Because of the scheduled extension of the Boeing Field runway, this initial flight of the YB-52 would terminate at Larson Air Force Base, Moses Lake, Washington.

Copilot Colonel Townsend and I had worked together during construction, preflight checkout, and taxi tests of the YB-52. Chase pilot Major Harley Beard of the Wright Field technical photo unit also attended preflight briefings to be well informed regarding test conditions and the airplane. He would keep close watch throughout the flight from the cockpit of his F-86.

F-86

The historic importance of this initial flight was in my mind as I taxied into position. Boeing Field's single runway stretched ahead past the company ramp, with city streets and hillsides crowded with men and women whose hopes and dreams hinged on the success of this airplane. With temperatures and pressures normal, all takeoff checks completed, and takeoff clearance, I advanced the throttles to 100-percent power and released the brakes. With an awsome eight-engine roar, the YB-52 sprang forward, accelerating rapidly, wings curving upward as they accepted the 235,000-pound initial flight gross weight. At V_2 (takeoff speed) the airplane lifted off the runway, because of the 6-degree angle of incidence of the wing, and at 11:08 a.m. we were airborne. The initial flight of YB-52 had begun.

Chase pilot Beard reported on test frequency that everything appeared normal. During climbout, I tried to apply lateral control and could hardly move the wheel. "They sure as hell prevented overbalance," I told Guy on the interphone. "Try the ailerons."

The wheel moved slightly. "You got that right," he agreed from his rear seat in the tandem cockpit. I reduced power and achieved a left turn by applying slight left rudder, thanks to the roll due to yaw of a swept-wing airplane.

We timed the retraction of the landing gear and flaps—right on the money. Chase pilot Beard reported the gear doors were all closed and flaps fully retracted. We extended and retracted the landing-gear again—no problem. All onboard systems except lateral control appeared to be operating normally. I transmitted running commentaries on what we were doing, including pertinent data, observations, and impressions.

With ground concurrence we departed for Moses Lake, climbed en route to 25,000 feet, and checked the operation of all systems. Colonel Townsend flew for some time, familiarizing himself with the airplane, before I took over to enter the Larson traffic pattern. Many ranking military officers and civilian dignitaries were gathered on the ramp at Larson to witness the initial landing. On final, cleared to land with the runway just ahead, the control tower suddenly announced an emergency scramble of fighters that were even then taking the active runway right in front of us. I applied full power and aborted the landing, climbed out, and established a second approach. This time we touched down without incident. Townsend deployed the drag chute, and I felt the deceleration and simultaneously retracted the flaps. Braking moderately, I turned off on a taxi strip, and Guy jettisoned the drag chute.

At three hours and eight minutes, the flight in the YB-52 was the longest-duration maiden flight in the history of aviation and introduced one of the world's great airplanes.

Before the second flight, the feel aileron control tab was adjusted to allow the pilot to achieve full aileron deflection using only one hand on the control wheel. However, during that flight, I found that the lateral control spoilers cut in at different times in sequence as the control wheel rotated. Turn entries and recoveries occurred in step functions rather than in a smooth, continuous operation. Boeing control system engineers modified the lateral control system, using a modulated pressure system to actuate all spoilers simultaneously, the degree of movement being proportional to control-wheel travel. It was an ideal solution. When the drag brake control was actuated, all spoilers extended simultaneously, providing effective drag while maintaining their lateral control function. No wing windup was encountered as with the XB-47, because the long outboard wing ailerons had been eliminated.

Boeing, in designing and building the B-47, pioneered and perfected semiflexible structures for large jet aircraft. Flexibility provides a smoother ride in rough air and increases airframe service life by reducing stress at points of high load concentration. The B-52, like the B-47, utilized a flexible wing. I saw the wingtip of the B-52 static test airplane travel 32 feet, from the negative 1-G load position to the positive 4-G load position.

Flutter

Aircraft are subject to two categories of flutter, which are of major consideration in the design and testing of new aircraft. Category one is a low-frequency visible sine-wave motion longitudinally through the fuselage or spanwise through the wings and vertical and horizontal stabilizers. Category two is an extremely high-frequency (buzz), small-amplitude flutter of aerodynamic control surfaces such as Cobra II's left elevator trim tab.

Don Knutson was copilot during the B-52 flutter tests. Engineering and Aerodynamics designed an electric-hydraulic multiple-mode flutter exciter mounted in the aft fuselage. The sequential test conditions, flutter mode, speeds, and altitudes were listed on my leg data board. Holding the transmit button down, I broadcast a continual narration of the test.

When the exciter was turned on, the sine wave that passed through the cockpit structure would have thrown us against the canopy if our safety belts and shoulder straps had not been tight. It was such a severe structural shock, I suggested a check of the recorder load data before continuing. Ground agreed. The data revealed structural loads near the limit. The mode machine was inspected and adjusted. After two more attempts produced near-limit loads, the machine was deactivated.

We completed the flutter program through the speed and altitude envelope using manual inputs: light, medium, and hard forward stabs on the control wheel, kicks on a rudder pedal, and hand cranks on the aileron control wheel. The manual excitations provided satisfactory data. It was interesting to observe and feel the sine-wave loads go outboard through the wing structure to the tip and see the engine pods wobble laterally in response. We also could see and feel the results of rudder stabs. In each case, we observed the decrease in amplitude and increase in damping rate as the test condition speed increased. The airplane was proved flutter-free throughout the speed and altitude envelope.

Don Knutson was also copilot during the YB-52 in-flight structural demonstration program. After the 3.5-G pullup he asked on the interphone, "Did you see the wing on that pullup?"

He knew I hadn't. I was busy with the airspeed, altimeter, and G meter (accelerometer). "What's the problem?"

"I think you should see it."

"Okay, repeat three point five G, but don't overshoot."

During the pullup, I looked out the window. The wingtips appeared about 35 degrees above level flight position. I mashed the mike switch and said, "You watch 'em. I can't stand it."

High Altitude

Townsend and I went to the aeromedical lab's altitude chamber at Wright Field to check out in the new flight crew high-altitude pressure suits and helmets, and we were issued suits for operational testing during high-altitude YB-52 test flights. The helmets were equipped with electrically defrosted faceplates to prevent fogging in case of cabin pressure failure and heat loss at 50,000 feet, where outside temperatures are −60 degrees Fahrenheit.

Later in the high-altitude test program of the B-52, Dix Loesch and I conducted tests at increasing operational altitude with depleting fuel. One day, at 52,500 feet, I encountered the identical condition I had experienced during the XP-59A testing. At 100-percent power in a slight climb, as the indicated airspeed dropped 15 mph, we experienced slight stall warning tremors. Then, when the nose was lowered slightly below the horizon, we encountered high-speed buffet when the speed increased 40 mph. We were flying in a speed corridor of 40 mph between stall and high-speed buffet. The engines, however, responded accurately to throttle adjustment, so it was not a problem as it had been with the XP-59A. The B-52 proved to be a truly magnificent airplane and is still on active service after 38 years.

The Correct Decision

Townsend flew copilot for General LeMay on the general's first flight in the YB-52. Boeing president Bill Allen and other Boeing officials were present as LeMay descended the steps to the ramp after the flight. "How do you like her, General?" Allen asked.

LeMay lit a cigar, placed the Zippo lighter in his pocket, looked Allen in the eye, and said, "You have a hell of an airplane, Allen. As soon as you put a side-by-side cockpit on it, I'll buy some."

All production B-52's had side-by-side cockpits.

Testing of the number one production B-52 was progressing on schedule. General LeMay arrived to fly it. I ushered him to the pilot's seat, gave him a cockpit briefing, and responded to his questions. As he reached for his helmet and oxygen mask, he said, "I'm ready when you are." I gave the crew chief the high sign, and he closed the nose belly entrance hatch. I assisted the general with the engine and air-driven alternator starts and then listened as he worked the tower. Turning to me, he said, "You all set?"

"Yes, sir," I said.

As he released the brakes, we were on our way. It was obvious that he had done his homework. The flaps were in takeoff position and the trim set when we were cleared onto the runway. As we became airborne, he retracted the gear and flaps and entered the climb at best climb speed. After experimenting with the lateral control spoilers and their effect as air brakes, he said on the interphone, "The spoiler lateral control is good, and the drag brakes a definite assist."

He leveled off at 30,000 feet, set up cruise power, and made several shallow turns. I pushed the mike button and said, "Let's go to forty-five thousand feet. I believe you will be surprised." He put the throttles against the stop, leveled off at 45,000, went to cruise power, and made a shallow turn. "General," I said, "may I demonstrate something?"

"It's all yours," he said.

I rolled to a 40-degree bank, executed a 180-degree turn, rolled to 40 degrees the opposite direction, and pulled her around another 180 degrees, and said, "It's all yours."

He wasn't bashful. He executed several identical maneuvers and said, "This is what we've been waiting for."

As we completed the flight, LeMay executed a good traffic pattern and landing. I pulled the drag chute.

President Bill Allen; senior vice president Beal; vice presidents Ed Wells, Schairer, Martin, and Woods; and resident Air Force personnel approached the plane as the engines wound down. The crew chief opened the hatch. I followed the general down the steps. Following a handshake, Allen stepped back and said, "What do you think of her now, General?"

Removing a fresh cigar from his pocket, he said, "Bill, now we have an airplane." He was right: I conducted the performance tests of the production model early in the program, and the data, within test tolerance, duplicated the YB performance data. The side-by-side cockpit did not affect speed or range.

Eisenhower

President Eisenhower and Secretary of the Air Force Talbot arrived to tour the B-52 production facilities. A viewers' platform was constructed on the flight ramp adjacent to the resident Air Force offices. The president, Secretary Talbot, their entourage, and Allen and his Boeing executives were assembled on the platform as the YB-52 sped down the runway on takeoff.

The partial fuel load resulted in a rather light gross weight. Employing 100-percent power, the climb angle was spectacular. To remain close to the airport, I executed a climbing left turn and quickly reached 3,500 feet. I was looking at 475 mph on the airspeed indicator as we came across the field at 300 feet and pulled up in a steep left chandelle. We were partially on our back at the top of the maneuver, and as the nose came down in a dive, we moved all throttles to idle. Advancing the throttles as we passed across the airport again at 300 feet, we were looking at 475 mph. It was difficult to remain in the area at that speed, requiring 3.2-G pullups and turns. After completing the demonstration maneuvers and landing, I taxied toward the observer platform. Cutting all eight engines, we rolled up to the platform as the turbines were decelerating, resulting in a significant reduction in engine noise.

Deplaning, I shook hands with President Eisenhower and Secretary Talbot. They were impressed by the performance of the airplane. I suggested a cockpit tour, which the president accepted, much to the alarm of the Secret Service agents. With the president seated in the pilot seat, I explained the cockpit and responded to questions. He made it clear that he was amazed that an airplane of such magnitude could execute the flight maneuvers he had witnessed. So were many other people.

⑭

Problems and Prospects

Commencing with early flights of the XB-47, Boeing's engineering management became convinced that the jet would revolutionize commercial aviation as it had the military. A classified, small engineering group was set up to study the potential for commercial applications. As XB-47 flight-test data accumulated, the jet's theoretical potential for commercial service was confirmed. The study group's effort was expanded to include an actual jet transport configuration and cost studies.

But the British had a head start. During the war British aircraft production concentrated on fighters and bombers. Transport types were built by American companies. So the British were concerned about their postwar role in commercial aviation and made several formal studies of the problem. One study proposed building a jet-powered transport the size of a DC-4/C-54.

In 1945, the idea of jet-powered transport aircraft had seemed impractical to many aviation authorities because of the jet's prodigious thirst for fuel. But the British believed that the fuel drawback was balanced by an important advantage: jet propulsion was one branch of aeronautics where they were far ahead of the United States, thanks to Frank Whittle's pioneering efforts. In 1947, the Ministry of Supply asked the De Havilland Aircraft Company, builder of the Vampire jet fighter, to develop a jet transport.

Sir Geoffrey de Havilland saw that a key to the fuel problem was to fly high. At 30,000 feet, jet fuel consumption is one third or one fourth that at 10,000 feet. So De Havilland's design incorporated a pressurized cabin to enable the aircraft to carry passengers in the rarefied upper air. In 1950 Boeing's president, William M. Allen, and chief of preliminary design, Maynard Pennel, went to England to see the fruit of that development, the de Havilland Comet, at the Farnsborough Air Show. Although impressed, the two men thought the Comet's small size a drawback. Boeing engineers were convinced that to be as economically successful as piston-engined planes, a jet transport should carry at least twice as many passengers.

Boeing's luxurious flying clipper ships—the trimotor biplane Airliner; the all-metal, twin-engine, low-wing 247 Airliner; and the double-deck, pressurized Stratocruiser—were well received. However, the company was best known for its military fighter and bomber aircraft. Bill Allen knew Boeing could not prosper by military business alone in the postwar world. Other developments also encouraged a Boeing decision to produce large, transport-type jet aircraft. The Boeing KC-97, the military version of the double-deck commercial transport, had been modified to an in-flight refueling tanker for jet fighters. In-flight refueling equipment and techniques were perfected. However, because the altitude of the KC-97's reciprocating engine was so limited, the jet fighters and the B-47 were forced to descend to the KC-97's low operational altitude to refuel, an inefficient procedure. Those concerns resulted in expansion of the classified jet transport effort to include a preliminary design group under the direction of engineer Jack Steiner. The Steiner group proposed an airplane, drawing number 367-80 (Dash 80), with tricycle landing gear, 35-degree swept wing, and four pod-mounted turbojet engines. The technical management and sales organization agreed unanimously: the future of commercial aviation was in jet transports.

The problem was dollars. Research and development money was not available from government or industry. The effort would have to be company-financed. Bill Allen proposed to the board of directors that Boeing fund, design, build, and demonstrate a prototype jet transport at an estimated cost of $15 million. At the annual meeting of April 22, 1952, in a leap of hope and faith, the board approved his proposal. The $15 million authorized for the project amounted to a quarter of the company's net worth. If the plane didn't sell, it could bankrupt the company.

Ten days later, on May 2, 1952, the Comet *Yoke Peter* took off from London Airport for Johannesburg, South Africa, via Rome, Beirut, Khartoum, Entebbe, and Livingstone on an impressive first revenue flight for British Overseas Airline Corporation (BOAC). The sleek jet carried 36 passengers and a crew of 6 at speeds just under 500 mph to make the normal 40-hour journey in 23½ hours—vivid proof that jets could shrink the world by 40 percent and make slower, less comfortable aircraft obsolete. De Havilland's Comets started scheduled commercial services in 1952 and impressed the world with their speed and comfort. From the start, they were a tremendous commercial success.

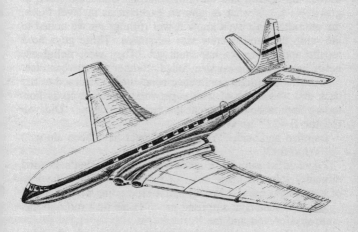

De Havilland Comet

Then, disaster after disaster. The thin skin, large spacing between fuselage circumferentials, and square windows, combined with in-flight pressurization cycling, resulted in metal fatigue, unimpeded tearing of the skin, and explosive decompression.

Animosity

The YB-47 was scheduled for special tests at Wright Field, and Dix and I flew this last company flight—our final salute to the many wonderful test hours we had flown in that beautiful bird. Completing the tests, and in a left traffic pattern, I said to Dix on interphone, "Let's show the ground crew what this lady will do."

"Why not" was the reply.

At full power in a climb I executed three left barrel rolls, extended the gear and flaps, and landed. A barrel roll is a climbing, lateral 360-degree roll maintaining 1 G by proper use of the aileron and elevator controls. Since the force of gravity (1 G) is what an aircraft experiences in level flight, the aircraft didn't even know it was rolling. As we taxied to the ramp the ground crew was all smiles. Those guys do a terrific and extremely important job. They were delighted, never having seen a bomber rolled. Neither had anyone else.

With the postflight conference concluded, I returned to my desk and was involved with paperwork. I looked up as Fornasero approached. I thought his face was drawn. "Did you roll the B-47?" he asked.

I smiled and said, "Yeah, you should have been along."

"What for?"

I looked at him for a second and said, "That's a good airplane, John. It made a lot of history, and it's a favorite of the ground crew's. We all had a little going-away party."

His next statement surprised me. "There isn't room in this company for you and me."

I looked him in the eye for several moments, my thoughts racing, and said, "I don't understand that statement, John." Then I added, "But you might be right."

Without another word he turned and left.

It was after 4:30. Most of the troops had departed. I leaned back in the swivel chair and cogitated. In my mind, John and I understood each other and were friends. We attended

QB together, played poker, went fishing, drank booze, and had flown together. I was surprised and confused by his attitude, particularly his last statement. Well, if that's the way it was, there was nothing to do but, as rodeo cowboys say in the bucking chute, grab a handful of hair and let her buck.

Family

DeLores loved the Northwest and particularly Bellevue. Judy and Gary were involved in school activities and Barbara Jean was walking. At dinner DeLores announced she had found the perfect home. It was precisely what we had been looking for, on the west shore of Hunts Point on Lake Washington, with a view to the west of the snow-crested Olympic Mountains. We were successful in negotiating a deal and moved yet again, but this time only three miles.

The Unexpected

Everyday it was a pleasure to buckle on that YB-52 and smell the odor of that wonderful machine. Listening to people who disliked or were bored with their jobs always saddened me. Never did I consider my activities in aviation a job. Each and every one combined challenge, opportunity, and pleasure, the gift of the Invisible Hand.

It was Sunday, October 6, 1953. DeLores was supervising my application of wallpaper in the master bedroom. She answered the telephone and said, "George Schairer wants to know if it's convenient for you to come to his home." Schairer was chief of technical staff.

"Sure, tell him I'll be right there." George lived a city block up Hunts Point Road.

We were seated in the living room when George said, "Tex, we want you to take on the chief of flight test duties."

I was truly shocked. My mind immediately recalled John's statement the day of the barrel roll. Looking at George, I said, "Thanks, George. I'm delighted and it's an honor, but what about Fornasero?"

"John wants to do more flying."

"George, that's going to be tough—not for me, for John."

"We understand that and believe you can make it work."

"Okay, George, I'll work the problem, but it's going to be tough." We shook hands and I departed.

I told DeLores what had happened. "I'm glad I'm not in your position," she said.

It was difficult to comprehend how the word spread so rapidly. Monday morning I received congratulatory calls from people throughout the company. John moved to my desk and I to his office. It was an unpleasant situation. The employees liked both John and me. They were not only surprised but embarrassed. I assumed an attitude that nothing had happened and continued the daily activities accordingly.

I called John into the office and said, "I was informed that you want to become active in test flying."

"That's correct," he said.

"Okay, proceed to Wichita for checkout in the production B-47. Build up a minimum of fifteen hours, more if you wish, in production testing. I will phase you into the B-52 when you return." He agreed, and I directed Lola to prepare the travel orders.

Reorganization

During the early B-47 program at Wichita, I was disturbed when I became aware that timely and accurate records on test-aircraft configuration control and other documents regarding equipment and configuration changes had not been maintained. My question was: How can a pilot diagnose in-flight problems and handle emergencies when he is not aware of existing configurations? I was also concerned that there were no standard procedures and paperwork for coordinating flight-test departments, nor was there a standardized system coordinating engineering projects with manufacturing, shop, and quality control.

The massive programs for the B-52, the prototype jet transport, the potential jet tanker, and jet transport certification made corrective action necessary. At my request, vice president Charles Beard supplied two company experts skilled in interdepartmental procedures. They—in concert with Fred

Woods, chief of the flight-test instrumentation department; Ben Werner, chief of flight-test engineering and data transcription; and pilots Dix Loesch and Jim Gannett—addressed the production of standardized flight-test forms compatible with all Boeing interdepartmental procedures. Finally they would produce a flight-test procedures manual, including planning, testing and report procedures, and flow diagrams. In addition to those procedural changes, unqualified personnel were transferred to other positions within the company commensurate with their skills.

In the meantime, responding to a Wright Field request, Boeing at the Renton plant was replacing turbojet engines with turboprop engines on a B-47. The combination of turbo engines with large paddle-blade props was new. The failure of a propeller to feather in the event of an engine failure would present a critical, if not uncontrollable, flight problem. My discussion with management concerning the program resulted in establishment of flight-crew hazard pay for first flights and phase-one proving flights.

John returned from Wichita qualified in B-47's. However, considering his background in large propeller-driven airplanes, I offered him the project-pilot assignment on the turboprop B-47. He rejected the offer. During the weekly pilot meeting I briefed the group and asked for volunteers for the job. I told them the bonus had been evaluated, it was not negotiable, and if no one wanted the job I would conduct the tests. Pilots Ray McPhearson and Lew Wallick accepted the assignment and proceeded with the initial flight tests.

The turboprop B-47 program proved unpopular in the Air Force and was terminated. I was delighted; the airplane was a giant step backwards.

Emotions

One of our weekly pilot meetings in my office was about to conclude when John said, "We are considering joining a union."

You could have heard a pin drop on a feather bed. I was completely surprised, and said, "Are you kidding?"

"No," he continued, "we are serious."

B-47

"What unions are you considering?" I asked.

"Air Line Pilots Association, possibly the Teamsters."

I looked at each pilot individually. I wanted to see their eyes. That was difficult. They were all studying the floor or looking out the window. "Okay, fellows, that's all for today." As they left, I asked John to stay. I rose, closed the door, returned to my chair, and proceeded with the most difficult task in my life. Looking him directly in the eye, I said, "John, you're fired."

"You can't fire me," he said.

"Clean out your desk and flight locker," I continued. "Give your travel card and Boeing credentials to Lola. I'll have Finance mail your salary plus severance to your residence."

When I walked out of the office everyone was absorbed in his or her paperwork. I recalled my statement to Schairer, "It's going to be tough," and it was. I wasn't angry; I was hurt. I liked John and considered us friends. He had helped me. It was a sorry situation. The chips were down. Every pilot in the organization was facing the greatest opportunities of his life: the B-52 and the Dash 80, the prototype of the future of air transportation until the supersonic age 25 to 35 years away.

The adverse effects of organized labor, already obvious to the objective observer, were eroding skills, self-motivation, and professional pride. I couldn't believe these pilots in their present status would consider unionizing, and they didn't. In thirteen years, the only time I heard it mentioned was when we started training members of the A.L.P.A. (Air Line Pilots Association) and encountered the union BS.

15

KC-135 Jet Tanker and the Dash 80 Jet Transport

The recently formed transport division under the direction of Boeing vice president Bruce Connelly was located at Renton Airport on the southwest shore of Lake Washington. The Dash 80 program manager Maynard Pennel and his staff of capable veteran engineers Dick Rouzie, aerodynamicist Bill Cook, structural engineer Don Finley, and a host of others dating back to the B-17 were hard at work. The Dash 80 prototype's beautiful lines were already taking shape on the factory floor.

Others outside Boeing were also interested in the possibilities of jet aviation. In response to a request by the Los Angeles chapter of the Institute of Aeronautical Sciences, I presented a paper on the B-52 before a packed auditorium. It was obvious the industry as a whole was genuinely interested in any and all information concerning new jet aircraft.

367-80 Preparations

Construction of the 367-80 was 95 percent complete. People, plans, and equipment for the airplane's preflight checkout were in the final stage of preparation. Senior vice president Wellwood Beal informed me that Reed Chambers, president of the United States Aviation Underwriters Insurance Group (USAIG), was arriving for a briefing. The insurance policy on the Dash 80 was destined to be the largest aviation policy written to date.

Although I had never met Chambers, I knew his background. He had an illustrious record as a World War I fighter pilot flying wing for Eddie Rickenbacker. After the war, he joined with Juan Trippe to form Pan American Airways. When a hurricane destroyed their fleet of three uninsured airplanes, Trippe promoted replacements while Chambers looked for airplane insurance in New York. Significant aviation insurance was not available. Chambers never returned to the struggling airline business but remained in New York, where he organized and developed USAIG.

In the boardroom at Boeing executive headquarters I gave Chambers a pilot description of the Dash 80, discussed the handling characteristics of the B-47 and B-52, and responded to his questions. We agreed to have dinner at the Rainier Club that evening, the start of a close friendship that continued until he departed from the earth-bound flight pattern. USAIG underwrote the $15 million insurance policy on the Dash 80 with the clear condition that one pilot, Tex Johnston, fly it. Later, after the Dash 80 had flown many hours, I was given authority to check out other pilots in the airplane.

The Dash 80 was towed to the Renton factory ramp area adjacent to the Lake Washington seaplane ramp and positioned so that the jet-engine tail-pipe blast would dissipate harmlessly over the water. Final system checks were made in preparation for engine runs.

At my office I had a call from DeLores. "Marge and Boo Paschall invited us for six o'clock cocktails," DeLores said. "Mr. and Mrs. Boeing will be there. They just returned from a cruise to Alaska on the *Tackanite*" (their personal yacht). Although Mr. Boeing had not been active in the company for many years, he took a keen interest in and closely followed company progress. Appropriately, Mrs. Boeing had been requested to christen the Dash 80. Marge produced Mr. Boeing's special chilled and diced raw-salmon cocktails, graced with a chilled red sauce of his own recipe and accompanied by chilled, dry, straight-up martinis with green olives and twisted lemon rind. Mr. Boeing's prize catch was an eighty-pound king salmon. During cocktails I was presented with a generous section of the huge fish. In recognition of

my position as chief of flight test and engineering test pilot
for the Dash 80, and because of her friendship with DeLores,
Mrs. Boeing had commissioned a jeweler to design and produce two gold pins, miniature replicas of the Dash 80, one
for DeLores and one for herself. It was an emotional moment
for DeLores and me.

Dash 80 Christening

As ground testing of the Dash 80 neared completion, I was
conducting simultaneous 100-percent power runs on all four
engines when I saw an automobile approach and park nearby.
The auto windows were closed, and inside I could see Bill
Allen and a visitor with their hands over their ears. Test
completed, I closed the throttles, shut down the engines, and
deplaned. Bill had a grim look on his face. "I pray it's not
that noisy in the airplane," he said.

I smiled and assured him it wasn't.

"Tex, meet Reuben Fleet," he said.

I told Fleet that Larry Bell had told me about him and that
I'd spent a lot of hours in Fleet trainers. (By now Fleet's
company had become the Consolidated Vultee Aircraft Corporation.) I ushered the two men to the pilot seats, explained
the cockpit, and said that one objective had been to keep the
flight crew to a minimum because of the absence of an emergency escape system. I then showed how the flight engineer's
movable panel swung to the secured position to allow access
by the pilot or copilot. "Good," Fleet said. As a design
engineer, he was impressed with the excellent cockpit layout
and external visibility. As I escorted them back to the auto,
Fleet stopped, faced the Dash 80, looked at Bill, and said,
"Allen, do you realize you have the answer to commercial
transportation for the next fifty years sitting on this ramp?"

The Dash 80 returned to the factory in preparation for
official rollout. On May 15, 1954 (during the shift change at
4 p.m. so the employees could witness the event), the airplane destined to reduce the size of the world by a factor of
two (measured by travel time) formally emerged from its
technical and mechanical birthplace. The ceremonial band
played. The speakers spoke, and Mrs. William Boeing ap-

plied the traditional champagne, saying, "I christen thee *The Airplane of Tomorrow.*" It was a misty-eyed event for Bill Boeing.

By May 21, 1954, proof testing of all onboard systems and equipment had been completed, and my copilot Dix Loesch and I had satisfactorily completed 98 percent of the ground maneuvering brake and taxi tests. It was time for the maximum high-speed taxi test, the final test before the maiden flight. Arriving at the airplane, Dix and I joined crew chief Don Whitford and the chief inspector for the walk-around visual inspection. With preflight inspection complete, we boarded and proceeded with system checks.

The control tower had closed the airport for our test activity, so after engine start I released the park brakes and taxied to runway 33 (the 330-degree runway). The flaps were left retracted for the high-speed taxi tests, to keep more weight on the wheels for better braking. Dix called the theodolite station and told them to stand by. Their sophisticated cameras, timers, and measuring equipment would record our acceleration and deceleration data. Holding the brakes while applying full power, I pushed the mike button and told them, "Brake release on the count of three. One, two, three."

I released the brakes; the airplane leaped forward. At 100 mph, I applied slight back pressure on the control wheel to lift the nose gear slightly and checked aileron effectiveness while maintaining heading with the rudder. At 110 mph, I moved all four throttles to idle, lowered the nose, and raised the drag brakes. I applied light braking pressure, which I increased as we slowed to an estimated 5 mph—a perfect test. I added a bit of power and taxied an additional 50 feet to the taxiway.

With throttles at idle as I completed the 90-degree right turn to enter the taxiway, I felt the airplane heel to the left. I looked out the left cockpit window. Number one engine was resting on the ground, the wing tip only a few inches above the turf. Dix notified the tower that we had a problem and would remain in our present location. I quickly closed engine fuel valves while Dix finished his transmission and then turned off electrical power. I opened the cockpit window, stuck my head out, and saw part of the left main landing gear protruding through the top of the left wing.

Airport emergency equipment and Boeing ground crew arrived as we opened the cargo hatch and deplaned. Everyone was devastated. Using a flight-line telephone, I informed program manager Pennel of the accident.

A long silence. "How bad is it?"

"The airplane is okay, just some damage to the number one engine cowling, but the left main gear failed. Two of its four wheels are protruding through the upper surface of the wing."

When I returned to the airplane, the ground crew had roped it off. Security guards were allowing only company engineering and shop personnel to approach the plane. Pennel and his crew of lead engineers and shop managers raised the left wing with inflatable bags, drove a flatbed truck under the wing to take the place of the left landing gear, and towed the airplane to the flight line for analysis.

I convened the postflight conference with the appropriate project personnel and described what I had observed during the incident. Afterward I went with Don Finley, the chief structural engineer, to his office. He sat down and stared at the wall. "Hey, Don," I said, "this is what taxi tests are for. What if that gear had collapsed on touchdown at the conclusion of the initial flight? Now that would be a real problem."

"Don't even mention it," he said. "As soon as they get it in the barn and jacked up, we'll see what the problem is."

On my way home, I listened to the newscasters' reports and felt sorry for my friends at the Boeing news bureau. Those guys really earned their money at times like those. Why is it the news media always emphasize the negative and not the positive, such as, how lucky it was that this structural failure didn't occur during landing or high-speed braking?

As I drove, I reviewed the taxi tests from slow ground maneuvering to final high-speed run. Nothing I could recall indicated the impending failure or any condition that could have contributed to that failure.

My mother and father were visiting. They had traveled from the Midwest at my invitation to be present for the initial flight.

"How bad is it?" DeLores asked as I came into the living room.

"Don't really know," I said. "The damage appears to be minimal. Turning to Mother, I said, "One good thing, it gives you guys a good excuse to stay for a while." Everybody laughed.

That night, the tension disappeared in the shower as it came to me that the incident, bad as it was, would be remembered at Boeing as a blessing in disguise.

Dawn, May 22, 1954. A sound! Jingling bells. My wake-up alarm. My eyes snap open: the eight o'clock meeting, the landing-gear conference. My feet hit the floor.

Pennel and his structural engineers had worked through the night. This morning they faced a sea of grim faces. However, the news was encouraging. The metallurgical laboratory had discovered flaws in the metal components of the failed left main gear, and preliminary structural tests of the right main gear indicated no problems. It was material failure, not design error. Repairs would take six weeks.

After repairs were completed and the left gear replaced, Dix and I executed repeated abusive ground maneuvers during taxi tests and made a maximum high-speed taxi run. There were no further problems.

On July 14, 1954, about two months after the accident, Engineering declared the airplane ready for flight.

The Breath of Life

July 15, 1954, the anxiously awaited first-flight date of America's first jet transport, dawned with unexpected low ceilings and poor visibility. At breakfast, I listened to the weather report from station KING Seattle. Clearing was predicted by noon. Our family plans were all arranged. DeLores, number one daughter Judy (17), son Gary (11), and number two daughter Barbara (3) were to meet me on the ramp at Renton after I completed my activities at the Boeing Field Flight Test Center.

En route I proceeded through Bellevue to Highway 10 and across Mercer Island and the Lake Washington floating bridge. As usual, morning traffic was bumper to bumper. Some passengers dozed, some read the morning *Post Intelli-*

gencer, others listened to Al Cummings, the morning disc jockey. My fellow commuters were various. Some appeared sad, worried, grim, bored, or passive, but not many appeared happy about going to work.

As on many past occasions, I thought how fortunate I was to be a test pilot with everyday work that was not only a challenge but a joy. How fortunate not to be confined to mundane tasks, repetitious procedures, and boring environments. But most significant to me was the challenge of the job, working with the most advanced states of the mechanical, electronic, and aeronautical arts to develop a product that would revolutionize travel habits, trade, and culture, and shrink the world by a factor of two.

That day, flight-test personnel were putting into motion plans perfected during the previous months. The day's preflight conference, which I chaired as project test pilot, included people from flight test, project management, technical staff, engineering liaison, plus those involved with air-sea rescue preparations and air traffic procedures. Dix and I had already prepared the test-condition cards for our leg databoards. The listed items were discussed in detail at the meeting. The meeting concluded with unanimous agreement on all flight arid support procedures and precautions. I adjourned the meeting, directing support personnel to report to their respective organizations and locations, all flight-test personnel to report to the radio-equipped test room, flight crew and support personnel to proceed to the Renton flight line, and the public relations people to notify top management and the news media that target takeoff time was 2 p.m. Dix and I then proceeded to the pilots' locker room to pick up our flight gear.

As we headed for Renton, I thought of the axiom framed on my office wall: "One test is worth a thousand expert opinions." Those words say it all.

At Renton, parked autos and pedestrians lined perimeter streets and jammed nearby hillsides and streets. The populace of the Seattle area was turning out to witness the maiden flight of Boeing's pride, its bid for the lead in the dawning jet age. The Dash 80, wearing new yellow and brown colors, gleamed in the sunlight on the south ramp adjacent to a flightline hangar. The wheels were chocked, engine inlets plugged with red covers, and flight-line crew chief Whitford and his crew in their white coveralls were standing by, eager to proceed.

Dix and I made our walk-around inspection of aerodynamic surfaces, flap actuators, flap screw drives, wheel wells, wheels, tires, and brakes and found no faults. Everything appeared in perfect order. Flight-test liaison reported all emergency crews were in position and ready, that Renton field was closed to all air traffic, and that the immediate airspace was cleared of airborne traffic. Boeing president Bill Allen joined Dix and me on the ramp by the lower entrance hatch. As we shook hands, our eyes met and I read his thoughts: "Is she ready?"

"Bill," I said, "the airplane is as good as we can make it. Project engineering and flight test are satisfied. I'm ready to fly."

He was quiet for a moment. "Good luck," he said, then turned and walked away—a little stooped I thought. At this point, that $15 million gamble was a heavy burden.

We entered the airplane. I closed and secured the hatch and toured the 128-foot length of the passenger compartment. Someday it would be upholstered and luxurious, but now it was empty, except for test instrumentation racks lost in a vast cavity of raw metal, endless circumferentials, and skin. I checked all doors, hatches, and instrumentation. The word was go.

We donned parachutes and settled in our seats. Dix adjusted the flight engineer's panel in the forward position to allow either of us to monitor and operate all systems. We secured seat belts and shoulder harnesses, donned crash helmets, and installed the radio and intercom connectors. I checked the landing-gear control in the down position and signaled the ground crew chief we were ready for ground-supplied electrical power. As the ground power engaged, the green light indicating "landing gear down and locked" came on, and the electrical power indicator showed power to the main buses. Depressing the transmit button, I requested an intercom check from the ground.

"Loud and clear," Whitford said.

I saw that the engine plugs were out and pitot cover removed. I turned to the flight engineer's panel and saw that the hydraulic system was full. Dix verified fuel quantity. Item by item, we completed the checklist. "Ready for engine start," I said on the intercom.

The ground crew started the turbine-powered, high-pressure air machine. As the turbine accelerated from a whine to a scream, Whitford announced: "Clear to start number one." As number one engine reached idle speed, the ground air source was disconnected and removed, and we used bleed air from number one to start engines two, three, and four. At my interphone request, the ground crew removed the landing-gear down locks, with long red streamers dangling, and laid them on the ramp where I could see them from the cockpit.

"Remove wheel chocks and disconnect interphone," I said.

Whitford placed the wheel chocks by the down locks. "Have a good flight," he said.

I released the park brakes. With left hand on the nose gear steering control and right hand on the four throttles, I added power as the ground crew gave the all clear. We were on our way.

I glanced at the crowds. People were cheering, waving, jumping up and down, or just staring at the airplane with hands over their ears.

I taxied to the very end of the runway before lining up for takeoff. I have a rule I meticulously follow: "Runway behind and altitude above are useless."

We completed our before-takeoff checklist, Dix worked the tower, and we were cleared for takeoff. I called the theodolite station: "Dash 80, Johnston, stand by, brake release on the count of three." At full throttle, the four Pratt and Whitney engines at 100-percent power, tail-pipe temperatures and oil pressure on the money, I said, "One, two, three," and released the brakes. The airplane leaped forward and accelerated rapidly. We obviously would be airborne by midfield. As airspeed passed the calculated V_1 speed, I applied back elevator. The nose gear lifted off. Dix called 130 mph, and we were airborne.

Eyeballing the airspeed, I continued to increase the climb angle to avoid exceeding the flap-down placard limit of 225 mph. We were at 1,200 feet as we climbed past the end of the runway. Dix commented, "Is this thing going to climb straight up?'' Over Lake Washington, I throttled back to climb power, sure that the spectators had never before witnessed takeoff performance and climb attitude like that. Later, Bill Allen and others confessed they'd feared we had control problems when they saw that steep climb angle.

I elected to proceed immediately to 12,000 feet for an initial evaluation of aerodynamic control and to test flap and landing gear retraction and extension. That altitude would give us time to work out any problems we might encounter. We were in constant radio contact with the F-86 chase pilot, Townsend. For the record, I transmitted a continual radio commentary on the test frequency as we performed the various tests.

With gear and flaps up, the airplane was a dream, extremely quiet and vibration free. The control forces and feel throughout the medium speed range were excellent. That substantiated and reemphasized the conviction I had held since the early testing of the XP-59A in 1945: jet propulsion would render the propeller airplane obsolete.

The low-speed gear and flap-down handling characteristics were satisfactory. The trim changes resulting from landing gear and flap retraction and extension were satisfactory. With gear and flaps down, I slowly reduced power and airspeed until a mild buffet provided a significant stall warning, demonstrating the built-in honesty of the airplane. However, there were disturbing signs of a typical 35-degree swept-wing Dutch roll characteristic when the airplane was slow and ''dirty'' (flaps and gear down). I made a mental note: low-speed stability and control testing should occur early in the test program.

Cockpit visibility was excellent during approach and landing at Seattle Boeing Field. I touched down main gear first, slowly lowered the nose gear to the runway, and braked moderately to taxi speed. The initial flight of the airplane destined to change the travel habits of mankind was history.

The area behind the roped-off Dash 80 parking space in front of the experimental flight test hangar was jammed with spectators and photographers. We shut down and, as the turbine noise diminished, deplaned. Allen, Beal, Wells, Schairer, Martin, Pennel, Cook, Rouzie, and others from sales, public relations, quality control, flight test, and manufacturing were all there. Without exception, joy, gratitude, and happiness were displayed on every face. This event had a special meaning for each, but to all it meant success.

DeLores, Judy, Gary, and Barbara and Dix's wife, Peggie, and sons Jamie and Andy were all present. Photographers had a field day.

Bill Allen stood straight and tall as we shook hands. That $15 million load had somehow become a bit lighter. The feel of his handshake and his words of congratulation will remain with me forever.

Testing

After the initial flight, we continued daily tests from 8 a.m. until dusk. As with any early-phase flight testing of prototype airplanes, the key targets during this period were "performance" and "stability and control."

During the second flight of the Dash 80, we ran into rough air while doing stability and control work at 2,000 feet, gear and flaps down, speed below 200 mph. Again, I noted the significant tendency to Dutch roll. In my test report, I recommended additional attention to directional stability.

Bendix and Goodyear brakes were being tested during the flight-test program. On August 4, 1954, as part of those tests, high-speed taxi runs terminated with maximum braking to determine minimum stopping distance and brake characteristics. The tremendous heat generated by the multiple friction plates within the brake assembly of each wheel is awesome, the product of converting the kinetic energy of a 240,000-pound airplane traveling at 120 mph into heat. The serious side effects are the extremely high temperatures induced in the hydraulic brake fluid, the brake expander tubes, and the wheels and tires. Our precautionary procedure with overheated brakes was to delay landing-gear retraction after takeoff. The high-velocity air passing around the extended gear and circulating in the open wheel wells expedited radiation cooling.

On this occasion, we climbed to 25,000 feet before retracting the gear and conducting a two-hour test flight. Following the letdown, approach, and touchdown on runway 36,

I applied light braking. Nothing happened. "Brake failure," I called out, and checked the nose-gear steering. "Steering okay," I said, as Dix operated the emergency brake control. No emergency brakes.

The runway ahead was shrinking. The parking ramps on the right side of the field contained private planes. The ramps to the left were packed with fueled B-47's and B-52's. I steered off the runway to the right hoping the turf would help slow us down. Steering close to the parked civilian planes, we continued north, speed decreasing. I planned to execute a left U-turn at the north end of the airport and proceed south past the parked B-47's and B-52's and roll to a stop. It was not to be.

Following completion of the recent runway extension, the contractor had dumped surplus concrete in the rough unused area of the airport. The heap of concrete, obscured by weeds, lay directly in the path of the nose gear. Just as I became confident my plan would work, the nose gear hit something solid and ripped from its mountings. The nose dropped into the weeds, and we slid to a stop.

We secured the cockpit. To save time, I opened the cockpit window, climbed out, hung by my fingers from the cockpit window track, and dropped to the ground. There was minor damage to the lower portion of the nose section and significant structural damage in the nose gear well. The nose gear and strut were lying near the culprit pile of concrete. Considering the situation we had faced, we were fortunate. Had the nose gear steering been inoperative, I would have been forced to apply power, take off, retract the landing gear, and make a belly landing. To have continued on the runway and off the end would have resulted in catastrophic damage.

The hydraulic engineers determined that the high-temperature foaming of the hydraulic fluid had triggered a safety valve designed to deactivate the brake system in case of pressure-line failure. The safety valve had misinterpreted the aerated hydraulic fluid as depletion and shut off the brake system. A system modification precluded further failures of that type.

The Dash 80 was receiving good press nationally and internationally. Meanwhile, the British Comet was experiencing two problems. First, the runways of many world airports were of minimal length for jet aircraft. In several cases, Comet pilots on takeoff roll, concerned by the rapidly approaching runway end, prematurely overrotated the airplane nose high to expedite takeoff. The increased drag of the wing's high angle of attack retarded acceleration and the aircraft ran off the end of the runway at less than takeoff speed with catastrophic results.

Jet transport pilots, as part of their preflight preparation, calculate the takeoff distance required and three critical airspeeds, based on the aircraft's takeoff gross weight (including airframe, fuel, and payload), ambient temperature, surface wind, and runway length: V_1, the decision speed at which the aircraft can either use the length of runway remaining to take off and climb out with one engine failed, or abort the takeoff and stop within the distance remaining; V_r, the takeoff rotation speed; and V_2, the speed 1.2 times the stall speed, which assures aircraft control and climb capability with one engine failed.

Problem 2: pressurized airplane cabins breathe. That is, they expand and contract as pressure is controlled by the cabin pressurization dump valves. These cycles can produce rapid metal fatigue in structures not resistant to the effects of such fluctuations. Failure can be catastrophic if the structure is not designed to prevent the spread of cracks once they start.

A deadly chain of design circumstances doomed the Comet. De Havilland built the plane as light as possible to achieve maximum performance. That does not mean that de Havilland cut corners. The Comet was the most stringently tested plane in British history. But the gauge of the fuselage skin was marginal, because the fatigue factor involved in pulsating pressurized structures was unknown. The square windows were also a mistake. Fatigue cracks started at the window corners. And the cabin's circumferential rib spacing was too wide. Once a skin crack developed, it rapidly progressed to catastrophic failure.

Boeing avoided those errors. Months before the Comet's tragic vulnerability became known, Boeing engineers specified aluminum skin of a significantly thicker gauge. In addition, they welded titanium "tear stoppers" at frequent

intervals inside the skin, included plug-type doors that sealed
tighter as the cabin pressure differential increased at higher
altitudes, switched to triple-strength round-corner windows,
and used spot welds (instead of rivets) and a twenty-inch
circumferential rib spacing. Boeing subjected a Dash 80 (707)
fuselage of that design to thousands of pressurization cycles,
proving the validity of the structure.

Boeing 707

The Comet accidents shook public confidence in the future
of jet transports. So beginning in 1955, a Boeing sales film
called *Operation Guillotine* offered visual proof that the Comet's problems would not afflict the 707. The film opened
with a shot of a Comet-like pressurized airliner fuselage on a
platform above which hung two large steel blades. In slow
motion, the blades dropped. At the two points of penetration,
the metal skin split and curled outward until suddenly the
entire fuselage burst, ejecting seats, dummy passengers, overhead bins, and even the cabin floor. The camera then focused
on a 707 fuselage. Five blades sliced through the skin. Puffs
of air escaped through the slits, but the damage did not

spread. There was no explosive decompression. Plainly, a 707 pilot would have time to descend to safe altitude as passengers donned automatically deployed oxygen masks.

Demonstrations

SAC, the Strategic Air Command, sorely needed the jet tanker proposed by Boeing. The propeller-driven KC-97 tankers, flying at slower speeds and lower altitudes, were not compatible with the jet fighter aircraft, B-47's and B-52's. The high-flying jets had to descend for in-flight refueling and then expend extra fuel and time to return to mission altitude.

Decision time was near. General LeMay again appeared at Flight Test, this time to fly the Dash 80. Again, I was impressed with his piloting skill. He simulated mission conditions at B-47 and B-52 in-flight refueling speeds and altitudes. He noted the inherent stability of the airplane and was impressed. Judging from what I observed and from his comments, he believed the airplane's characteristics would meet Air Force requirements for a jet tanker.

16

Public Relations,
Hot Brakes and Flutter,
and the 707 Barrel Roll

The roar of Lockheed and North American jet fighters and the Boeing B-47's and B-52's created a public backlash. Opposition to aircraft noise grew in every major U.S. city. Residents of areas near Newark Airport, New Jersey, transported their livingroom divans and chairs onto the active runway and staged a sit-in protesting aircraft noise. Whenever I spoke in public concerning the Dash 80, someone always asked, "What about noise?"

The Dash 80 was in lay-up to install special instrumentation when the public relations department requested that I speak at a dinner for members, wives, and guests at the Santa Monica Chamber of Commerce. The subject was to be the Boeing prototype jet transport. Santa Monica was right in Donald Douglas's back yard, and more interesting, my co-speaker was Donald Douglas, Jr., who would speak on the proposed DC-8. It was an ideal assignment—Boeing had a jet transport flying; Douglas had a paper DC-8.

A similar situation had occurred a short time before in Chicago at a dinner meeting of A.L.P.A., the Air Line Pilots Association. The speakers were Donald Douglas, Jr., on the proposed DC-8, a Lockheed engineer presenting that company's proposed turboprop Electra, and myself describing the flight characteristics and performance of Boeing's prototype jet transport, Dash 80. In each case, during the question and answer session, the predominant question was "What about noise?"

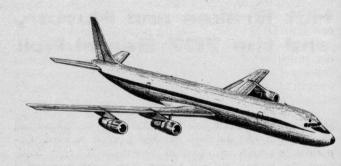

DC-8

My answer began by noting that Boeing recognized two major problems regarding the jet transport. First was jet noise, and second was the need for thrust reversers to provide early and rapid deceleration after touchdown. Such deceleration would rapidly reduce lift and thus increase the weight on the tires for better braking. The combined effect of reverse thrust and improved braking would greatly reduce landing roll. With regard to the first problem, I said that Boeing was experimenting with variously configured noise suppressors and was confident a substantial reduction in jet engine noise could be accomplished. With regard to the second problem, Boeing's comprehensive testing of thrust reversers attached to engine tail pipes indicated that efficient thrust reversers would be achieved, significantly reducing the landing roll distance.

Mach II

The morning following the Santa Monica soiree, Phil Coffer, a former Seattle businessman and dear friend, insisted I attend a party at the Kona Kiya Club in San Diego. Seattle friends Colonel "Hoolie" Wayne and Colonel Carter Arnold and numerous Lockheed and North American troops would be present. Indicative of the nature of the festivities, at the height of the party Hoolie and I dove fully clothed from the high board into the pool. I had a new pair of cowboy boots made for every prototype experimental airplane I flew, so my new Dash 80 boots went into the pool with me.

The next morning, about noon, we were in the bar getting our hearts started with Bloody Marys when a TV newscast announced that the Boeing Company had been awarded a contract to build an undisclosed number of jet tanker aircraft, military designation KC-135. I bought the next round.

Returning to Santa Monica, we checked in at the Miramar Hotel. I chose a cabana on the lawn across the street from the beach and departed for an appointment to be measured for a made-to-measure crash helmet. When I returned to the cabana at 6 p.m., a surprise awaited me in the form of a one-quarter-grown lion in a heavy cage against the far wall. I had told the guys about Inman's Flying Circus and Thor. The lion looked at me, in a friendly way, I thought. Slowly I moved my hand close to the bars. It snarled a bit and turned so that I saw it was a female. "Okay, Babe, it's time for you and me to get acquainted," I said.

I carefully slid the door up, latched it in the open position, then slowly retreated to the bed and placed a pillow on my lap to distract her if the need arose. Speaking in a normal tone, I coaxed her to come out and get acquainted. She stuck her head out, inspected the room, retreated, then ambled out. First she checked the bathroom, investigating the tile floor, then strolled over and lay down in front of me. I stood up slowly, moved to the bathroom while continuing to talk, removed my shirt, freshened up, put on a fresh shirt, then stepped back into the bedroom with an ashtray full of water. She had returned to her cage. I eased the ashtray in and lowered the door.

En route to the bar, I selected a name, "Mach II"—twice the speed of sound. I crawled up on a bar stool, ordered a Scotch and watched my friends' faces in the back bar mirror as I criticized the leisurely attitude of the helmet people. The guys seemed puzzled. Hoolie said, "Is it hot in that cabana?"

"It's not too bad," I said, "but Mach Two thinks it's a little cramped."

DC-3

Mach II reached Seattle Boeing Field the following Thursday evening via military C-47 transport escorted by a lion trainer from the Thousand Oaks Wild Animal Farm, and she arrived at the house while I was at a QB meeting. By the time I arrived home at 1 a.m., DeLores had made her comfortable in a carpeted cage. The following day, DeLores terrified the news photographers when she demonstrated her newly acquired ability to coax Mach II out of the cage.

I partitioned off part of the basement two-car garage with heavy mesh wire supported by studding. Mach II loved it. Every night she stood waiting at her gate to greet me. I would put on an old flight jacket, enter the cage, and romp with her. Soon she was consuming fifteen pounds of horse meat, half a dozen eggs, and a quart of milk a day. When I became involved with the 707 sales effort in Europe and the Far East, I reluctantly donated her to the Seattle Zoo, reserving the right to her first cub.

We received one of her first litter, a male, while it still

required bottle feeding. Daughter Barbara pushed Mach III around the house and lawn in her doll buggy. Eventually, he also returned to the Seattle Zoo, making me known as a major wild-animal contributor.

A Hot Problem

Jim Gannett, an Air Force pilot with engineering background, was Townsend's copilot during the Air Force B-52 service testing program and a test pilot at the Air Force test base at Muroc. When his Air Force hitch expired I hired him as a Boeing experimental test pilot. Jim flew with me as copilot for Dash 80 high-speed brake tests at high gross weight and for high-gross-weight, high-altitude performance work.

The severe brake test conditions called for two maximum performance stops from 110 mph. Representatives of the brake company were present to measure brake temperature after each stop. After the first stop they reported temperatures within the predicted range. After the second stop, I was concerned for their safety. They were leaning over the extremely hot tires inserting electronic temperature probes through the cooling space to the brake disks. A blowout could be fatal. On interphone they reported the temperatures were near maximum but considered acceptable for flight.

I commented to Jim, "I don't believe the tires can accept this amount of heat." On interphone, I asked to speak with the lead engineer, who assured me the temperatures were acceptable. "I've heard those words before," I thought.

We left the gear down after takeoff to expedite cooling during the climb to 20,000 feet and delayed gear retraction another fifteen minutes after reaching altitude. After I retracted the gear and was setting up the first test condition, there were three consecutive explosions. "What's that?" Jim said.

"Those damn tires are on fire and exploding," I said. As I lowered the gear, there was another explosion. "Go aft and see if you can observe fire or smoke under the trailing edge of the wing." I maintained the gear-down placard limit speed of 305 mph so that the air blast would extinguish the fire and informed Flight Test of our problem. Jim returned and reported seeing slight smoke at first, but that it had dissipated.

Flight Test asked if I wanted foam on the runway. I declined. "The fire is out. I'm sure we have six or seven flat tires and any inflated burned ones will probably fail on touchdown. Foam won't solve anything."

The landing was normal, but the bare wheel rims were noisy and the ride a bit rough. Pieces of burned rubber flailed the insides of wheel wells and gear doors. I refrained from braking; the metal wheels would merely lock and skid. The airplane decelerated rapidly anyway and required added power to reach the taxiway and clear the runway.

After that incident, I conducted many more brake investigations but never again flew with superheated brakes. The possible time saved was not worth the risk.

Flutter: A Dash 80 Example

Aerodynamic flutter occurs without warning. A perfect example was the elevator trim tab flutter that caused the instantaneous loss of the entire left elevator aft of the hinge line on Cobra II. Another example occurred when my friend Colonel Guy Townsend and several officers from Wright Field involved with the KC-135 tanker program were aboard the Dash 80 for a flight demonstration. Colonel Townsend was in the pilot's seat and I in the copilot's. We leveled off at 35,000 feet.

Up until this flight, the maximum Dash 80 speed tested had been 0.72 Mach, so I had set that figure as limit speed for the flight. I had turned sideways in the seat to converse with some of the observers when suddenly I noticed increased airflow noise. I turned, saw the Mach needle approaching 0.74, jerked the throttles to idle, and pulled the nose up. Simultaneously, the entire airplane began shaking violently—so violently that the flight engineer's panel partially ripped from its moorings. With the speed reduction, the shaking ceased, having lasted only two or three seconds. I suspected rudder flutter, and Guy reported an unusual feel in the rudder pedals.

Postflight inspection revealed no structural damage except

to the flight engineer's panel. Inspection of the rudder aerodynamic balance cavity revealed no problem. However, a
change was made in the mass balance of both the rudder and
control tab. Subsequently, I conducted tests to 0.76 Mach
with no flutter problems.

Later in the program, Dix also experienced severe rudder
flutter. In that case, postflight inspection revealed that a hand
tool had been left in the rudder, upsetting the balance. Fortunately, the violent flutter caused the tool to jam the rudder
in the streamline position, terminating the potentially catastrophic condition.

Bill Allen

At 8 a.m., Lola buzzed. "Mr. Allen wants to see you," she
said. As I entered his office, he motioned me to a chair, and
sat looking at me for a moment before he spoke.

"I wish I were at forty thousand feet," I thought.

"Tex," he said, "I want to congratulate you. This is the
first time in the history of the Boeing Company that flight
test has operated within its budget. Also, the test airplanes
are flying four times the historical monthly average of five-
and-a-half hours per month each. The YB-52 and XB-52 cost
was running fifty-four thousand dollars per flight hour, and
that has decreased to twenty-eight thousand per hour. Good
work. Keep it up."

I departed on cloud nine.

Flight Test had gained prestige with engineering during the
B-47 and early B-52 programs. Management now regarded
Flight Test as a contributing organization, not just a testing
function of engineering. Our new procedures manuals, record
keeping, and objective operations were paying off.

Based on my experience at Bell, and so far with Boeing,
I was convinced that the flight-test organization should report
directly to the chief engineer, not to the respective project
engineers. I viewed the latter case as equivalent to allowing
a student to grade his own final exam. So I was pleased when
an organizational change was formally implemented. Flight
Test now reported directly to the VP of technical staffs.

Jet Travel Preview

The world's airlines recognized that propeller-driven aircraft were obsolete. Airline managements accustomed to thinking in terms of hundreds of thousands of dollars for an aircraft were now having to think in terms of millions. Even so, increasing numbers of prospective airline customers visited Boeing.

Meanwhile, Douglas had the DC-8 under construction and had mounted an aggressive sales program. It had one advantage. In the past, when airline companies thought of transport airplanes, they thought of Douglas. Boeing, historically, was considered mainly a military manufacturer.

Senior vice president Wellwood Beal and Englishman Vernon Crudge, a naturalized U.S. citizen and prominent in world airline circles, prevailed upon Frank Gledhill, Pan American senior vice president, to return to New York from Santa Monica via Seattle for a 707 briefing and a flight demonstration in the Dash 80. I demonstrated for Gledhill an airline-profiled takeoff and climb to 35,000 feet, then took a time hack over Seattle and another over Portland, Oregon. The elapsed time was thirteen minutes. Returning to Beal's office, Gledhill called New York and ordered a Pan Am engineering team to Seattle. Their assignment was to develop a theoretical jet airplane route structure in concert with Boeing. Pan American became our first 707 customer.

On October 16, 1955, with president Bill Allen and guests aboard, we departed Seattle on a demonstration nonstop flight from Seattle to Andrews Air Force Base, Washington, D.C. Dix and Jim Gannett alternated as copilot and flight engineer. Three hours and 48 minutes later, we landed at Andrews Air Force Base. Boeing's public relations and news bureau had arranged a press conference at which Allen said, "This flight is a tribute to the International Air Transport Association convening today in New York City." I briefed the assembled reporters on the flight—altitude 35,000 feet, flight time 3 hours and 48 minutes, maximum speed 620 mph, average speed 595 mph—and responded to their questions. By the time the press conference adjourned, the Dash 80 was refueled.

The return flight required 4 hours and 8 minutes, for an overall round-trip flight time half that of propeller airplanes. The press coverage was extremely positive.

Management School

Boeing management had scheduled me for a two-week management course conducted by the American Management Association at the Astor Hotel in New York City. I returned from the Andrews Air Force Base demonstration flight the evening of October 16 and boarded a United DC-7 for New York at seven the next morning.

The United captain was aware of my presence and announced the speed and elapsed time of our Dash 80 coast-to-coast round-trip over the P.A. system during his climb. Shortly a stewardess told me that he requested my presence in the cockpit. As I went forward, the captain introduced me over the P.A. system. I was flabbergasted at the number of passengers who wanted to shake hands. When I arrived at the cockpit door, the captain announced, "Tex has agreed to fly the airplane to New York."

There I was in the DC-7 pilot seat with the captain on the jump seat. It was perfectly legal, as I carried an airline cockpit pass issued by the Civil Aeronautics Authority. It was a great flight. I checked my watch and kidded the pilot, "I hope these engines don't wear out before we get there."

School convened at 7 a.m. with 49 classmates who were vice presidents and department heads of businesses throughout the U.S., including pharmaceuticals, steel, automobiles, and electronics. After first-day classes adjourned, Bill Allen telephoned. "Can you give Bob Six a briefing on the Dash 80 at 8 p.m.?" he said. Six was president of Continental Airlines.

"Yes, sir. Where is he?"

"The Plaza. Get the suite number at the desk. Tex, this is important. Ralph Bell has been with them. They want to talk to you. Wells, Schairer, and Ralph Bell from sales are with me at the Park Avenue address. Call me when you finish."

I didn't know Six, but I liked what I had heard about him

DC-7

from his chief pilot. Six opened the door, and I liked him right away. He looked you in the eye and almost welded your fingers together with his grip. He introduced me to his treasurer and said, "Tell us what you think we need to know about the 707 airplane." Three hours later they'd heard it all: design concept, performance envelope, handling characteristics, and safety factors. We had a Scotch while I answered further questions. "Good, Tex," he said as we shook hands. "Have you seen Ethel's show?" Ethel Merman was Mrs. Bob Six. "Here're two tickets. It's a good show. Take a friend."

In the Plaza lobby I called Allen's apartment on Park Avenue, then grabbed a cab. On arrival, I gave them a full report, adding, "Bob is sending his chief pilot to fly the Dash 80 as soon as I return." Despite my good news, the other men were tense. I sensed a problem. As the conversation continued, I learned that United Airlines' president Patterson had ordered 25 DC-8's and 20 of our 707's. C. R. Smith, American Airlines' president, would not accept the 707 passenger cabin diameter. The DC-8 was larger.

Boeing, in the interest of dollars, had a financial arrangement with the government to use the KC-135 tooling for 707 construction. It had a smaller body diameter than the DC-8. That smaller diameter may also have resulted in United's split order. Allen bit the bullet the next morning in a meeting with Smith. "C.R.," he said, "what size body do you want? We'll build it." That decision turned the tide.

To accommodate Australia's Qantas Airline, Boeing tailored the body length.

Meanwhile, my attendance at the management course added to my knowledge of business administration and management plus gave me opportunities to meet business leaders from around the country. While I was in New York, TV star Arthur Godfrey invited me to appear on his morning show. On camera, we discussed the Dash 80 Seattle-Andrews round-trip, giving the new Boeing jet yet another plug. Our get-together also spawned an enduring friendship.

Aerobatics

Seattleite Ted Jones, a keen marine engineer, designed a revolutionary speedboat, the hydroplane, supported at high speed by two sponsons—streamlined, buoyant, lateral extensions—attached to the forward sides of the boat's wide, flat body. The hydroplane was powered by an Allison aircraft engine identical to the one I modified for Cobra II.

Stan Sayer, a successful automobile dealer in Seattle and my neighbor on Hunts Point, was owner of Jones's first hydroplane, named *Slo-Mo I* for "slow motion." *Slo-Mo I* completely vanquished the displacement-hull speedboats and received extensive national and international publicity. The success of *Slo-Mo I* resulted in construction and sales of additional hydroplanes, a homegrown industry.

Seattle billed itself as the boating capital of the U.S.A. Recognizing the tourism and sporting potential of hydroplane racing, city leaders established a yearly Seattle extravaganza, Seafair Week, whose major attraction and final event was the renowned hydroplane Gold Cup race. The Gold Cup trophy became the coveted prize of all hydroplane drivers. Another annual attraction on Gold Cup day was the outstanding tight-formation aerobatics of the Navy's Blue Angels.

Through the years Seafair and the Gold Cup, like Mardi Gras in New Orleans, grew in fame and magnitude. In 1955 two renowned international organizations, the International Air Transport Association (whose members included every airline company in the world) and the Society of Aeronatical Engineers, elected to hold their annual meetings in Seattle during Seafair Week. The result was an assembly of the most important people in world aviation—airline executives, design engineers, and aircraft and engine manufacturers—right on Boeing's doorstep. The collective number of aircraft industry attendees was probably a first in aviation history and presented a historic opportunity to promote the Dash 80.

I had driven one of Ted Jones's hydroplanes, *Miss Thriftway,* whose sponsor was a major supermarket chain. Driving and maneuvering at speeds well over 100 mph was great sport, and the sound of the Allison engine was music to my ears. I thought seriously of participating in the Gold Cup, but early in the week Bill Allen called. "Tex, can you conduct a test flight on Gold Cup day and conclude with a pass over the Gold Cup racecourse?"

"Yes, sir."

"Good, Carl Cleveland in public relations will arrange the time." That ended my hydroplane aspirations. Cleveland called Friday evening and said the Dash 80 fly-by was to follow the Blue Angel show and gave me a time hack.

The weather on Gold Cup day was impeccable. My flight crew included Jim Gannett, copilot, and Bell Whitehead, test engineer. We completed our test over the Olympic Peninsula, and as I turned to a 90-degree heading for Lake Washington, I told Jim, "I'm going to roll this bird over the Gold Cup course."

Jim's head snapped around, his eyes wide, his mouth slightly open in surprise. "They're liable to fire you."

"Maybe," I said, "but I don't think so. There are more than two hundred thousand spectators. Everyone in the airplane and airline business in the world is here. This is the airplane that's going to dominate the industry for forty years. We're going to get their attention and make this airplane famous.'' I pulled the nose up and executed a leisurely climbing left barrel roll, and then began the descent to Lake Washington.

I observed the Blue Angels' last pass and their departure for Sand Point Airport four miles north of the racecourse. Approaching from southwest of the lake on a northeast heading, speed 490 mph, altitude 200 feet, we passed over the racecourse, pulled up in a left chandelle, pulling 3.5 G in the vertically banked left turn to 1,500 feet altitude.

Proceeding on a southwest heading in a shallow dive across the racecourse to 300 feet altitude, speed 490 mph, I established a 35-degree climb and released the back pressure. The airplane was climbing at 1 G, the same as level flight. I applied full left roll control and, as the airplane approached the inverted position, applied slight back pressure, bringing the nose down slightly to maintain 1 G, continually holding full left roll control. The roll was completed in level flight at 1,500 feet altitude.

Executing a 180-degree nose-down turn, we again passed over the racecourse at 490 mph and executed the second climbing roll. During the two barrel rolls the airplane never knew it was inverted. The entire roll maneuver was executed at 1 G, the same gravity force as at level flight. Whitehead, the test engineer, knelt by a passenger cabin window and snapped the today-famous photo of the Dash 80 inverted over the Gold Cup course.

DeLores, aboard one of the Boeing chartered guest boats, was seated at a bridge table. Her companions left to witness the Dash 80. Her response to her friend's question ''Don't you want to watch?'' was, ''What's new? I've been watching for twenty-five years.''

A friend of mine aboard Bill Allen's boat told me the following day that ''Mr. Allen, while conversing with Larry Bell, had observed Larry taking a heart pill. Following the rolls, Bill turned to Larry and said, 'Larry, give me one of those pills. I need it more than you.' Larry laughed and said, 'Bill, you don't know Tex very well. He just sold your airplane.' ''

Monday morning, Lola buzzed and said, ''Mr. Allen wants to see you.'' When I arrived, Beal, Wells, Schairer, and

Martin were present. Everyone nodded as I entered and selected a chair. Allen said, "What did you think you were doing yesterday?"

"Selling the airplane," I said, and explained the loads the airplane experienced during the 3.5-G chandelle and 1-G barrel rolls. "The airplane does not recognize attitude, providing a maneuver is conducted at one G. It knows only positive and negative imposed loads and variations in thrust and drag. The barrel roll is a one G maneuver and quite impressive, but the airplane never knows it's inverted."

Allen's response was, "You know that. Now we know that. Don't do it anymore."

Monday evening, after a postflight conference, I arrived at my office to find a note, "Dinner at Bill Allen's at 6:00."

"It's five-thirty now," I said to myself.

Fifteen minutes later I was showered and en route. Arriving twenty minutes late, I stepped on the patio adjoining the guest cabana, and instantly Bill's guest jumped out of his chair, ran across the patio, grabbed my Stetson by the brim with both hands, and jerked it down over my ears, saying, "You slow rollin' S.O.B. Why didn't you let me know? I would have been ridin' the jump seat." It was Eddie Rickenbacker. Eddie had been delayed and missed the Gold Cup. Allen was his normal self, at ease and joking. Eddie said, "Bill, that's the way to get attention with a new airplane. I wish I could have been there."

It was a terrific evening, just the three of us, talking about the airline conversion to jets.

The Wings Club

The subject of my March 1955 luncheon address at the renowned New York City Wings Club was the Boeing jet transport. It was an impressive group, or rather, crowd: airline executives; airplane manufacturers; state, county, city, and federal airport executives. My presentation was a review of technical concept, flight characteristics, performance envelope, safety, and progress on noise abatement and thrust reversers. It was an eager audience, there for information, and I presented the hard facts.

The afternoon's technical discussions concluded with cocktails and dinner in a private dining room at Mama Leoni's, hosted by George Weiss of Sperry Gyroscope. In attendance were Herman Pusin of the Glenn L. Martin Company, R. P. Kroon of Westinghouse, Fred Chamberlain and Duke Krantz (previously a pilot with Gates Flying Circus) of Bendix, C. A. Rheinstrom and L. L. Brabham of Republic Aircraft, and Herb Fisher with the New York Port Authority.

'Round the World

On January 16, 1957, five B-52 bombers departed Castle Air Force Base, California, on a nonstop flight around the world. Two aircraft were forced to abandon the mission because of mechanical difficulties, one with my friend and copilot on the YB-52 initial flight, Deputy Air Commander Guy Townsend, Command Pilot. The remaining three aircraft touched down on March Air Force Base, California, 45 hours and 19 minutes later with Major General Archie Old, Jr., air commander of the 15th Air Force, aboard the lead airplane. They had traveled 24,325 statute miles at an average speed of 543 mph, to make the first nonstop globe-encircling jet aircraft flight.

Bill Allen and I traveled to March Air Force Base on January 17 to observe the arrival of the record-breaking B-52's. During his speech at the ceremonies, Allen said, "There was also another record established—by the tail gunners. The three B-52 tail gunners were the first and only three humans to fly nonstop around the world backwards."

During the return trip to Seattle our discussion included the 367-80 decision. He was extremely concerned with the projected cost. "Bill," I said, "the vast majority of the civilized population of the world are in a hurry. Example: this B-52 trip. There are people in the freight business at this moment thinking about that potential. The limited British Comet experience is proving it every day. Our job is to build, test, and deliver a better airplane."

Acceptance

Production Air Force KC-135 jet tanker and 707-120 aircraft were progressing down their respective assembly lines. The flight-test schedule was heavy: XB-52, YB-52, two production B-52's, and Dash 80 testing, plus local and cross-country demonstrations.

The demonstrations kept me busy. At Dash 80's first appearance at Los Angeles International Airport, senior Boeing vice president Beal and potential customers were aboard. We were cleared for landing on runway 27 left. Halfway down final, with gear and flaps down, the tower changed our clearance to 27 right. At my request, they approved a landing on 27 right from our present position. Applying required power, I executed rapid right and left turns and landed on 27 right. The Dash 80 again demonstrated its remarkable maneuvering capability.

The word of the Dash 80 arrival spread rapidly, and like magic, Douglas engineers appeared, equipped with their yo-yo measuring tapes. At their request, Beal permitted them to inspect the airplane. A bright-red, fur-covered Ford Thunderbird convertible arrived graced by numerous Hollywood starlets. I terminated the Douglas inspection. The cockpit photographs included in the starlets' publicity photos testify to the mundane life of a test pilot.

The 3:48 flight of March 11, 1957, from Seattle to Baltimore, Maryland, received the most sensational and complimentary press of the Dash 80's glorious history. The passenger manifest read like a Who's Who of newspaper and magazine executives and journalists. William Randolph Hearst, Jr., Bob Considine, and fifty other writers including Carl Cleveland, the Boeing public relations officer, enjoyed the record speed dash that averaged 612 mph.

On March 12 we conducted demonstration flights for military and civilian dignitaries. March 13, we flew to Chicago with fifty more journalists and were the first jet transport to land at the new, and still under construction, O'Hare Airport. Approaching Chicago, 100 miles out, we contacted Chicago air traffic control for control-zone entry instructions. "Proceed to Midway Airport for hand off to O'Hare," was the reply. The Midway tower, aware of our airplane type, requested a fly-by. I informed them we would be happy to, providing they received approval from the Chicago Airport Authority and the F.A.A.

"Stand by," was their reply. We were in the letdown, and considering the Midway traffic problem, I doubted they would be successful. We were 25 miles out when Midway reported, "Approval granted."

I couldn't believe it. Picking up the mike, I said, "How about your traffic situation?" The answer was, Midway was holding all takeoff and landing traffic, and we were cleared to O'Hare. "How low and how fast?" I asked.

"As you wish," was the answer.

Copilot Lew Wallick notified the passengers of the request and of our intentions. Midway received its first jet buzz job and probably the last. Our pass was east to west at 200 feet altitude and 500 mph on the clock. As we passed the tower, I closed the throttles and pulled the nose up, and we zoomed power off to 12,000 feet, extended the gear, and proceeded to land on O'Hare's partially completed runway 9. Our elated passengers deplaned to view O'Hare's unfinished terminal building. The O'Hare management people were genuine and professional. On a subsequent trip I was indoctrinated by them into the virtues of Chicago nightlife.

With a new group of guests aboard we were en route to Denver. One hundred miles out, Wallick worked Denver approach. Denver cleared us for letdown and a straight-in approach on 27. I believe there is no use in worrying about what's going to happen. It usually does, and it did. With gear and flaps down as we approached, I could see it was snowing. Also, I was holding 10 to 15 degrees of right crab to maintain track with the runway. That meant a 90-degree crosswind, and now we were in heavy snow and marginal visibility. It was decision time.

I opened the throttles and requested Wallick to "tell the tower we're going around for landing on thirty-six." After landing and braking to a stop, I said, "Request a truck to lead us in." The combination of darkness and heavy snow reduced the visibility to the point that we couldn't find our way to the ramp. The truck led us to the ramp in front of one of the Continental hangars. Bob Six was present to greet us as we deplaned. "You guys should do something about this weather," I said as we shook hands.

"I ordered rain so you'd feel at home. The order got garbled," he replied.

It was difficult to get ahead of Six. Looking at the airplane, I said, "Is there a hangar available? We cold-soaked at thirty-five thousand feet, and that wet snow is freezing right where it lands."

"Right here," he said, motioning to the hangar.

Continental public relations people were handling transportation for our departing guests and notifying the arriving group of the new departure time, nine the next morning.

Bob spoke to a mechanic: "Remove the cover from Ethel's car." He turned to me and said, "You use Ethel's car.'"

In Bob's office, I called public relations in Seattle. I briefed them on the situation and quoted an estimated arrival time the next day. As we entered the office, I had observed a three-foot-square, sweep-second-hand clock and anticipated Bob's plan. He removed a single-action handgun and gunbelt from a desk drawer. "Know anything about fast draw?" he asked.

"A little," I replied, "never with a timer."

"It's the only way. Come on, I'll check you out. Stand facing the impact target, gunbelt in place, finger of left hand on clock switch, and gun hand poised over the gun butt. When you are ready to draw, simultaneously release the clock switch, clutch the gun butt, draw, and point the gun at the target, holding the trigger back with index finger, and fan the gun hammer with the heel of your left hand. The gun fires, the projectile strikes the impact target, and the sweep second hand stops, all in a fraction of a second." Bob demonstrated several times. He was fast.

I fired several times and hit the target, but the time was slow. "Not bad," he said. "Where'd you shoot?"

"I've practiced," I said, "but never against the clock."

"All you need is practice. I'm going to a competitive meet in L.A. this weekend. Come down. Hell of a group of fellows. You'll enjoy it."

"I'd like to," I replied. "I'll check the schedule tomorrow and call you."

"Where you going to stay?" he asked.

"Motel up the road," I replied. "I don't want to fight the traffic in the morning."

"Okay, we're having dinner downtown. Come by the house for a drink on the way. Here's the address." He handed me a card.

I fired up Ethel's Chrysler Imperial, checking the mileage. It was slightly over 500 miles total. I checked into the motel, showered, dressed, and called a cab. Bob answered the bell as the cab departed. "I don't know this part of town," I explained. "The cab is a lot simpler."

He was nursing a drink, and I had the impression he was preoccupied. Placing his drink on the coffee table, he said, "I'm canceling our 707 order." In shock, I waited for him to continue. "Allen's going to have to do something about his sales department. I cannot accept the head man's attitude and methods."

"Bob, I don't know what the problem is, but I'm sure it can be corrected. It can't be worth a bad decision."

He looked me in the eye for a moment and said, "I have notified the board of directors. Tex, I want you to inform Bill Allen upon arrival."

"Bob, my position doesn't involve this category of problem. I suggest you sleep on this one. You're making a serious mistake." Six insisted, and to end the session I agreed.

The flight to Seattle was routine. The guests were impressed and complimentary. I was deeply concerned regarding the Six conversation, but it was a problem between Bill Allen and Bob Six, and I eliminated it from my mind.

Two days later Six called. "Did you talk to Allen?"

"No, Bob. I haven't mentioned it to anyone, and I don't intend to."

There was silence. "It's okay, Tex. I talked with the board. We're going to stay with the 707. I'll work the other problem."

"That's great, Bob, and a good decision."

San Remo, Italy

The 1956 convention of the International Air Transport Association (I.A.T.A.) was scheduled for San Remo, Italy, a picturesque village nestled on the coast below terraced mountain vineyards. I leased a lovely hillside chalet. The veranda overlooked the village and the blue Mediterranean. Ken Luplow, Boeing European resident representative, and Don Buck, Seattle sales representative, were also present.

Air India was exhibiting significant interest in the 707, and early in the session I met Adi Gasdar, the 6-foot-1, 200-pound Air India chief pilot. He was well educated and, I discovered later, a competent pilot. A congenial working friendship with Gasdar and his group, which included seven well-qualified aircraft engineers, developed. Midweek I hosted a cocktail party at the chalet for the Air India group. Included was the vice president of public relations, Bobby Kuka, a recent recipient of an I.A.T.A. award for his outstanding performance in the development of international air travel. Gasdar informed me that Kuka was also a big-game hunter. Luplow presented movies of the Dash 80. I discussed travel comfort, speed, and safety and responded to questions.

I understood the selection of San Remo as the convention location when I learned of the running of the Monte Carlo Grand Prix the next Sunday. At my suggestion, Luplow obtained Grand Prix tickets for the Air India and Boeing group. We chartered a bus for transportation and reserved a private dining salon for dinner at the casino after the race. The formula cars were awesome, and the race through the streets of Monaco was an impressive event. That evening was my introduction to the casino, and I must confess the reputation is justified.

Gasdar and Kuka, learning that I enjoyed big-game hunting, suggested that in the event Air India purchased 707's and I delivered the first airplane, they would arrange a tiger shoot. That captured my attention. During a private conversation I suggested to Adi that he come to Seattle as early as feasible and fly the prototype. He was genuinely pleased and said he would when appropriate.

Friends

A Dash 80 flight demonstration required an R.O.N. in Los Angeles. I telephoned my friend, Bill Lear, now chief executive of Lear Siegler, Inc., in Santa Monica. Lear Siegler produced electronic aircraft products, including autopilots. My hotel was the Hyatt House adjacent to Los Angeles International Airport. He agreed to stop by for a short conference en route to another commitment.

Following a handshake, I said, "Bill, how are the autopilots doing?"

"Good," he replied, "we have a proposal submitted to the Air Force for the KC-135 autopilot."

"What are you doing about automatic approach-to-touchdown equipment?" I asked.

"We've studied it. It's a tough job."

"Bill, we now have an airplane that doesn't worry about weather. The engine inlets and wing and tail leading edges are thermally de-iced. Bill, it's impractical and too expensive today to sit on the ground and wait for visibility."

"You're correct," he said. "Have you heard of any research money?"

"No, but Sperry is financing their own research."

"I'll think about it, and thanks." Within one year, Bill Lear had prototypes of automatic takeoff and landing equipment operating experimentally in Europe. The Air Force selected his production autopilot for the KC-135.

The phone rang. It was Fish Salmon. He and a group of Lockheed and North American test pilots were in the lobby. "What are you doing in there?" I said. "Come on. I'm in a poolside room." Before they arrived, I called the desk. Fortunately the room next door was available. I ordered ice and glasses. This was going to be a rough night.

I recognized the entire group except one North American fighter pilot, Jack Waddell, and Fish's female companion. The bar was set up in the adjoining room. Someone, probably Fish, made some phone calls, and the place filled with lovely ladies.

Later in the evening Waddell and I proceeded to the coffee shop and discussed his technical and pilot background. By the time we returned to the party I had offered him a job, and he had agreed to visit our Seattle operations. Our flight-test workload was increasing. There were three new 707 configurations: the 707-220 (the Braniff airplane with J75 engines to provide the increased power required for the high-altitude airports in South America), the 707-320 (for the long non-stop intercontinental routes), and Qantas Airline's short-body 707. We also faced a massive, worldwide pilot-training program. I was looking for experienced pilots to train as instructors. Loesch, Gannett, and I developed a 707 pilot-training manual—an essential for a standardized worldwide program to train airline pilots.

Slim Lindbergh

Testing of the 707-120's performance, stability and control, and flight characteristics had been completed. We were preparing for the certification program. Just before takeoff one day, public relations called requesting my personal attention to a prominent passenger who would join us on the flight. No name was given. I delayed engine start—no passenger—so after a short wait, I left the cabin entry steps in place and started all four engines.

A solitary figure in an overcoat, with his felt hat pulled low, hurried from the hangar and entered the plane. The flight engineer closed and locked the entrance door. The visitor came forward and removed his hat. I was stunned but managed to say, "Captain Lindbergh. Welcome aboard."

He reached over my seat back and shook hands, and I introduced him to Loesch. Dix vacated the copilot seat. "Fly copilot, Slim," I said.

"The jump seat is okay."

"Come on, you're closer to what's going on up here."

After takeoff, when the climb was established, I removed my hands from the wheel. "She's all yours. Level off at thirty-five thousand feet."

Lindbergh made shallow climbing turns to 25,000, then said, "Go ahead. I'll observe."

When level at 35,000 feet, I rolled into a steep turn so he could see Seattle directly below. "We will be recording data during a stabilized run," I said. I trimmed the airplane at 98-percent power on a south heading, identified mounts Adams, Rainier, St. Helens, and Hood, then rolled into a steep right turn. "That's Portland, Oregon," I said. "Twelve minutes from Seattle."

"Very impressive," he said.

I offered him the controls again, but he preferred to observe. We recorded performance data at 25,000 feet while returning to Seattle. Over Seattle, Lindbergh assented to my offer of an emergency descent demonstration. I closed the throttles, raised the air brakes, extended the landing gear, and let her dive. In three minutes we were at 7,000 feet. He was impressed. "Follow through on approach and landing to feel how the airplane responds to the controls," I said.

After we parked, he thanked us for the flight, shook our hands, donned overcoat and hat, and deplaned. He had asked not to be escorted. I watched him disappear alone into the hangar.

Lindbergh was technical advisor to Pan American, and later in the test program he reappeared for a second flight.

17

707 Certification and Pan Am Route Survey

Dick Slith, certification pilot for the F.A.A. Western Region, arrived to monitor and fly the 707-120 during the certification program. He had never flown jet aircraft before, so he had some initial difficulty with low-speed Dutch roll. However, he quickly mastered the corrective control technique and he, Dix, and Gannett worked together during the remainder of the program.

Early on, Director Alcorn of the F.A.A. Western office arrived for a flight demonstration. I offered him the pilot seat, but he declined and took the copilot position. In the climb I said, "I don't believe you remember me."

He looked at me again and said, "I know the name but don't recall a meeting."

"It was a long time ago. You gave me my first pilot license in 1933 at Spartan in Tulsa."

"Al Johnston! Sure I remember. You're the sideslip, spot-landing guy."

After the flight, he was complimentary regarding the Dash 80 and said, "The industry is facing a major task to prepare for this equipment."

Adi Gasdar

Sales escorted Adi Gasdar, Air India chief pilot, to Flight Test. After giving him a technical explanation of the Dash

80, I walked him through an external inspection and checked him out in the cockpit. "It's an airplane," I said. "Fly it like you do your Connies" (Lockheed Constellations).

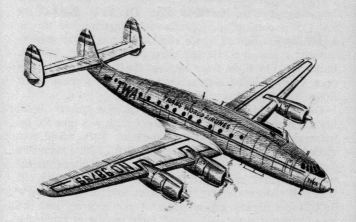

Lockheed Constellation

I coached him through the engine start, taxi, and takeoff check lists. In takeoff position, he held the brakes and applied full power. All temperatures and pressures were in the green. "It's all yours," I said.

He released the brakes. The airplane accelerated rapidly. I called V_r (rotation speed), he rotated the nose to takeoff attitude, and we lifted from the runway. With gear and flaps retracted, I pulled the wheel back a bit more. He couldn't believe the steep angle and the 270-mile-per-hour best climb speed. I adjusted the throttles to climb power and said, "Don't worry, Adi. Everyone falls a little behind this airplane until you adjust to the performance."

He nodded his head in amazement. After our postflight discussion, I was positive he would support an Air India 707 decision.

KC-135

I looked across the desk at Loesch. "Dix, you've come a long way since the revetment days. The initial flight of the KC-135 is coming up. Effective immediately, you are assigned project pilot. I'll ride copilot for you." Dix was delighted. I was also. He had earned it. When we flew the initial KC-135 flight from Renton, the field perimeter was once again crowded with spectators eager to witness a first flight. The flight was a complete success.

General LeMay was eager to get the new tankers. Proof flight testing was nearing completion, and it was time for the incremental maximum gross weight tests. They would conclude with a maximum gross weight takeoff with a simulated outboard engine failure at V_2. Because of the hazardous nature of the tests, we moved the program to the Edwards test base in the Mojave, my old home away from home. Edwards' 15,000-foot runway adjoining the 10-mile-wide dry lake bed greatly increased the odds in our favor in case of problems. I elected to pilot the aircraft during these tests and assigned Lew Wallick as copilot.

On the Friday night of my first week at Edwards, I attended a QB meeting at the Hollywood Roosevelt. I knew many of the L.A. Hangar QB members, but at one table was a man I felt I knew but couldn't place. Then he turned full face toward me. It was Art Inman. I hadn't seen him since he roared away in the Ford Tri-motor into the predawn darkness that long-ago day in Missouri. I hurried over and grabbed his hand. Startled, he looked up, then slowly stood up, shaking his head. "Al Johnston. I don't believe it," he said as we embraced.

In a quiet corner, with two fresh Scotch and waters, we reviewed the intervening years. Art had retired from flying and was in L.A. real estate. Smitty, whose crash had precipitated our hasty departure from Plattsburg, Missouri, recovered quickly, but the Travel Air was a total loss. Inman's Flying Circus prospered as President Roosevelt's New Deal took effect and the economy improved. Then World War II ended the era of barnstormers and flying circuses. Rawley Inman became a Pan American contract ferry pilot ferrying

B-24's over the North Atlantic to England. On a return trip in a C-47, while he was getting a much-needed rest in the crew bunk, his copilot flew into a Pennsylvania mountain. Don Inman was killed in an unsuccessful emergency landing; he was a passenger with a pilot friend in a J-5 Travel Air in Texas. During the war, Art was a flight instructor and ferry pilot. After the war, Smitty became an Alaskan bush pilot. His performance in that hostile environment with primitive equipment became legendary. After many years of Alaskan flying, during which he was known as Mud-Hole Smith, he retired as chief executive and major stockholder of Alaska's Cardova Air Lines.

When Art and I moved to the bar, Tony LeVier and Fish Salmon slapped me on the back. As I suspected, they and Art were old friends. Fish asked, "Do you know a gal named Wilma?" That gave me a start. I knew that Wilma Caldwell, our barnstorming ticket seller, had gone to Hollywood.

Fish's story was that a week before, at a party in Beverly Hills, an attractive blonde had singled him out and said, "I understand you're a Lockheed test pilot. Do you know Tex Johnston?"

"Maybe you should leave town," Art interjected, and Fish joked, "I told her that every place I go the gals ask if I know that S.O.B." Everybody laughed. Then Fish told the real story as she had told it to him. Following our last meeting, Wilma had gone to Hollywood and a successful movie career. She was seriously injured during the filming of an action movie, and in the hospital she met a young doctor, whom she married. His career prospered, and he became a prominent neurosurgeon. Fish described her Beverly Hills residence as elegant.

The next morning, I called Wilma's residence. A maid gave me her office number at the Hollywood recording studios of RCA. I dialed, and the answering hello seemed familiar. "How would you like to go barnstorming?" I said.

Silence for a moment. "Al, is this really you? Where are you?"

"Hollywood Roosevelt."

"Come over immediately. I cannot believe this."

During a three-hour lunch at Trader Vic's, we reviewed the 22 years since last we met. Her father, mother, and married sister, Lucille, now lived in Glendale. Wilma and the doctor were divorcing, and she was starting a new career in the music business.

The following week, at my invitation, Wilma visited the test base. That evening we made introductory visits to Willow Springs and Juanita's in Rosamond before arriving at Pancho Barnes's place. Pancho joined us during dinner and expounded on the virtues of test pilots in the distinctive, colorful, and salty vernacular for which she was famous. "Now I understand the movie-crowd stories," Wilma said after Pancho left the table.

The following Monday morning, the KC-135 maximum gross weight takeoff with number four engine cut at V_2 was beautiful. The directional control needed to compensate for the loss of number four engine was significant but not excessive. With gear up and incremental flap retraction, the three-engine performance satisfied specifications. The KC-135 tests were complete. Soon, KC-135 tankers were arriving at tactical B-47 and B-52 bases, greatly improving mission performance and efficiency.

Arthur Godfrey and the KC-135

After good friends General LeMay and Arthur Godfrey returned from an African safari, Boeing public relations informed me that Godfrey, his camera crew, and support personnel would be arriving to produce a prime-time show featuring the KC-135. They would shoot at the flight-test experimental hangar.

The endless take, retake, retake, for each scene soon destroyed the glamour of movie-making for me. When we finally wrapped it up, I invited Arthur on a KC-135 test flight. Arthur, a certificated pilot, occupied the copilot seat. I completed the test at 35,000 feet, descended to 20,000 feet, increased the power to 98 percent, entered a climb, and commenced a continuous series of climbing barrel rolls. Art didn't know what was happening until we were on our back. Then he laughed and said, "This is the best, the very best." While inverted after several consecutive climbing barrel rolls, I felt a small tremor and glanced at the altimeter. We were at 31,000 feet. For years after, Art told the story of being on his back at 31,000 feet in a KC-135.

707 Certification

The 707 certification process was complete except for an operational cross-country flight to give F.A.A. officials a firsthand look at line operation of the airplane. The flight was made on a South American run in the first Pan American 707-120. The onboard observing group included Pan Am captains Waldo Lynch and Scott Flower and Eastern Airlines' Dick Merrill, in addition to the F.A.A. officials.

During final approach for landing at Caracas, Venezuela, some of the observers expressed apprehension about the slightly downhill slope of the runway. I touched down on the first 300 feet, applied light braking, progressing to heavy as we decelerated, and added power to reach the taxiway. That performance increased everyone's confidence in and respect for the 707's landing and braking characteristics.

We returned to Seattle with the certification program completed. The Boeing 707-120 became the first certificated jet transport in the U.S.A.

First Delivery to Pan American

I officially delivered Pan Am's first 707 to San Juan, Puerto Rico, after a stop en route in Miami to pick up airline officials. The next morning an airline flight crew trained by Boeing took off from San Juan on Pan Am's first jet transport flight, a nonstop to New York. I observed from the jump seat.

The first group of Pan Am pilots had been trained and certificated at Seattle. My assignment now was to give 707 flight crews route checks between New York, London, and Paris. The next day, equipped with shave kit and sleeping bag, I again climbed aboard the number one Pan Am 707, this time with a New York–based flight crew bound for London and Paris. Thereafter, I completed three consecutive New York–London-Paris round-trips, six crossings of the North

Atlantic with a crew change at each turnaround. Minimal rest periods were spent in the sleeping bag on the floor of the empty passenger cabin. The airplane performed perfectly, requiring only fuel and food service at each turnaround.

Next, at Pan Am's request and in the airline's DC-7's, I made a "quick" round-the-world survey of airports and facilities with projected 707 commercial operations. The trip was an eye-opener. To upgrade airports to accommodate the 707's 275,000-pound gross weight, its sheer physical size, and its fuel and passenger capacity was a real problem for the affluent nations and a nightmare for developing nations. Pan Am focused immediate attention on Istanbul, Beirut, Karachi, Bombay, Bangkok, Hong Kong, and Tokyo.

The Beirut stop was of particular interest. Halfway to the airport on my day of departure, there was a burst of automatic weapon fire. The occupants of our first taxi, with the exception of the driver, hit the floorboards. It was a wild ride. Our car took two rounds, one through a side window, which showered us with glass—no injury—and one in the trunk. The other car took no hits. The captain said there had been one previous attack of the same type.

On final approach to Karachi, Pakistan, the control tower informed the captain that the glide-slope equipment had been stolen during the night—a frequent occurrence, the captain said. The ramp was covered with a mixture of accumulated engine oil, which had dripped from the parked airplane engines, and sand. The terminal had no air conditioning, and the rest rooms were a disaster. My impression was that my friend McNiece, stationed at Karachi during World War II flying the Hump in B-24's, was correct when he said, "If they ever decide to give the world an enema, Karachi is where they'll place the hose."

At Bombay's Santa Cruz Airport, the runway extension to 10,000 feet was under construction. The runway felt rough on landing, and I understood why when I watched the concrete being poured in 10-foot-square sections, one square at a time. Freshly mixed concrete was carried in small containers on the heads of male and female laborers and dumped in the 10-foot section. When full, it was leveled and troweled by hand. Occasionally, the height of a completed square would not precisely match the adjoining ones, resulting in a rough runway. The male laborers received 35 cents per day, the females 25 cents per day. Originally a small mountain had existed south of the airport. Extending the runway to accommodate the soon-to-arrive jet transports mandated the removal of the mountain. The task was accomplished in the same manner—one basketful of dirt and rock at a time on the heads of hundreds of male and female laborers.

In Bangkok I was pleased to find that the combination of Pan Am's planning and the cooperative attitude of Thai officials had resulted in satisfactory facilities to accept the inaugural jet passenger service.

In Hong Kong, I didn't know a soul. However, I remembered a popular observation: "A total stranger cannot sit in the leisure area adjoining the Peninsula Hotel lobby for one hour and not see someone he knows." Checking into the Peninsula, I deposited my gear in the room and proceeded to the prescribed area. I sat at a table for two, enjoying a beer and watching people come and go. Suddenly a voice from behind said, "Tex, are you lost?" It was my oil-exploration buddy Paul Cary, from Houston, Texas. I looked at my watch. It had been 35 minutes.

It's an occasion when two old-time pilot buddies get together, just as it is when two old-time doodlebuggers find each other, but the combination of both calls for a real wingding. It was a time when coolie-drawn rickshaws were the paramount mode of tourist transportation in Hong Kong. Paul and two of his employees, Jim and Lyle, chose three from the large group of rickshaws at the hotel entrance and climbed aboard. I took my time.

"What are you waiting on?" Paul said.

"I'm looking for a driver with a good pair of legs," I said. "This may be a long trip. I suggest we rent four rigs till six a.m. and get these boys on our side. It might come in handy. I picked up a few good pointers on this in Bangkok."

I made a deal for $20 U.S. apiece for all night. Later in the evening, Lyle said, "Tex, this rickshaw deal is all right. I believe these guys would haul us up that mountain at the end of the runway if you asked them." (The Hong Kong runway extended from the bay to the base of a significant hill. All landings were toward the hill and takeoffs toward the bay.)

It was an all-around evening, including getting measured for new suits. Our last stop was Paul's favorite Eastern hotel and club. It was 3 a.m. Our rickshaw drivers had spent most of the night asleep in the rigs waiting for us. "Boys," I said, "we're going to have a race to the Peninsula. We're putting five dollars each in a pot. The winner takes all. Okay?" They were eager. It was one and a half miles to the Peninsula and slightly downhill a portion of the way. It was close for about a mile, then my lad's long-muscled legs began to pay off. We won by half a block. My driver received the pot, and Paul gave the other three five each. They were delighted. I assure you we never waited on a buggy when we stepped out of the hotel.

I returned to Seattle and submitted a detailed report to Pan American management concerning requirements for the fast-approaching 707 round-the-world service.

(18)

The Russian Tu-104 and the 707 European Round-robin

Although the Russian Tu-104 four-engine jet transport had been much reported in the world press, little technical information was available. In response to world interest, the Russians agreed to exhibit a Tu-104 at the Vancouver Air Show in British Columbia, Canada.

Boeing arranged to display the 707-320, our intercontinental model. The passenger list for the short flight to Vancouver included Boeing public relations and sales representatives, 707 project engineer Maynard Pennel, and international aviation consultant Vernon Crudge. At Vancouver's municipal airport, we were directed to park adjacent to the Tu-104. As we did so, I noted that the Soviet plane was roped off as though off limits to visitors. The plane had eye appeal, but the body diameter appeared smaller than the 707's.

During that evening's gala invitational cocktail party at the Vancouver Hotel, an interpreter introduced me to the captain of the Tu-104, who spoke no English. I thought it strange that the Soviets had not sent someone like Kerchetkoff, my Russian pilot friend at Bell, who spoke excellent English. Through the interpreter, I came right to the point. "I would be pleased for you to fly with me tomorrow, and I would enjoy flying with you. Your airplane looks very interesting." The captain seemed nonplussed when the interpreter relayed my proposal. The two men adjourned for a short conference, after which the interpreter (who was also the Tu-104 flight engineer) said the captain was happy to accept.

237

Shortly after nine the next morning, captain and mouth-piece arrived at our boarding stairs. I escorted them through the passenger cabin and pointed out the automatically available passenger oxygen masks in case of a pressure loss, the lounges, the galley, and the multiple johns. Other guest passengers accompanying us on this demonstration flight were already seated. In the cockpit, the captain occupied the copilot position, the interpreter the jump seat, and Dix the flight engineer's position. Cleared for takeoff, I applied full power and, with temperatures and pressures checked, released the brakes.

Because our load was relatively light, the acceleration was sensational. At rotation, we were immediately airborne. I retracted gear and flaps simultaneously and established a steep climb at 270 mph; the altimeter spun like a runaway clock. The captain checked the instruments, looked at the earth falling away below, glanced at the downhill angle of the passenger cabin aisle, looked at his interpreter, and shook his head slowly from side to side. He was clearly amazed. Removing both hands from the control wheel, I said, "Tell him to fly the plane."

The captain grasped the wheel with both hands and continued the climb. As we climbed through 25,000 feet, I motioned for him to turn left. Doing so, he grossly overcontrolled, probably because of being accustomed to the Tu-104's high control forces. I motioned for him to remain on the controls while I leveled out at 30,000 feet, set cruise power, then rolled at maximum rate into a 60-degree banked turn to the left. At the 180-degree point I reversed the turn to a 60-degree banked turn to the right, rolling out on the original heading while maintaining a constant altitude throughout the maneuver. "Ask him how he likes the performance," I said.

The relayed answer was, "Good."

"Good?" I thought to myself. "It's the best in the whole damn world, and he knows it."

"Tell him we are going to execute a simulated emergency descent."

The captain nodded his head. I closed the throttles, extended the gear and air brakes, and entered the steepest dive possible, maintaining the maximum gear-down placard speed of 305 mph. I worked the tower, entered the downwind leg of the traffic pattern, turned on base leg and then final approach, touched down on the first 200 feet of the runway, retracted the flaps, extended the air brakes, employed medium to heavy braking, and turned off at the mid-runway taxi strip. As we parked in our assigned position and cut the engines, I said, "Tell the captain I'm interested in his comments concerning the 707."

They conversed briefly in Russian, and then the interpreter said, "We thank you for the flight demonstration. The captain said he enjoyed the flight very much."

"Any questions?" I asked. There were none.

"When are we going to fly the Tu-104?" I asked.

"We will check and inform you."

At 11 a.m., as stipulated, the guests invited for the Tu-104 flight arrived at their boarding stairs. The interpreter met us and said there would be a slight delay, so I invited everyone to relax in the 707. The outside air temperature was in the upper eighties, and the 707's ground air-conditioning unit was keeping its interior comfortably cool. Boeing sales people were already hosting visitors.

Forty-five minutes later the interpreter announced we could board the Tu-104. Pennel, Crudge, and I entered the passenger cabin together. It was hot—no air conditioning. The walls of the partially compartmented passenger area were covered with ornately patterned material in red, gold, and rose. The windows were adorned with companion curtains with ball fringes. "This reminds me of a Klondike whorehouse," I said to Crudge and Pennel.

Pennel, slightly embarrassed, smiled. Crudge belly laughed. "Precisely, old boy."

The captain, copilot, and flight engineer were already buckled in their respective seats. A fourth crew member sat at a shelf desk surrounded by electronic gear. In accented English he said he was the navigator and would answer any questions. I glanced around the cockpit. There was no jump seat, and all crew positions were occupied. "Ask the captain what happened to our agreement that I could fly as copilot, as he did in the 707?"

"Sir, that's impossible," the navigator replied.

Glancing around the cabin and wiping the sweat out of my eyes, I said, "Where am I supposed to sit?"

"If you remain in the cockpit, you must stand. You can hold to the cleat," he said pointing to the overhead. Bolted to the ceiling was a cleat similar to the handle of a toolbox. I grabbed the cleat, thinking to myself, "If these bastards think I'm going to back down, they're crazy."

Turning to the navigator, I asked, "Why don't you fire this S.O.B. up and turn on the air conditioning?" I thought he looked a bit strange. I understood why fifteen minutes later after the engines were started. There was no air conditioning. During taxi, the brakes chattered each time they were applied. The take-off roll was unreasonably long and the gear retraction time excessively slow. With no air conditioning, I expected at least some old-fashioned ram air, but when the flight engineer turned the air inlet on, I wasn't sure there was enough to blow out a candle. Instead of climbing to 20,000 or 25,000 feet for temperature relief, they leveled off at 10,000 feet. I say "they" because both pilot and copilot clung to their respective control wheels throughout the flight, like children clinging to security blankets. I strolled through the passenger cabin. The male guests, their jackets removed, were perspiring through their shirts. The ladies' makeup was running.

During the entire flight, the steepest bank was 15 degrees. I clung to my ceiling cleat during the approach, determined to witness the landing. At one point, I reached over the captain's shoulder and tried to sample the force required to move the control wheel. The captain slapped my hand away, and the cockpit atmosphere became downright unfriendly.

The Russian pilots flew an unprofessional traffic pattern and turned to final so far out I could hardly see the airport. They carried power all the way to the ground and overflew a significant amount of usable runway before touchdown. It was obvious the brakes were being applied because they were chattering; however, the runway ahead was shrinking rapidly. I seriously considered retreating to the passenger cabin to occupy an aft-facing seat. But at this point I suspected the pilot and copilot were both on the brakes, as the deceleration rate increased slightly. When we turned to taxi back, the wing extended beyond the end of the runway.

The unusually slow taxi speed, the brake chatter, and the almost unbearable heat would be unacceptable in any competitive commercial air operation. When we were parked on the ramp, the deplaning stairway in place, the engine noise diminishing, I turned to the navigator and said, "I have a message for the captain. Please tell him that in my twenty-one thousand hours of piloting time, the Tu-104 is the sorriest damn airplane I have ever had the misfortune of flying in." He sat and looked at me. "Go ahead. Tell him exactly what I said."

I'm not sure, but I believe he did. The captain's head snapped around, his eyes hostile. I returned the hostility and departed.

Rome, Paris, Frankfurt, London

Canadian Pacific Airlines was close to decision time: 707 or DC-8? Ralph Bell, director of Boeing's sales department, called my office. "Canadian Pacific is close to a decision," he said. "Allen wants to make a European round-robin with Chairman Brian McConnachie aboard—Rome, Paris, Frankfurt, London, and return. Depart Friday, return Sunday."

On Friday the forecast weather for our near great-circle course was good except for head winds over the north Atlantic. Boeing pilots Johnston, Gannett, and Wallick, a Pan Am navigator, and two stewardesses were aboard. McConnachie, a six-foot, 210-pound Canadian, who had been a Canadian bush pilot, President Allen, and Boeing's international consultant Vernon Crudge boarded.

While climbing to altitude, I saw the fuel pressure on number one engine pulse, then slowly drop. I shut down number one and notified crew and guests that we were returning to Boeing Field and would be dumping fuel to the allowable maximum landing weight. After dumping fuel over Puget Sound, I landed and taxied to the flight-test hangar, where mechanics replaced a malfunctioning fuel regulator during the time it took to refuel. It was an unfortunate incident, but McConnachie, being a pilot, was impressed by the simplicity of fuel dumping and the easy access to the engine.

Over the North Atlantic I asked Allen and McConnachie to the cockpit to watch as dusk faded rapidly to darkness. Forty-five minutes later I called them back to see the sun rising above the distant eastern horizon. It had been a short night—only 45 minutes from sunset to sunrise at jet speed at our latitude and altitude.

Eight hours and five minutes from the Seattle takeoff we landed at Rome's Campeche Airport. McConnachie was impressed.

Ken Luplow, Boeing's European representative, had arranged receptions at Rome, Paris, Frankfurt, Brussels, and London, each a festive occasion with local dignitaries and masses of interested observers.

Gannett and Wallick flew the London-Seattle leg and gave me an opportunity to converse with McConnachie. He told stories of bush flying and of later developments in Canadian aviation. During the course of a long flying career that began in the early twenties, he played a significant role in bringing air transport services to the Canadian far north.

Bill Allen loved to travel in the 707. After that trip he often bragged, "We were in five countries, crossed the Atlantic two times, spent one night each in Rome and London, all in a total elapsed Seattle time of fifty-three hours."

Transition Problems and Sales Trips

When the safety records of various commercial transportation modes are compared on the basis of fatalities versus passenger miles, commercial air transportation is the world's safest way to travel. Flight crew physical standards, mandatory flight training, F.A.A. flight crew certification, and periodic flight checks have tended to assure competent flight crews. Appropriate regulations and periodic inspection of aircraft and operational procedures by government control agencies have assured certified equipment and standardized operating procedures.

But the jet age gave rise to new problems. In the era of propeller-driven transport aircraft, flight crew transition from single, to twin, to four-engine aircraft had been relatively routine. The transition to turbine-powered aircraft was proving more difficult for the following reasons: Jets routinely fly at altitudes above 30,000 feet. Previously, most flight crews had never flown above 20,000 feet. The gross weight of the big jets was many times that of previous airliners. Takeoff and landing speeds, which vary with gross weight, had to be calculated in every case. Takeoff gross weights vary widely, both because of variations in payloads and because of variations in fuel requirements for flights of varying lengths. Landing weights vary widely, being based on takeoff gross weight less the weight of fuel consumed en route. Accustomed to the high drag of propellers when power is reduced, transitioning crews had trouble losing excess speed in a timely fashion for approach and landing. Power reductions had to be anticipated and drag brakes used when required. Determining speed at altitude by Mach number (percentage of the speed of sound) in place of indicated airspeed was also a change. Because of factors like these, Boeing's training program for customers became a massive undertaking.

American Airlines lost a 707-120 in a training accident on Long Island. The airplane crashed during an approach and landing simulating the loss of two engines on one side; the accident was strictly pilot error. Subsequently, Jim Gannett and I arrived at American Airlines at New York's La Guardia Airport to monitor the flight crew training program. We embarked on a training flight with an American Airlines student captain in the pilot seat, the instructor in the copilot seat, Gannett in the jump seat, and myself standing in the forward passenger cabin aisle conversing with a student captain. The instructor initiated Dutch roll. The student was to apply corrective control. Feeling the oscillation increasing, I turned with haste to the cockpit and saw Jim jam his left arm over the student captain's shoulder, seize the control wheel, and apply corrective control while simultaneously closing all four throttles with his right hand. I had never before seen a professional pilot allow an airplane to yaw in excess of 10 degrees. I am confident Jim's quick action prevented a catastrophe. In a later meeting with American Airlines management and instructor pilots we reemphasized the hazards of allowing the yaw angle to exceed 15 degrees.

At our hotel, Jim and I reviewed the problem. It had seemed inconceivable that experienced pilots would allow a pilot-induced flight mode to develop to a dangerous condition when simple use of rudder and aileron would establish normal flight. Immediately I directed Boeing instructors to spend additional time on Dutch-roll control technique.

Meantime, Pan American was enjoying 100-percent load factor on all trans-Atlantic flights, and reports indicated the jet-aircraft revenue was amortizing one 707 per month, a clear indication of the traveling public's acceptance of the jet transport. But Pan Am had a learning experience too.

A westbound night flight from Paris was progressing on schedule midway over the Atlantic at 34,000 feet with the airplane on autopilot. Captain Lynch left the cockpit for the rest room. The copilot, a senior captain based in San Francisco, was executing his paperwork. Captain Lynch, returning to the cockpit, stopped just outside the cockpit door to answer passenger questions. Suddenly the sound of faster airflow alerted him to trouble. Opening the cockpit door, he was horrified to see the flight attitude indicator showing a steep diving left turn. He snapped the throttles closed as he slid into the captain's seat, grasped the wheel, and carefully corrected the bank angle and pulled the nose up to level flight. Checking the altimeter, he was shocked. They had lost 28,000 feet.

Mechanics at Gander, Newfoundland, found minor damage. Pan Am dispatched another 707 to pick up the passengers. Temporary repairs allowed Lynch to fly his plane to Seattle for further examination. There, Boeing engineers discovered that the plane had approached the speed of sound in the plunge and been subjected to stresses during the pullout that slightly exceeded design-limit load, causing a slight permanent set to the wing. Fortunately, structural integrity was not affected. The airplane returned to scheduled service after repairs.

An investigation concluded that the autopilot had become disengaged, possibly when the copilot or his papers accidentally hit the autopilot disconnect button. The airplane entered the dive so slowly that the copilot, absorbed in his paperwork, was oblivious to what was happening until Captain Lynch recognized the danger.

Soon after the North Atlantic episode, Pan Am experienced another in-flight incident. During a pilot-training flight near Paris, France, flight instructor Captain Howard Cone allowed a pilot-induced Dutch roll to exceed the recommended yaw and roll limit. The airplane thereupon rolled so violently to inverted flight that an outboard engine strut failed. The engine separated from the aircraft and fell to the ground. Cone recovered to level flight and returned for a successful three-engine landing.

I was seriously concerned by the incidents. The Dash 80 and the production 707 had been thoroughly flight tested. The stability and control were good, with one minor exception: the slightly positive directional stability, which was considered acceptable.

Dutch roll is an inherent characteristic of swept-wing air-craft. The F.A.A. certificated the airplane with the consideration that Dutch roll control is a required piloting control function, just as stall recovery and engine-failure control are a necessary part of a pilot's perfected technique. "Could it be," I reasoned, "that the airline pilots were so confident, because of the overall performance and good control characteristics of the airplane, that they failed to recognize the necessity for early application of corrective control when Dutch roll occurred?" If so, our rigid flight-training program should solve the problem.

Distinguished Guests

Lord W. S. (Sholto) Douglas, a renowned aviator in the early days of English aviation, was chief executive of British European Airways. Well aware of the jet airplane's potential, he was keenly interested in the 707. He and Lady Douglas were guests of Bill Allen when Boeing sales executive Clarence Wilde escorted them to the flight hangar for a briefing on the Dash 80. Following the briefing, I escorted them to the airplane for a demonstration flight and invited Lady Douglas to occupy the jump seat and Lord Douglas the copilot seat. The flight was the beginning of a long friendship. I last visited their Kirtleside residence in London during Sholto's illness just before his passing.

London

During the early period of the trans-oceanic, large flying boat, the British developed a procedure for engine power changes that later caused problems. The captain would request a power change; the flight engineer would acknowledge and then adjust the throttles. Because the BOAC captains clung to that procedure during Dash 80 demonstrations and early flight training, they experienced some embarrassing and potentially dangerous situations. The fact was, they had forgotten how to integrate power changes with the right hand on the throttles while simultaneously controlling pitch and roll with the left hand on the control wheel. Once they realized they could not consistently land on an airport using their old system because of undershooting or overshooting, they accepted the recognized standard technique and developed the necessary piloting skills.

The BOAC 707 was equipped with Rolls Royce turbojet engines. I attended the ceremony at the Rolls Royce plant celebrating the delivery of the first engine under that contract. During my first visit, I was particularly moved by the immaculate World War II Spitfire fighter plane (powered by a Rolls Royce Merlin) poised gracefully on the shining marble floor of the plant's entrance lobby. What a potent reminder of the bitter, but glorious, not-too-distant past.

After the delivery ceremonies at Rolls, I departed for an appointment with Brian Trubshaw, chief test pilot for Vickers Aircraft. Trub had flown the British Comet, and in Seattle, when I took him on a Dash 80 demonstration flight, he flew the 707 well, adapting quickly to its characteristics. Trub had scheduled two flights for me: one in the four-engine turboprop Vickers Viscount, and one in the Vulcan jet bomber. The Viscount was a satisfactory airplane, a significant improvement over reciprocating-engine machines, but doomed to a relatively short service life by the arrival of the turbojet. For pilots accustomed to the B-47, B-52, and Dash 80 handling characteristics and performance, the Vulcan was a disappointment. By our standards, the high control forces and slow control response were unacceptable.

After the flights, I arrived at the Savoy Hotel in London and received an invitation to Saturday lunch and dinner with Sir Charles and Lady Housdon. Sir Charles, a friend and business associate of Reed Chambers's, the Dash 80 insurance underwriter, was an executive officer of Lloyds of London, and Reed had previously introduced me to him in New York. During our time together, Sir Charles questioned me closely regarding 707 training accidents and seemed to accept my explanations and our training objectives. The next morning, at the invitation of Sir Charles, I visited the Lloyds of London trading floor and inspected its huge bell, which had been used to announce the loss of each ship at sea during the era of tall sailing ships. The trading floor itself seemed in pandemonium to me, with scores of traders waving sheets

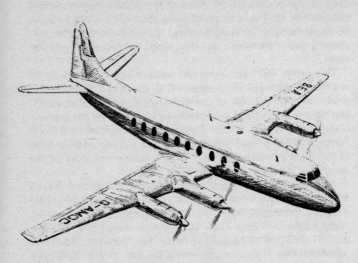

Vickers Viscount

of paper and using finger language. It reconfirmed my good fortune in being involved in the flight testing of high-performance airplanes.

Air France

In Paris, Ken Luplow's fluent French and well-established rapport resulted in productive meetings with Air France. At the conclusion of the meetings, we were optimistic regarding Air France's forthcoming equipment discussions. It did turn out as we hoped, and subsequently I had challenging, and on occasion exasperating, flight-training experiences with Air France.

American Airlines

Back in New York I met with Red Mosher, an American Airlines senior vice president and a veteran in the airline business. Red said the increase in the number of passengers transported by the 707's was taxing the capacity and capability of airports, airlines, and airways. American Airlines' load factors were running in the high 90-percent bracket, and aircraft utilization was averaging ten hours per day. Already the system was suffering flight delays, and the number of jet transports in service was small compared with the number on order. The people problem was becoming greater and greater as the numbers of flights and numbers of passengers increased. Problems were not confined to surface activity. Air traffic control required upgrading of methods and procedures, personnel, and equipment to satisfy jet airplane conditions.

Mosher was concerned about the possibility of midair collisions, particularly in high-density areas, and was considering a four-man flight crew, the fourth member to act as visual lookout. I disagreed with him on that one. On many occasions I had seen maps and newspapers attached to windshield frames as sun shades. A conscientious captain and first officer could satisfactorily scan for other aircraft. The fourth crew member would be too expensive. American implemented the four-man system, but results were inconclusive and the costs excessive, and the system was terminated.

20

Air India

I telephoned Arthur Godfrey and proposed that he join me with his camera crew on the delivery flight of the first 707 to India as guests of Air India. Bobby Kuka, Air India's vice president and director of public relations and sales, had authorized the invitation and was setting up a tiger shoot to follow the delivery ceremonies. The plan was for a week of tiger hunting followed by a trip to Mysore for an Indian bison hunt as guests of the maharajah of Mysore. "We shall reside in the fifty-five-room guest house and hunt from the back of the maharajah's elephants. How does that grab you?"

"Tex, I can't believe it."

"There is adequate space on the airplane for you to take your TV equipment and personnel to photograph whatever you think would fit in your show."

"You're right on target. We'll make a great show and work in some plugs for Air India. I'll check with CBS."

Pending the trip to India, I was back on the job as a test pilot. It is difficult, if not impossible, to describe the satisfying odor of an airplane cockpit—a mixture of paint, leather upholstery, acoustical material, lubricants, aftershave lotion, and, yes, some honest sweat, thoroughly combined to achieve that special cockpit aroma—for me, the ultimate atmosphere in the greatest combination office and workplace in the world.

In the climb to 35,000 feet, our test altitude, the thoughts of past flights flashed through my mind. Although technical presentations, sales pitches, and travel were always a challenge, sometimes disappointing, sometimes rewarding, they never approached the challenge, the continually changing conditions, hazards, problems, achievements, and pride the test pilot enjoys in that special place called the cockpit. If only it could continue forever.

Chopsticks, Jets, and Saki

I was afraid it was too good to last—test flying every day—and it didn't. The sales department requested my participation in a sales effort in Tokyo and Hong Kong. Boeing was represented in Japan by the Nissho Company, a major multiendeavor organization. Arriving for our 8 a.m. appointment in Tokyo, we were introduced to Mac Shimada and Stanley Maeda, two well-educated English-speaking Nissho representatives. Mac Shimada said the Japan Air Lines (J.A.L.) agenda would require two days. A dinner at an exclusive club hosted by five officers of the Nissho Company would conclude the second day. Our presentations were well received and the work sessions with the various J.A.L. departments resulted in mutual understanding.

Mac Shimada and I became good friends during my numerous visits to Tokyo. On several occasions we arranged weekend parties at quaint villages on the shores of the Sea of Japan and the Pacific, where several small and exquisite hotels were perched high on the near-vertical cliffs with the waves crashing at their bases. The dainty Japanese architecture, the infinite variety of delicious cuisine, and the baths integrated into the natural rugged landscape supplied by constantly flowing natural hot springs provided a perfect party atmosphere.

In Hong Kong, my previously enterprising rickshaw boys smiled and waved a friendly welcome upon our arrival at the Peninsula Hotel. Cathay Pacific, a fledgling airline expanding its route structure, would soon require jet transport equipment to remain competitive. Our technical presentations, movies of the 707, and suggestions that the chief pilot and technical people visit Seattle for a flight demonstration and in-depth economic route analysis were well received.

Flight to Bombay

The certification of the larger intercontinental 707-320 was complete. Production 320's were rolling off the line. Boeing flight instructors, pilots, and flight engineers were busy at customer bases instructing flight crews. Donna buzzed. "Mr. Godfrey on the line," she said.

I gave Arthur the good news. The delivery date of Air India's number one 707 was firm. We would arrive Idlewilde at 3 p.m., February 20, and I would meet him at six the next morning at the Air India office for an 8 a.m. takeoff. We'd refuel at London and depart immediately nonstop to Bombay.

Acquisition of the 707 aircraft was a nationally celebrated event for the Indian government and Air India International. Fifty government and airline officials, some with wives, chief pilot Adi Gasdar, an Air India navigator, and two lovely Air India stewardesses in their colorful saris assembled in Seattle for the acceptance of the first Air India 707 and the delivery flight to Bombay. Boeing flight instructor Bob Mattison and flight-engineer instructor Dick Smith, en route to assignments as 707 instructors in Bombay, were included.

Predeparture ceremonies completed, Gasdar triumphantly occupied the first officer (copilot) seat, and I taxied to takeoff position. On the P.A. system I briefed the passengers that we would cruise at 36,000 feet nonstop to New York with an estimated four hours, ten minutes, en route. Established in the climb at 270 mph, I turned to Adi and said, "She's all yours. Level off at thirty-six thousand and take us to New York." Four hours and thirty minutes later we were on the ground at New York's Idlewilde Terminal (now John F. Kennedy International Airport) taking part in Air India's 707 reception ceremonies.

Next morning at seven I introduced Arthur Godfrey to the passengers assembled at the Air India departure gate. The plan to film motion pictures in India for the *Arthur Godfrey Show* surprised and delighted them. Air India's planning and the professional performance of Arthur's technicians resulted in proper coordination with customs officials and the efficient loading of the voluminous video, sound, lighting, and support equipment. My friend Vernon Crudge was also a passenger.

During climbout, I invited passengers to visit the cockpit two at a time under stewardess supervision. Turning to Gasdar in the copilot seat, I said, "Captain Gasdar, as our guests arrive, please give them a detailed cockpit briefing."

"I'm not ready for that, Tex."

"Sure you are. You've completed ground school, and you flew the airplane from Seattle to New York yesterday."

Apprehensively, he glanced aft through the open cockpit door and with a tortured look said, "Here they come."

"Relax, Adi, our guests are basically interested in the cockpit. Don't forget, these people are strangers to this environment."

The first two were an Air India official and his wife, and they recognized Adi. I introduced Boeing flight engineer Dick Smith and instructor pilot Bob Mattison. The visitors stared in awe at the instruments, switches, and electronic displays on the pilot and copilot's forward and overhead panels, the similar complexity of the flight engineer's panel, the circuit-breaker panels, and the other cockpit controls. Their reactions were typical of laymen during a first visit to the front office of a multi-engine jet airplane. I gave them a nontechnical briefing and responded to their questions. They thanked us and returned to the passenger cabin. Adi, now completely relaxed, said, "Thanks." Adi and I alternated in briefing our visitors. Introducing passengers to the sophistication of a modern airplane and helping them understand its operation not only relieves the monotony of trans-ocean flight but also, for me, is a source of personal satisfaction.

The arrival ceremonies at the Air India International passenger area of London's Heathrow Airport were reminiscent of the New York festivities, but with an added attraction. I was introduced to J. D. Tata, chairman of Air India International, an extremely aristocratic and articulate gentleman, who was scheduled to go with us to Bombay. Chairman Tata had used his English legal and technical education to achieve business success in a number of Indian industries. In addition, as an early pilot in India, he had achieved a measure of fame by flying a British Gypsy Moth single-engine, open-cockpit biplane from Bombay to London.

Following the style of many successful industrialists, our conversation consisted mainly of my answers to his questions, but I did manage to suggest that he occupy the copilot seat during the flight to Bombay. During the preflight cockpit check and engine starts, I gave him a continuous description and explanation of our procedures and activities, addressing him as "Mr. Tata." I was grateful when he interrupted and said, "My name is Jay."

In the climb out of Heathrow, I said, "She's all yours, Jay. Climb on this heading to thirty-five thousand, hold two hundred seventy miles an hour. We'll fly Mach number when we get to altitude. When you wish, I'll engage the autopilot." Jay leveled off at 35,000, and I set cruise power and instructed him in the use of the longitudinal trim control. Fifteen minutes later he requested autopilot. As I checked the trim, engaged the autopilot, and selected altitude hold, Jay complimented the airplane. He was most impressed with the high rate of climb at 270 mph and the light flight-control forces.

Over Athens at 35,000, cruising 592 mph, we looked down on the ancient ruins of the Acropolis and the Parthenon. Again I marveled at man's progress with time.

At 150 miles from Bombay I said, "Get on the controls, Jay, and we'll establish the letdown for Bombay." Disengaging the autopilot, closing the throttles to idle, and trimming to the letdown attitude, I said, "She's all yours. You will see Bombay over the nose soon." Working Bombay radio, I gave them our location and estimated time of arrival. I had suspected Jay was a true airplane driver, so I said, "Jay, would it be appropriate to show the residents of Bombay their new airplane—a good buzz job before we land?

"Why not?" he said.

I informed the passengers of our intentions. Bombay was visible in the distance. "Increase the letdown angle a bit, Jay. We don't want to overshoot."

"I can't believe it. The engines have been at idle for over a hundred miles," he replied.

"It requires a little getting accustomed to. There is a lot of kinetic energy involved."

I called Bombay's Santa Cruz Airport, gave a position report, and was informed there was no traffic in the Bombay area. I grasped the controls and said, "Follow through on the controls if you care to."

Increasing power to 100 percent, I approached Bombay on a 90-degree heading from five miles offshore over the Arabian Sea. At full throttle, we flashed over downtown Bombay at 500 feet and 500 mph, made a steep climbing left turn to 3,500 feet over North Bombay, entered a steep power-reduced dive on a south heading, and recrossed the city, again at full throttle at 500 feet and 500 mph. We completed the run with a climbing left turn east of Santa Cruz Airport and slowed to traffic-pattern speed with drag brakes.

Retracting the drag brakes and extending the landing gear, I entered base leg, extended half flap, and turned on final approach, working the control tower all the while. On final, I extended full flaps, touched down on the first 300 feet of runway, raised the drag brakes, employed moderate braking, executed a 180-degree turn on the runway, and with control-tower direction taxied to and parked in the designated area for the 707 receiving ceremonies. Before leaving the cockpit, Jay shook my hand and said, "Congratulations. This is truly a remarkable airplane, and your precision flying demonstration is the pinnacle of my flying experience."

Arthur, Crudge, and I were the last to deplane and were immediately escorted to a position in front of the airplane adjacent to the nose gear. Sri Prakasa, governor of Bombay, officiated. At his request a beautiful lady in a flowing sari lightly struck a cracked coconut on the nose-gear strut and christened the number one Air India 707 with a gush of coconut milk. Simultaneously, three sari-attired maidens, each bearing a large floral wreath, appeared before Godfrey, Crudge, and me and gracefully placed the wreaths over our heads and around our necks. It was truly touching—a feeling intensified by the sharp thorns in the flowered wreaths. Tata praised the 707 and said, "Today we traveled the five thousand miles from London to Bombay in eight hours. Thirty years ago I flew the same course in reverse, Bombay to London. My time was the same number, eight, but measured in days, not hours. Our 707 covered the eleven thousand miles from Seattle to New York to London to Bombay in nineteen hours and fifteen minutes flight time."

The sun was a molten mass sinking into the Arabian Sea when our entourage invaded the Hotel Taj Mahal lobby. The desk clerks were more interested in describing the vibration of the hotel, the tremendous roar, and the pandemonium that followed the 707 arrival than in the registration of their most recent guests. Surveying the lobby, I was rewarded. There she was, Carole Chourbaji, the Indian version of our Betty Grable, the schoolteacher, tutor, linguist, and cover girl I had met during my last visit to India. As I approached, she rose, clasped both my hands in hers, and said, "I expected something, but nothing like that. People were jumping out of windows, crawling under parked cars, children screaming, old men crying, and women praying. Then the word spread—"It is our new airplane"—and everyone wanted to celebrate. It was scary at first, but now it's so funny. If only there were movies taken."

The next morning at six-thirty, Mattison, Smith, and I were in a taxi on our way to the Santa Cruz Airport in an effort to avoid the unbelievable morning traffic, the thousands of pedestrians, bullock carts, pushcarts, autos, and buses. At the maintenance hangar, we contacted Vish Vishvanath, Air India's aircraft-maintenance director, and a Boeing customer service representative. Vish produced the airplane service record and flight training schedule. At nine I boarded their first 707 training flight to observe the conduct of training and the Indian pilot's initial reaction to the 707.

During this delivery visit to Bombay, Boeing's service department people assigned to Air India reported that Indian technicians and maintenance personnel were well trained and capable. However, the Air India personnel lacked confidence and requested constant supervision in servicing and maintaining the newly arrived 707. Attention and consideration were necessary. The machine age in general had not arrived in India (reference my previous description of airport runway construction). But a study of India's history and of Air India's performance and safety record showed the skills were available. What the country needed was an expanded educational system.

After coordination of the flight-simulator program and meetings with Gasdar and Vish, I arrived at the Taj Mahal at 5:30 p.m. The desk clerk produced a message: "Dinner, Kuka's residence, time 7:00 p.m., join you at 6:00," signed, Carole.

The Jungle

Our hunting adventures in the jungles of India are fond memories, but their telling must be saved for another time and place. One anecdote, however, reveals something of the contrast between village India and the world of the jet-age airline.

Carole Chourbaji and I walked toward a village well to help carry water for our camp. We had gone but a short distance when I remembered I'd left my .375 magnum leaning by the bed. The camp was deserted except for the cook. I retrieved the rifle, and hung it on my left shoulder by the sling. As we approached the well, we saw three typical jungle men arguing with the women waiting to fill their water bags. Carole was listening. "What's the deal?" I asked.

"I have never heard of this. The three strangers are demanding the people pay them for the water."

"What with?" I asked. "They don't have any money."

"Some do," she replied, "but they are demanding their bracelets and earrings."

"Come on," I said, as I swung the rifle around in position. "Tell those bastards I said to get the hell out of here. This water is for everyone, free."

"Are you sure?" she said. "I don't trust them."

"Tell them," I repeated.

We were about ten feet from the troublemakers when Carole spoke. They turned and stared at me. I concentrated on each in turn. They spoke softly to each other.

"What did they say?"

"I couldn't hear," she replied as they approached.

"Back up and get out of the way, now," I said, and heard her retreat. The one on the right grabbed at me, and he took the gun butt right in the pit of his pot belly. As the one on the left came at me, the rifle barrel made a dimple in his belly all the way to his backbone. While the two on the ground writhed in agony, I placed a .375 slug between the third one's flat feet. He appeared paralyzed. "Carole, tell him to go, and if he returns, I'll blow his guts out."

The muzzle was one inch from his protruding belly button.

He turned and disappeared into the jungle at full bore, never looking back. I looked at the assembled crowd as Carole spoke to them. "They want to thank you," she said.

"Tell them it's okay. They won't have any more trouble."

The word spread, and at every village we visited we were greeted with smiles and hand-waving. What a contrast: these natives in the bush, and two hundred miles away people building airports by pick and shovel and wicker baskets while multimillion-dollar airplanes take off for and land from transoceanic flights at near 600 mph. What a massive problem, incomprehensible until one has the opportunity to witness it.

Following a joyous farewell at the airport terminal, the Godfrey entourage boarded an Air India Lockheed Constellation destined for New York. I returned to work with Air India, whose crews were adapting well to the 707. I flew several route checkout flights to Cairo, Zurich, and London.

21

Accidents and Consequences

I was booked on a late afternoon 707 flight out of Hong Kong for Tokyo and Honolulu. I visited friends at the Pan Am engine overhaul facility, then dropped by the flight crew dispatch office, met the crew, and presented my F.A.A. cockpit pass. They were friendly but did not invite me to join them in the cockpit. I checked the weather and noted that a weather system extended from a hundred miles east of Hong Kong almost to Honolulu. I met a friend in the boarding lounge, a vice president of the airline, who was returning to New York. The flight was filled to capacity, and we sat in the two most aft passenger seats.

The takeoff and initial climb were routine, but as we gained altitude the airplane began to Dutch roll. "What is causing this motion?" my friend asked.

"We're on autopilot, and I suspect the rudder indexing to the autopilot is misrigged," I said.

"Can't something be done?"

"The captain should disengage the autopilot and hand-fly the airplane," I said. "The oscillation is not excessive, we just feel it more in these aft seats."

The condition did improve slightly at cruising altitude. During the instrument approach in heavy rain at Tokyo, I watched for the runway threshold lights. As we crossed them, I realized we were too fast. The excess speed carried us far down the runway before touchdown. I felt the antiskid cycling as the tires hydroplaned on the water-puddled runway and said to my friend, ''Tighten your belt. We may run off the end of the runway.'' When we turned around to taxi back I could see the wing extending beyond the runway end.

Finishing my cup of coffee in the terminal coffee shop, I excused myself and went to take a look at the brakes. I presented my credentials, proceeded to the airplane, and found a pool of hydraulic fluid under the forward outboard wheel of the left truck. I identified myself to a ground crewman and told him of the problem.

''What can we do?'' he asked.

''First determine if there is a brake assembly and balanced wheel and tire available.''

''How do we remove and install the wheel? We don't have jacks to handle this weight.''

''Get the tow tractor and some planks. We'll tow the inboard wheels up onto a ramp.''

Fortunately, the required spares were available, and at 3 a.m. we departed Tokyo in heavy rain. The plane was now at maximum gross weight with a full load of passengers and fuel for the flight to Honolulu. The tendency to Dutch roll increases at high altitude with a maximum load. As altitude increased, the increasing oscillation resulted in airsick passengers, particularly in the aft section of the cabin. The resulting odor aggravated the nausea. Soon most of the passengers became ill, including those in first class, where the stewardess had one elderly lady lying in the aisle and was administering oxygen.

I unbuckled my belt and started forward to the cockpit. On the way, the perturbed chief stewardess grabbed my arm and said, ''The captain wishes to see you.'' I opened the cockpit door. The airplane was on autopilot, the control wheel oscillating right and left with the Dutch roll. The coatless captain, shirt wet with sweat, hands clenching the seat armrests, was almost in shock. The copilot and flight engineer were in a similar state.

I slid into the jump seat as the captain asked, ''What can we do?''

''Disconnect the damn autopilot,'' I said.

''No, no,'' he said. ''We'll lose it.''

''There is nothing wrong with the airplane. The autopilot is misrigged,'' I said. ''Disengage it.''

"Could you fly it?" he asked.

"Sure," I said, "let me in there."

He stood watching as I fastened my safety belt and reached for the autopilot disconnect button. He grabbed my arm. "We'll lose it," he cried.

"Sit down," I said. "Let me show you something." As he eased into the jump seat, I grasped the control wheel, pushed the autopilot release, and with two slight control movements we were flying straight and level, altitude 35,000 feet.

The cockpit door swung open and the chief stewardess entered saying, "Thank God. Thank God." Looking at her, it was obvious she was also ill.

The captain said, "Would you fly for a while? I need some rest."

I nodded and said, "My seat's back in the tail."

Addressing the copilot, I said, "Want to get some flying time?"

His answer was precise. "No."

"How much 707 time do you have?"

"This is my first flight since training."

"How about the captain?"

"He just made captain. This is his second trip as captain."

"We must check these guys' training program," I said to myself.

The captain didn't show up during the letdown. Consequently, I continued the approach and landed at Honolulu. While taxiing to the terminal, the captain appeared and said, "I better taxi to the terminal. If they see you in the seat they'll fire me." I kept my thoughts to myself.

When we were parked with engines shut down, I said, "Hand-fly this thing to San Francisco. I have squawked the autopilot in the log, requesting the autopilot directional axis be rerigged prior to the next flight."

Futures

In Seattle the flight-test schedule was awesome. Certification tests of Braniff's 707-220 equipped with the higher-thrust J75 P&W engines and Qantas Airline's short-body 707 were nearing completion. The developmental tests of noise suppressors and thrust reversers were progressing with gratifying results. Production predelivery flight tests of B-52 bombers, KC-135 jet tankers, and commercial 707's placed severe demands on the organization led by chief production test pilot Clayton Scott. Jack Steiner, a prolific design engineer, and his organization had three new airplanes in final design, the four-engine 720, the three-engine 727, and the two-engine 737—three new jet transport configurations to satisfy the multiple route structure requirements of the world's airlines.

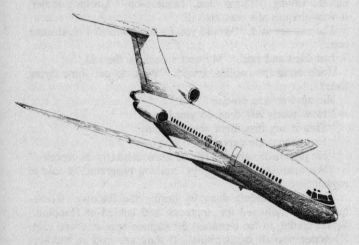

Boeing 727

I assigned instructor pilot Allsop to Air India. Mattison returned to Seattle to prepare for the Air France training program. The ever increasing domestic and foreign aircraft sales had resulted in a major expansion of the training program for customer flight crews, now the largest such program in the history of the industry. When I arrived in Paris to initiate the Air France pilot qualification program, I was disturbed that there was no French equivalent of the U.S. Federal Aviation Administration. As in India, there was no government regulatory agency for aviation. My instructions to instructor pilots

Mattison and Tom Lane and flight engineer instructor Jim Mathison were, "Customer crews meet our standards. Period."

To obtain maximum airplane utilization, preflight briefings were scheduled at 6:30 a.m., first flight 7:30 a.m. But Air France flight crews were habitually late, and on occasion the airplane was not serviced. Eventually, with diligent effort, flight crew punctuality improved. However, the less than aggressive and enthusiastic attitude was disappointing. On occasions flight training was interrupted when the trainee crew requested a landing at Marseilles for lunch.

After much extra and, in my mind, excessive flight training, the chief pilot failed to qualify. It was an uncomfortable situation. In a private meeting with the airline chief executive, I informed him of the problem and stated I did not believe the captain capable of qualifying in the 707. I confirmed the conversation with a letter the following day.

Upon delivery of additional Air France aircraft, I increased the number of Boeing flight instructors in Paris and returned to Seattle. Eventually, Air France flight instructors' techniques were perfected and approved by Boeing instructors.

Following the departure of the Boeing instructors, an Air France instructor qualified the chief pilot. On his second 707 trip as captain, he missed an inclement weather approach at an airport in the Lesser Antilles and on the go-around for a second approach failed to climb to minimum altitude and crashed into a mountain on an adjacent island.

More Problems

I occupied the jump seat as check pilot on the delivery flight of Air India's number four 707. The arrival at Bombay's Santa Cruz Airport was routine, except for the enthusiastic welcome I received from my Indian friends.

Allsop, the Boeing instructor pilot based in Bombay, briefed me and said that Air India flight crew training had been completed except for three marginal captains. I flew with the three exceptions. Two improved with a change of instructor; the third did not.

Taxiing in from a round-trip check flight to London, I was exasperated to see an Air India 707 parked with the rubber seals around the landing-gear doors hanging in strips and hydraulic fluid pooled on the ramp. I knew the problem. The 707 uses Skydrol, a fire-resistant hydraulic fluid that is extremely corrosive and deteriorates rubber. After parking, I immediately went to the maintenance manager, Vishvanath. "Vish, the 707 with the hydraulic leak is deteriorating rapidly. The landing-gear door seals and various decal service instructions in the wheel wells are being destroyed and structural damage is possible. Skydrol is water soluble. Let's get with it." Without a word he was on his way.

At Jay Tata's office, Jay told me he and the board were extremely happy with the 707. He asked about flight crew training. I told him of my concern about the remaining marginal captain. He studied my face and said, "Unfortunate. I am confident you will provide him with every opportunity." As I left he said, "I understand you are going on a tiger shoot. Good hunting."

Returning to the damaged 707, I saw 25 workers with goat-hide waterbags on their shoulders standing in line to dribble water on the $30 million airplane. Operating conditions in India were not the world's best, but we persevered.

A successful tiger hunt finally gained for me the trophy I had dreamed of for almost three years. However, my lifelong interest in hunting began to decline after the leopard and tiger shoots in India and finally terminated one and a half miles off the Russian coast on the polar ice when I took my polar bear, in the most unsportsmanlike hunt I ever experienced. When I returned from that Alaskan hunt, I sold my entire collection of fine hunting rifles and never hunted again.

With the tiger hunt behind me and Air India on track, I once again bid farewell to my Indian friends and boarded a Lockheed Constellation for the long flight to Hong Kong and on to Honolulu via Tokyo. Out of Honolulu bound for Seattle, the DC-7 flight crew, whom I knew, invited me to occupy the jump seat. As we were completing the letdown for landing at Seattle 35 miles off shore, we monitored the departure chatter of a Northwest Airlines Stratocruiser departing Seattle for Honolulu. Suddenly the Stratocruiser pilot called, "May Day. May Day. We are experiencing severe vibration throughout the airplane." Shortly, he reported that he considered the airplane unairworthy and was going to ditch in Puget Sound near Vashon Island.

"That's right on our course," our captain said. He altered course slightly, and we circled overhead as the Stratocruiser, spray flying, came to rest on the waters of the sound. Three passengers drowned.

An accident investigation revealed that the "severe vibration throughout the airplane" had been caused by wide-open engine cowl flaps, a setting designed for engine cooling on the ground, not for use in flight. It was a period when airlines exchanged aircraft as an economy measure. The Northwest crew was flying another airline's Stratocruiser in which all electrical switches operated in the reverse of the system adopted by the balance of the airline industry. A perfectly sound airplane was ditched because the flight engineer, accustomed to another aircraft, placed the cowl flap switch in the wrong position. The captain failed to recognize a known characteristic of the airplane (severe buffeting with engine cowling flaps full open), neglected to check the cowl flap position visually, and made an unwarranted decision, the result of unprofessional cockpit knowledge and discipline.

New Horizons

Daughter Judy was married. Son Gary was making miniature rooster tails with his small hydroplane on Lake Washington. Daughter Barbara was showing her horse Kalif in equitation and hunter jumping competition. DeLores was busy with Barbara at the horse shows and with philanthropic organizations. For me, it was the ultimate in satisfaction and challenge to step each day into the cockpit, strap on a 707, and take off on an engineering test mission.

Major progress had been achieved. Approved engine noise suppressors and thrust reversers were in production. Certification of the Braniff 707-220, equipped with Pratt and Whitney's increased-thrust J75 engines for the high-altitude airports of South America, and the Qantas short-body 707 was complete.

Then, tragedy. On October 19, 1959, a Braniff 707-220,

with Boeing instructor pilot Russell Baum and trainee flight crew aboard, perished in a training accident near Bellingham, Washington. Flight instructor Allsop, an observer aboard the flight, recognized the catastrophic condition, retreated, and secured himself in an aft seat in the passenger cabin and survived the crash. An in-depth accident investigation and Allsop's statement concluded that instructor Baum, during Dutch roll training, allowed the yaw angle to exceed the established 15-degree limit. The resulting crosswind on the vertical tail forced the rudder to full deflection, overpowering the authority of the rudder control tab. The resulting extremely high roll rate created severe centrifugal loads, which caused engine attaching structures to fail, and three engines separated from the airplane.

For two days I reviewed previous customer near-catastrophic incidents, the Braniff accident, and our intensified training effort. The facts showed that all such incidents had occurred during training. Considering the future training requirement throughout the world, I was deeply concerned.

During dinner DeLores said, "What's the problem? The roast tastes okay to me."

"Discussion time," I replied.

Friday morning I called Wellwood Beal. "What's up?" he said.

"Wellwood, we need a meeting regarding the 707."

"Whom do you want in attendance?" he asked.

"Wells, Schairer, and you," I said.

"Okay, I'll set up a meeting for tomorrow."

I interrupted. "No, Wellwood. I want a meeting now."

"How about in five minutes?" he replied.

"Perfect. I'll be there."

Wellwood was seated at his desk with Wells and Schairer on his right and left. Seating myself in front of the desk, I placed the folder of pertinent pilot reports on the desk as we greeted one another. "It's your meeting," Wellwood said.

"I'm here because of the Braniff accident." They were silent.

Picking up my papers, I said, "Here are my Dash 80 pilot reports regarding marginal directional stability and Dutch roll beginning with flight number two." I reviewed the data. "We have emphasized Dutch roll training and stressed the yaw limits. It is obvious that training and establishing limits are not solving our problem. I cannot continue to endorse the 707 airplane unless we correct the problem.''

It was very quiet. Wells spoke. ''What are your recommendations?''

One by one, I reviewed a high-aspect-ratio vertical tail, a full-time irreversible boosted rudder with reduced rudder pedal force, and a ventral fin to augment directional stability. The ventral fin would have the additional advantage that the ventral structure beneath the tail would preclude overrotation on take-off. Following my responses to their questions and our agreement, Wells said, ''We will proceed accordingly.''

Addressing me, Beal said, ''Does that satisfy you?''

''No, sir,'' I replied.

''What else?''

''When?'' I replied.

Wells answered the question. ''Now,'' he said.

Late that afternoon, my friend Bruce Connelly, vice president and director of the transport division, telephoned me at the flight-test office. ''Tex, can you attend a meeting in my office at nine in the morning?''

''Sure, what's the subject?'' I asked.

''I don't know,'' he said. ''It's Ed Wells's meeting.''

I arrived for the meeting. Being Saturday, there was no secretary in the outer office. I opened the door and stepped into Connelly's office. The desk chair was vacant. Wells, Schairer, and Connelly were seated on one side of the office. Project manager Pennel, assistant manager Rouzie, chief aerodynamicist Bill Cook, and other 707 program engineers were seated around the room. As I sat down, Wells, without rising, announced, ''Tex has something to say.''

Completely surprised, I slowly rose, my thoughts racing. ''What is the meaning of this? In my position as chief of flight test, in the best interests of my employer, I had presented a serious company problem, which definitely fell within my realm of responsibility.'' I recalled my father's advice: ''When in doubt, check the facts. If you're sure you are correct, press on.'' I stepped behind the desk to the wall blackboard and reiterated in detail the 707 problem and my recommendations. Wells interrupted at various points to request comments from aerodynamicist Cook, who at Wells's request joined me at the blackboard to draw comparison data curves depicting the characteristics of the present 707 versus the Douglas DC-8 and a modified 707 vertical tail and rudder control system. The discussion concluded with an agreement that the proposed changes were appropriate. As the meeting adjourned, I was relieved. The one built-in marginal characteristic of the 707 would be corrected; the future of the airplane was assured.

Surveying the faces of my departing colleagues, I became uneasy. Did I see animosity and no enthusiasm for correcting this deficiency?

The following week, vice president Connelly called and requested I proceed to Europe to brief our customers on the proposed changes to the 707. "The Braniff accident repercussions from the customers are serious," he said.

The first presentation in London was to BOAC. A grim-faced group assembled in the conference room. "The basic cause of the Braniff accident was pilot error, allowing the aircraft to exceed the established fifteen-degree maximum yaw angle," I said. I described previous near-accidents and details of the Braniff crash, then outlined the changes to be incorporated in 707 aircraft. "Those changes will improve the directional characteristics of the 707 and eliminate the possibility of future accidents of this type," I said.

Congeniality had been slowly returning to the room. The vice president of finance stood and said, "Thank you for providing the details we required. The question is, who pays for these modifications?"

In an instant my mind recalled Wells's words, "We will fix it," and my reply was, "Boeing."

My presentations to our other European customers corrected serious adverse customer relations. The financial burden at that point was no doubt significant. However, without the technical and financial commitment, the future of the 707 program was in peril.

Soon after my return to Seattle, Connelly informed me that customer reaction to the company explanations regarding the Braniff accident and Boeing's corrective action were well received. Meanwhile, the preliminary design group was completing the design of a four-engine, long-range, double-deck transport, with increased passenger capability, that would become the 747. A second group had completed a feasibility study for a supersonic transport and had moved on to cost analysis.

As the fifties ended, the space age was dawning. On October 4, 1957, the Soviet Union launched *Sputnik*, the first man-made satellite to orbit the earth. On July 29, 1958, president Dwight D. Eisenhower signed into law the National Aeronautics and Space Act, which led to the establishment of the National Aeronautics and Space Administration (NASA) on October 1, 1958. On April 12, 1961, Soviet space technology made another major leap into the future by launching Russian cosmonaut Yuri Gagarin into low earth orbit, making him the first man in space. After one orbit, he reentered the atmosphere and landed safely. The series of Soviet successes, combined with some humiliating U.S. failures, jolted Americans into the space race. President John F. Kennedy correctly assessed the national mood. On May 25, 1961, before a joint session of Congress, he proposed a historic national goal: ''I believe that this nation should commit itself to achieving the goal before this decade is out of landing a man on the moon and returning him safely to earth.''

Boeing was already involved with space. With previous experience in producing the Bomarc unmanned, preprogrammed winged missile and the Minute Man intercontinental ballistic missile, and nearing completion of the lunar orbiter designed to obtain high-resolution photographs of the lunar surface for the Apollo mission, Boeing was named winner of the Dyna Soar competition.

Dyna Soar was to be a space vehicle manned by one pilot, capable of reentering the earth's atmosphere and landing on a conventional runway. The fixed-wing airplane was to use conventional controls for flight within the earth's atmosphere and reaction controls (high-pressure gas jets) in space. The small nose cone of the airplane would be protected by ablative material (extremely heat resistant), while the rest of the airframe would be designed using new technology and materials promoting radiation cooling of the structure. Dyna Soar would be launched by booster rocket from Cape Canaveral, Florida. Once in space, the spent rocket would be jettisoned. Thereafter, the pilot would use reaction controls to fly his mission and reenter the earth's atmosphere. After reentry, he would use conventional controls for descent and landing at Edwards Air Force Base, or at Cape Canaveral as an alternate. I could see that the future frontiers of flight lay in supersonic flight, the development and test of space-age vehicles and new forms of propulsion.

As I returned from a postflight test conference, Donna buzzed and said, "Mr. Tory Gamlin, line one." Gamlin, a VP in the Wichita engineering organization, had recently been transferred to the transport division in Renton. I had met him on one occasion in Wichita.

Placing the telephone to my ear, I said, "Hello, Tory."

Without acknowledgment, he said, "Tex, there is going to be an organizational change. Flight Test will report to the respective project engineers."

Shocked, I replied, "What are you talking about, Tory? We went through this exercise several years ago. The present organization is more effective and productive. I'll be over immediately. We must discuss the situation."

"No," he replied, "there is nothing to discuss."

Hanging up the phone, I was devastated. It was difficult to realize the words I had heard. By the time I was en route to Renton, I was over the initial shock and mad. Ignoring Gamlin's secretary, I knocked two times, opened the door, and stepped into his office. I was under control, but firm in my statements.

He refused to reply to my questions regarding the reason for such an organizational change. His attitude and conduct were completely at odds with the normal and established way of handling such matters at Boeing.

On my way to the dining room at the Seattle executive headquarters building, I reviewed the facts. The situation violated Boeing Company operational procedures. Gamlin had no jurisdiction over the flight-test organization. A competent executive does not conduct business of that type by telephone. Was his unorthodox action the result of animosity within the transport division's engineering organization? Considering the less than enthusiastic attitude displayed by several attendees at the conclusion of the rudder boost meeting, that seemed possible. The entire situation seemed clandestine, particularly with the meeting being conducted by vice president Wells.

Recalling the early Dash 80 test program, I had identified the marginal directional stability of the airplane on flight number two and obtained substantiating data on numerous subsequent flights, which were presented in the individual flight-test reports. The early training incidents and near-incidents (previously described) had also been documented. Those flight-test reports went directly to the respective project engineers. Now I was in a jam because I had insisted on a solution to the problem. Thinking farther downstream, regardless of the outcome of the situation, it was inevitable that the previously excellent working relationship among departments and their mutual professional respect would be affected.

When I entered the executive dining room, a group of my friends, vice presidents George Martin, Lyle Wood, George Schairer, and George Stoner, asked me to join them. The conversation was typical, and there was definitely no indication of any special concern by any of the group. I was positive not one of them knew of my problem. Seeing George Stoner made me think of the attractions of the Dyna Soar program. When the others departed, only George Martin and I remained at the table.

"George, is there a position within the company that will fit me?"

With surprise he said, "What do you mean?"

"I'm thinking of hanging up my parachute, George."

"I can't believe it. Are you serious?"

"I'm serious."

Shaking his head, he said, "I'll give it some thought, Tex, and get back to you," and added, "I still don't believe it."

Later Stoner called me. "Is it true what Martin tells me; you're looking for another job?"

"That's correct," I replied.

"This surprises me. Are you familiar with Dyna Soar?"

"Not really, George, only the press releases."

"Tex, it is an interesting and technically challenging program and right in your field. I need an assistant program manager. Would you be interested?"

"Yes, George, I'm interested because it is a hypersonic airplane, not a capsule, and a new technology. When can we discuss it?"

"I'm available now," he said. "I'll brief you on the total program."

It was six when Stoner and I shook hands. I had accepted the Dyna Soar job as assistant program manager. I dearly loved the chief of flight-test position, but I had thoroughly analyzed the facts. The greatest era of advancement in the history of aviation was over. Additional increases in aircraft performance, speed, altitude, range, and payload would be in small increments compared with the advent of the jet engine and swept-wing airplanes. Yeager and the X-1 ushered in supersonic flight. Now numerous research airplanes and late-model fighters were routinely flying supersonic. I was one of the first civilian pilots to exceed Mach 1 in a specially prepared F-86 at the Air Force's invitation. The Anglo-French Concorde SST (supersonic transport) would fly soon, but calculations of its economics indicated it would not be financially successful. The challenge for Boeing and other manufacturers was similar to that faced in the mid-forties. Develop an economically feasible aircraft powered by new-technology engines and fuels capable of operating at altitudes, speeds, and ranges many times those of today's aircraft.

Before leaving Flight Test, I appointed Jack Waddell project pilot for the forthcoming 747 double-deck transport and Jim Gannett project pilot for the supersonic transport under study. I also recommended Dix Loesch for chief of flight test.

My flying activities and long-ago childhood dreams were not yet fulfilled, but once again, the effect of the Invisible Hand was giving me the opportunity to move on.

22

Dyna Soar and Apollo

From 1960 to 1963 I was assistant program manager for Boeing's X-20 Dyna Soar program in Seattle. During its development, we built an open-frame mockup of the Dyna Soar vehicle mounted on a tripod base fifteen feet high. The mockup was attached to the base with a single, frictionless air bearing mounted precisely at the center of gravity.

On the day I tested the mockup, I climbed to the cockpit by ladder, fastened the safety belt, called for high-pressure air to the air bearing and reaction flight controls, and tried the controls. The ship's rate and degree of attitude change were proportional to control application, but the feel during banked turns was unrealistic because of the absence of G forces.

The air-bearing Dyna Soar mockup became popular with the assigned military pilots as well as with military visitors from Wright Field and Washington, D.C. Famed rocket scientist Wernher von Braun observed a mockup demonstration after I briefed him on the Dyna Soar mission. The visit by Braun was the start of a professional relationship that prevailed throughout my later work in the space program. On two subsequent occasions, while relaxing from Apollo duties on the Cocoa Beach sand, Braun intrigued Stoner and me with his thoughts and predictions regarding deep-space exploration.

The Dyna Soar project was progressing well. The first vehicle was near completion, and the Cape Canaveral launch facilities, equipment and personnel, the down-range facilities, and the Edwards Air Force Base preparations were on schedule and on budget. However, after Secretary of Defense McNamara received a Dyna Soar briefing at our Seattle facility, Wright Field terminated the program, an unexpected disappointment.

I made a realistic postcancellation analysis. On the positive side, Dyna Soar utilized heretofore unused technologies: metals resistant to high temperatures and a first-of-its-kind radiation-cooled structure that eliminated the need for high-temperature ablative material except for the small nose cone. On the negative side, although Dyna Soar would pioneer those new technologies and a new kind of space flight, it was limited to a one-man crew, small payloads, and short missions.

On the other hand, the Saturn program that was being planned involved a vehicle capable of lifting a huge payload in both volume and weight, of carrying a multiple-member crew, and of staying in flight for extended periods. Thus Saturn was a significantly more productive program. Dyna Soar's one-man crew with limited mission length and data-acquisition capability was simply not worth the cost.

Apollo

In 1963 NASA selected Boeing as prime contractor to produce the giant five-engine first stage of the multistage Saturn booster for the Apollo lunar landing mission. Boeing management named vice president George Stoner director of the Saturn booster program. Stoner assigned Richard "Dick" Nelson to manage the booster manufacturing facility in New Orleans and named me manager of the Boeing Atlantic Test Center (B.A.T.C.) in Cocoa Beach, Florida.

When I arrived at B.A.T.C. in mid 1964, Boeing test activities consisted of test firing instrumented Minute Man ballistic missiles from two underground silos and the final laboratory testing of the Boeing-built lunar orbiter. I was disappointed by my initial inspection of the management, administrative, and technical offices in Cocoa Beach and the shop and laboratory facilities at Cape Kennedy. Although the director's office, supervisor offices, conference rooms, and work areas were adequate, the entrance lobby, furniture, and decor were mundane and substandard. The most obvious and unprofessional condition was the substandard esprit de corps of the employees and the leisure-type personal attire.

I called a meeting with all B.A.T.C. supervisors, identified myself, and emphasized the importance of the two Boeing programs. Minute Man was vital to U.S. security. The lunar orbiter was paramount in supplying lunar surface information for the fast-approaching Apollo lunar landing mission. In discussing the complexity of the Apollo mission and the serious nature of B.A.T.C. responsibilities, I emphasized the importance of punctuality, both in-house and with contractor and NASA personnel, and that personal attire should meet established professional business standards. "The opportunities for the Boeing Company and its employees are substantial," I said. "The degree of our success therefore is a function of our professional performance."

My first meeting with the formal Dr. Kurt Debus, director of the NASA Cape Kennedy organization, was congenial and objective and initiated an excellent working relationship. At that time, pile drivers were driving miles of piling to stabilize the sandy location of the vertical assembly building, destined to be the largest building in the world. There the 526-foot-tall Apollo vehicle would be assembled on the gigantic crawler transporter before moving to the launch pad for final checkout and launch. Nearing completion were the launch and mission control facility, launch pads, and reinforced concrete roadways for the mobile transporter and support vehicles.

As facilities were completed, Apollo equipment and components began arriving. Simultaneously the prime contractors' head count increased, along with coordination problems. Because of inadequately detailed schedules for prime contractor assembly and checkout, the Apollo program faced potential schedule slides, quality-control problems, and escalating costs. I briefed Stoner and received permission to approach Debus with a Boeing proposal to solve the ever-increasing contractor interface problems. Debus agreed to evaluate a proposal. I called Seattle and obtained a team of technical program planners on loan. I directed them and selected B.A.T.C. systems engineers and technicians to develop the Boeing proposal, which would include two attachments:

Attachment one would propose conversion of the number three launch control auditorium, which was not scheduled for use in the foreseeable future, to a program-schedule and status-review facility for Apollo contractors and NASA. The existing auditorium included three large motion picture screens suspended high above a theatrical stage with behind-the-screen slide and film projectors. It would be ideal for NASA, contractor, and political presentations and reporting. I also proposed a small podium equipped with microphone, remote-control movie and slide projector controls, a light-beam pointer, interphone to the movie and slide technicians, and a carpet in the bowl auditorium to improve acoustics.

Attachment two would propose using the huge vacant room behind the number three auditorium stage to accommodate representatives of each Apollo prime contractor in one location. That would alleviate communications problems resulting from geographic separation and promote a team atmosphere. I instructed the B.A.T.C. facilities department to provide a detailed layout of the proposed integrated program scheduling room, including secretarial desks, clerical equipment, files, and telephones.

Within eight weeks, the proposal and the two attachments were completed and approved by Boeing management. We started preparing A-frame flip charts for a presentation date with Debus. Several days before the scheduled presentation, I was hospitalized with severe abdominal pains. The long hours and tensions of the period had taken their toll. On the morning of our eight o'clock presentation to Debus, I rose from my hospital bed at six, shaved, showered, and dressed. As I walked down the hall, I saw my nurse approaching, placed my hand up to my face, and turned my head slightly as we passed. The presentation was well received. After numerous subsequent meetings and the incorporation of changes required by NASA, Boeing was selected to implement the new program. Our resulting requirements for additional personnel were met by employment ads in major U.S. newspapers. With the assistance of the Seattle personnel organization we acquired well-qualified people to handle the new responsibilities.

Necessary additional working space was acquired by taking over two office complexes in Cocoa Beach from departing contractors. Later, as the B.A.T.C. head count exceeded 5,000, we added to our original management complex and took over a vacated NASA office building in Cocoa Beach.

The Boeing lunar orbiter made a successful and spectacular launch and was soon transmitting informative photos of the moon surface from lunar orbit.

On Januaury 27, 1967, a catastrophic Apollo command module fire during a simulated launch countdown took the lives of veteran astronauts Virgil Grissom and Edward White and rookie Roger Chaffee. The catastrophe resulted from an electrical short in the cockpit wiring in the cockpit atmosphere of 100 percent oxygen, A redesign of the command module hatch to assure rapid opening, a cockpit atmosphere with standard oxygen content, and flame-proof wiring insulation and personal garments eliminated the contributing factors in the tragedy.

Numerous Saturn V launches with various payloads proved the reliability of the Saturn booster for the long-awaited lunar landing mission. The world was poised for the scheduled July 16, 1969, blastoff.

The morning of July 15, I received a call from Neil Armstrong inviting me to join Michael Collins, Buzz Aldrin, and the other astronauts and himself for dinner at their facility at the cape. It was a typical airplane driver get-together, no one uptight. Everyone there had experienced his share of hairy situations and understood, in detail, the hazards of the mission. Yet, every man there would jump at an opportunity to be aboard, while also being delighted that Neil, Michael, and Buzz were going to make this most significant exploratory mission in the history of mankind.

DeLores, my bride of 34 years; John Johnson, Apollo program planning engineer; and his wife Bobbe, my secretary, were present at the designated area near the launch pad at 7 a.m. Eastern Standard Time to avoid as much as possible the predicted crush of one million spectators. The 36-story-high Apollo 11 vehicle glistened in the morning light. The last minutes of the countdown ticked away. Eight seconds before the launch, the five rockets of Saturn's first stage roared to life, and at precisely the scheduled launch time, 9:32 a.m., the hold-down clamps released, and Armstrong, Collins, and Aldrin were en route to the moon.

The successful moon landing and moon surface exploration by Armstrong and Aldrin, ascension and rendezvous with Collins in the control module, return to planet Earth, and splash-down July 24 in the Pacific Ocean southwest of Hawaii became history.

After completing the four-year assignment as director and principal executive of the Boeing Atlantic Test Center at Cape Kennedy, Florida, which included managing the Saturn S-IC and Apollo integration programs for NASA, I went into business for myself. From 1968 to 1971 I headed Tex Johnston, Inc., TIFS (Total-In-Flight-Simulator), Inc., and Aero Spacelines, Inc., in Santa Barbara, California. Aero Spacelines engaged in the manufacture and certification of an outsized cargo airplane known as the Guppy.

In 1975 I became chief pilot and director of the test department at Stanley Aviation Corporation, the company Robert M. Stanley formed after he left Bell Aircraft. Stanley's company developed, manufactured, and tested personnel escape systems, actuated by a tractor rocket, for fixed- and rotary-wing aircraft. I was responsible for the scheduling and piloting of company aircraft and the management of the Denver test laboratory and suburban test site. I also directed aerospace advanced technology testing at Stanley's high-velocity test facility at Hurricane Mesa, Utah. The equipment included a rocket-powered sled on a heavy-gauge, railroad-steel track, capable of ultrahigh velocity. Strategically located ultrahigh-speed cameras provided infinite detail of the action during a crew member's escape, at high velocities and zero altitude, using a tractor rocket to propel him to adequate altitude for parachute deployment and safe descent. The technology was also applicable to escape from high-performance aircraft and rotary-wing machines at altitude.

Looking back on a long and satisfying career, I am grateful for key test pilot assignments during the most prolific technical achievement period in the history of aviation and for executive assignments involved with preparing for mankind's first trip to the moon. From biplanes to rockets, it all took place within the span of one man's career.

The workings of providence have played a major role in my life. I thank almighty God for the opportunities, personal skills, and guidance I was provided.

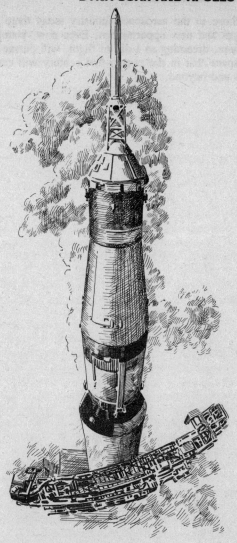

Apollo Liftoff

For those in the aerospace industry today there are new challenges and new opportunities. Even now, young people somewhere, dreaming as I did of flight, will pursue a career in aerospace that in the twenty-first century will carry them to Mars and beyond.

Index

ABOUT THE AUTHORS

A. M. "TEX" JOHNSTON:

As a child on his first flight in a barnstormer's cockpit, "Tex" Johnston knew that flying would become his life. Later a paper route financed his first flight lessons.

A barnstormer himself during the lean years of the depression, Johnston was forethoughtful enough to attend an aviation college to gain the theoretical know-how he would need to fly the highly evolved planes that were soon to fill the sky. He tested our first jet fighter and the rocket-powered Bell X-1 that Chuck Yeager flew through the sound barrier.

Johnston's later career involved the development of the huge jet transports we know today. Then, after working as director of the Boeing Test Center at Cape Kennedy, he went on to develop several major aeronautical businesses of his own. Now retired, Johnston lives in Seattle, Washington.

CHARLES BARTON:

A freelance writer and former naval aviator, Barton is the author of the book HOWARD HUGHES AND HIS FLYING BOAT, named best nonfiction aviation book of 1982 by the Aviation/Space Writers Association.

A NOTE ABOUT THE BANTAM AIR & SPACE SERIES

This is the era of flight—the century which has seen man soar, not only into the skies of Earth but beyond the gravity of his home planet and out into the blank void of space. An incredible accomplishment achieved in an incredibly short time.

How did it happen?

The AIR & SPACE series is dedicated to the men and women who brought this fantastic accomplishment about, often at the cost of their lives—a library of books which will tell the grand story of man's indomitable determination to seek the new, to explore the farthest frontier.

The driving theme of the series is the skill of *piloting*, for without this, not even the first step would have been possible. Like the Wright Brothers and those who, for some 35 years, followed in their erratic flight path, the early flyers had to be designer, engineer, and inventor. Of necessity, they were the pilots of the crazy machines they dreamt up and strung together.

Even when the technology became slightly more sophisticated, and piloting became a separate skill, the quality of a flyer's ability remained rooted in a sound working knowledge of his machine. World War I, with its spurt of development in aircraft, made little change in the role of the flyer who remained, basically, pilot-navigator-engineer.

Various individuals, like Charles Lindbergh, risked their lives and made high drama of the new dimension they were carving in the air. But still, until 1939, flying was a romantic, devil-may-care wonder, confined to a relative handful of hardy individuals. Commercial flight on a large scale was a mere gleam in the eye of men like Howard Hughes.

It took a second major conflict, World War II, from 1939 to 1945, to provoke the imperative that required new concepts from the designers—and created the arena where hundreds of young men and women would learn the expertise demanded by high-speed, high-tech aircraft.

From the start of flight, death has taken its toll. Flying has always been a high-risk adventure. Never, since men first launched themselves into the air, has the new element given up its sacrifice of stolen lives, just as men have never given up the driving urge to go farther, higher, faster. Despite only a fifty-fifty chance of any mission succeeding, *still* the dream draws many more men and women to spaceflight than any program can accommodate. And still, in 1969, when Michael Collins, Buzz Aldrin, and Neil Armstrong first took man to the Moon, the skill of piloting, sheer flying ability, was what actually landed the "Eagle" on the Moon's surface. And still, despite technological sophistication undreamed of 30 or 40 years earlier, despite demands on any flyer for levels of performance and competence and the new understanding of computer science not necessary in early aircraft, it is piloting, *human* control of the aircraft—sometimes, indeed, inspired control—that remains the major factor in getting there and back safely. From this rugged breed of individualists came the bush pilots and the astronauts of today.

After America first landed men on the Moon, the Russian space program pushed ahead with plans for eventually creating a permanent space station where men could live. And in 1982 they sent up two men—Valentin Lebedev and Anatoly Berezovoy—to live on Solyut-7 for seven months. This extraordinary feat has been recorded in the diaries of pilot Lebedev, DIARY OF A COSMONAUT: 211 DAYS IN SPACE.

The Bantam AIR & SPACE series will include several titles by or about flyers from all over the world—and about the planes they flew, including World War II, the postwar era of barnstorming and into the jet age, plus the personal histories of many of the world's greatest pilots. Man is still the most important element in flying.

APRIL 18, 1942

The 16-ship Navy task force centered around the aircraft carriers *Hornet* and *Enterprise* had been steaming westward toward Japan all night. I had given my final briefing to the B-25 bomber crews on the *Hornet* the day before. Our job was to do what we could to put a crimp in the Japanese war effort with the 16 tons of bombs from our 16 B-25s. The bombs could do only a fraction of the damage the Japanese had inflicted on us at Pearl Harbor, but the primary purpose of the raid we were about to launch against the main island of Japan was psychological.

The Japanese people had been told they were invulnerable. Their leaders had told them Japan could never be invaded. Proof of this was the fact that Japan had been saved from invasion during the fifteenth century when a massive Chinese fleet set sail to attack Japan and was destroyed by a monsoon. From then on, the Japanese people had firmly believed they were forever protected by a "divine wind"—the *kamikaze*. An attack on the Japanese homeland would cause confusion in the minds of the Japanese people and sow doubt about the reliability of their leaders.

There was a second, and equally important, psychological reason for this attack. America and its allies had suffered one defeat after another in the Pacific and southern Asia. Besides the devastating surprise attack on Pearl Harbor, the Japanese had taken Wake Island and Guam and had driven American and Filipino forces to surrender on Bataan. Only a small force of Americans was left holding out on the island of Corregidor. America had never seen darker days. Americans badly needed a morale boost. I hoped we could give them that by a retaliatory surprise attack against the enemy's home islands launched from a carrier, precisely as the Japanese had done at Pearl Harbor. It would be the kind of touché the Japanese military would understand. An air strike would certainly be a blow to their national morale and, furthermore, should cause the Japanese to divert aircraft and equipment from offensive operations to the defense of the home islands.

The basic plan for the raid against Japan was simple. If the Navy task force could get us within 400 to 500 miles of the Japanese coast, the B-25 medium Army bombers aboard the *Hornet* would launch, with carefully trained crews, against the enemy's largest cities. Although the carrier's deck seemed too short to allow the takeoff of a loaded B-25 land-based Army bomber, I was confident it could be done. Two lightly loaded B-25s had made trial takeoffs the previous February from the *Hornet* off the Virginia coast before the carrier had joined the Pacific fleet. All of the pilots had practiced a number of short-field takeoffs at an auxiliary field near Eglin Field, Florida.

I would take off first so as to arrive over Tokyo at sunset. The other crews would leave the carrier at local sunset and head for their respective targets. I would drop four 500-pound incendiary bombs on a factory area in the center of Tokyo. The resulting fires in the highly inflammable structures in the area would light up the way for the succeeding planes and steer them toward their respective targets in the Tokyo-Yokohama area, Nagoya, and the Kobe-Osaka complex. The rest of the B-25s would be loaded with four 500-pound bombs each—two incendiaries and two demolition bombs. After launching the B-25s, the Navy task force was to retreat immediately and return to Hawaii.

We would not return to the *Hornet*. After bombing our targets, we were to escape to China. The planes would be turned over to the new Air Force units being formed in the China-Burma-India theater.

There were five crew members in each airplane—pilot, copilot, bombardier, navigator, and gunner. One crew had a physician aboard—Dr. (Lieutenant) Thomas R. White—who had volunteered and qualified as a gunner so he could go. This was a fortuitous choice, as it turned out, for four members of another crew.

The State Department had tried to get permission from the Soviets for us to land in Soviet territory for refueling. This flight would have been an easy 600 miles or so after bombing the Japanese targets. But permission was denied because the Soviets were neutral vis-à-vis Japan and did not want to have another Axis power at their back door invading their country from that direction.

Therefore, after dropping its bombs, each plane was to head generally southward along the Japanese coast, then westward to Chuchow, located about 70 miles inland and about 200 miles south of Shanghai. After refueling there, we were to proceed to Chungking, 800 miles farther inland. The greatest in-flight distance we would have to fly was 2,000 miles. With the fuel tank modifications we had made and extra gas in five-gallon cans, there was enough fuel on board to fly 2,400 miles, provided the crews used the long-range cruising techniques we had practiced.

Our planes had been positioned on the deck for takeoff the evening before. The mechanics had run up their engines and made last-minute adjustments. I wanted the crews to get a good night's sleep, but few heeded the advice of an oldster who, at 45, was twice the age of most of them. Some of the officers played poker with the Navy pilots who had been unable to fly since leaving California because our planes took up all the space on the deck. The Navy pilots and our crews wanted to recoup their individual losses before we left.

The *Enterprise* launched scout planes at daybreak for 200-mile searches, and fighters were sent up as cover for the task force. The weather, which had been moderately rough during the night, worsened. There was a low overcast and visibility was limited. Frequent rain squalls swept over the ships, and the sea began to heave into 30-foot crests. Gusty winds tore off the tops of the waves and blew heavy spray across the ships, drenching the deck crews. At 6:00 A.M., a scout plane returned to the *Enterprise* and the pilot dropped a bean bag container on the deck with a message saying he had sighted a small enemy fishing vessel and believed he had been seen by the enemy.

Admiral William F. Halsey immediately ordered all ships to swing left to avoid detection. Had the enemy vessel seen the aircraft? No one knew. The question was answered about 7:30 A.M. when another patrol vessel was sighted from the *Hornet* only 20,000 yards away. A Japanese radio message was intercepted by the *Hornet*'s radio operator from close by. One of the scout planes then sighted another small vessel 12,000 yards away. A light could be seen bobbing in the rough sea. Halsey ordered the cruiser *Nashville* to sink it.

Unknown to us, the Japanese had stationed a line of radio-equipped picket boats about 650 nautical miles out from the coast to warn of the approach of American ships. I went to the bridge where Captain Marc A. Mitscher briefed me on what had happened. "It looks like you're going to have to be on your way soon," he said. "They know we're here." I shook hands with Mitscher and rushed to my cabin to pack, spreading the word as I went.

Some of the B-25 crews had finished breakfast and were lounging in their cabins; others were shaving and getting ready to eat; several may have still been dozing. A few had packed their bags, but I think many were completely surprised because they thought they would not be taking off until late afternoon.

At 8:00 A.M., Admiral Halsey flashed a message to the *Hornet:* LAUNCH PLANES X TO COL DOOLITTLE AND GALLANT COMMAND GOOD LUCK AND GOD BLESS YOU.

The ear-shattering klaxon horn sounded and a booming voice ordered: "Now hear this! Now hear this! Army pilots, man your planes!"

The weather had steadily continued to worsen. The *Hornet* plunged into mountainous waves that sent water cascading down the deck. Rain pelted us as we ran toward our aircraft. It was not an ideal day for a mission like this one.

The well-disciplined Navy crews and our enlisted men, some of whom had slept on deck near their planes, knew what to do. Slipping and sliding on the wet deck, they ripped off engine and gun turret covers and stuffed them inside the rear hatches. Fuel tanks were topped. The mechanics pulled the props through. Cans of gasoline were filled and handed up to the gunners through the rear hatches. Ropes were unfastened and wheel chocks pulled away so the Navy deck handlers could maneuver the B-25s into takeoff position.

Meanwhile, the *Hornet* picked up speed as best it could in the rough sea and turned into the wind. The 20-knot speed of the carrier and the 30-knot wind blowing directly down the deck meant that we should be airborne safely and quickly. This ability of an aircraft carrier to turn its "airfield" into the wind is a distinct advantage. Rarely do Navy pilots have to worry about cross-wind takeoffs and landings. However, a rough sea such as the one in front of us could ruin a pilot's day if he ignored the signals of the deck officer and tried a takeoff when the bow of the ship was heading into the waves. It was like riding a seesaw that plunged deep into the water each time the bow dipped downward.

Lieutenant Henry L. "Hank" Miller, the naval officer assigned to us at Eglin Field, Florida, to teach us how to take off in minimum distances, said good-bye to each crew. He told us to watch a blackboard he would be holding up near the ship's "island" to give us last-minute instructions and the carrier's heading so our navigators could compare our planes' compasses with the ship's heading and set their directional gyros. The navigators were very concerned about our magnetic compasses. After more than two weeks on the carrier, they would be way off calibration, especially on those planes that were tied down close to the carrier's metal structure. With an overcast sky, the navigators wouldn't be able to take shots of the sun or stars with their sextants. It would be dead reckoning all the way to the Japanese coast. A check on the accuracy of the compasses was essential.

My crew emerged quickly from their quarters below decks. Sergeant Paul J. Leonard, our crew chief, was one of those skilled mechanics who knew instinctively what to do. He already had his barracks bag and toolbox stowed in the rear and was helping the deck crews get our ship into takeoff position. In the air, he would be the top turret gunner. During our training at Eglin, he had proven he was a marksman with the twin .50s. Born in 1912, he had dropped out of high school in Roswell, New Mexico, and enlisted in the Army Air Corps in 1931, at the start of the Depression. He was one of those rare individuals who applied himself and became one of the most outstanding mechanics with whom I ever served. Men like him were the backbone of the nation's air service when war began and were highly regarded for their dedication and expertise. They set high standards for the enlisted men who served with them.

Sergeant Fred A. Braemer, of Seattle, Washington, was another "old-timer." He had joined the infantry in 1935 and transferred to the Air Corps in 1939. He had completed both bombardier and navigator training but was serving on our crew as the bombardier.

Our copilot was Lieutenant Richard E. "Dick" Cole, from Dayton, Ohio, who had completed pilot training in July 1941. Dick was a quietly competent pilot who had attended Ohio University for two years before enlisting as a Flying Cadet. If anything happened to me, I was confident that he would take over the controls of the aircraft and the leadership of the crew without hesitation.

Lieutenant Henry A. "Hank" Potter, of Pierre, South Dakota, was our navigator. Like so many young men in those days, he had also completed two years of college, the minimum for entry into flying training, and had graduated from navigator school in 1941.

I was proud of my crew and all the other volunteers who were willing to lay their lives on the line for a risky mission that I could not tell them about until we were on the carrier. Every man had proven his competence during our training at Eglin. I felt completely comfortable and confident as our B-25 was placed in takeoff position and the wheels chocked.

I knew hundreds of eyes were watching me, especially those of the B-25 crews who were to follow. If I didn't get off successfully, I'm sure, many thought they wouldn't be able to make it either. But I knew they would try.

I started the engines, warmed them up, and checked the magnetos. When satisfied, I gave the thumbs-up sign to the deck launching officer holding the checkered flag. As the chocks were pulled, he looked toward the bow and began to wave the flag in circles as a signal for me to push the throttles forward to the stops. At the instant the deck was beginning an upward movement, he gave me the "go" signal and I released the brakes. The B-25 followed the two white guide lines painted on the deck and we were off with feet to spare as the deck reached its maximum pitch.

We left the *Hornet* at 8:20 A.M. ship time. The carrier's position was about 824 statute miles from the center of Tokyo. Its position: latitude 35°43′N, longitude 153°25′E.

I signaled Dick for wheels up and as the plane gained flying speed, I leveled off and made a 360-degree turn to come over the carrier. This gave Hank Potter a chance to compare the magnetic heading of the carrier with our compass and align the axis of the carrier with the drift sight. The course of the *Hornet* was displayed in large figures from the gun turret near the island. Through the use of the airplane's compass and directional gyro, we were able to set a fairly accurate course for Tokyo.

As we headed toward Japan at low altitude, I thought about how easy the takeoff had been. If everyone followed instructions, they should have no trouble. A night takeoff would have been easy and practicable. That was something I wanted to report to Washington when I got home. It might be useful for future operations.

I began to wonder about the arrangements in China. Generalissimo Chiang Kai-shek, China's ruler, had not wanted us to land in China after bombing Japan for fear of extensive retaliation against his people by the Japanese, who had occupied China's coastal areas and Manchuria for several years. The Chinese had been slaughtered by the thousands whenever marauding Japanese troops invaded an area. American military personnel in China reported that leaks of classified information were common; we were told that secrecy was almost impossible to maintain in Chiang's headquarters. As a result, it was decided in Washington that he would not be informed of our plans until we were at sea and the mission could not be recalled.

As we droned on at about 200 feet above the water, Dick Cole and I took turns at the controls. We were all concerned about gas consumption, and everyone on the flight deck was continually checking the gauges against our estimates. A half hour after takeoff we were joined by the second B-25 to depart, which flew a loose formation with us. It was piloted by Lieutenant Travis Hoover. About an hour later, we sighted a camouflaged Japanese ship that we thought might be a light cruiser. About two hours out we flew directly under an enemy flying boat that just loomed at us suddenly out of the mist. We don't think they saw us. It was heading directly toward the task force.

The weather improved gradually as we got closer to Japan. We changed course briefly several times to avoid various civil and naval surface craft until we made landfall north of Inubo Shima, about 80 miles north of Tokyo. This was the first time Hank Potter was able to get an accurate fix on our position. Trav Hoover promptly turned off toward his target area.

Since we were somewhat north of our desired course, I decided to take advantage of our position and approach the target area from a northerly direction, thus avoiding anticipated antiaircraft batteries and fighter planes located in the western part of the city. We stayed as low as we could and saw many flying fields interspersed among the beautiful scenery. People on the ground waved at us. There were many planes in the air, mostly small biplanes, apparently trainers.

It was shortly after noon in Tokyo. About 10 miles north of the city we saw nine enemy fighters in three flights of three. Dick Cole kept Paul Leonard advised of the enemy aircraft he could see ahead and at one time counted 80. The fighters didn't attack us, but flak from antiaircraft ground batteries shook us up a little and might have put a few holes in the fuselage.

When we spotted the large factory buildings in our target area, I pulled up to 1,200 feet and called for bomb doors open. Fred Braemer toggled off the four incendiaries in rapid succession. It was 12:30 P.M. Tokyo time.

I dropped down to rooftop level again and slid over the western outskirts of the city into low haze and smoke, then turned south and out to sea. We saw many barrage balloons over east central Tokyo and passed over a small aircraft factory with a dozen or so completed planes on the flying line. Unfortunately, we had no bombs left and I didn't want anyone to do any strafing with our machine guns. If we had done that and were downed for any reason, we would surely have been dealt with severely by our captors.

As we sped toward the coast, we saw five fighter planes converging on us from above. There were two little hills ahead. I swung very quickly around the hills in an S turn. The fighters turned also, but apparently they didn't see the second half of my S. The last time I saw them, they were going off in the opposite direction from us.

We stayed low off the coast and Hank Potter plotted a perfect course to Yaku-shima. The ceiling gradually lowered along the route and got down to about 600 feet. We then turned west over the China Sea and encountered a headwind. Hank Potter estimated we would run out of gas about 135 miles from the Chinese coast. We began to make preparations for ditching. I saw sharks basking in the water below and didn't think ditching among them would be very appealing. Also saw three naval vessels and many small fishing vessels. None of them fired, so they probably didn't see us.

Fortunately, the Lord was with us. What had been a headwind slowly turned into a tailwind of about 25 miles per hour and eased our minds about ditching. Trav Hoover had followed us nearly all the way to the Chinese coast. However, he left us as the weather deteriorated and it began to get dark. Visibility was reduced drastically by fog and light rain. As we crossed the Chinese coast, I went on instruments and pulled up to 8,000 feet through the overcast. Our maps showed the mountains to be about 5,000 feet above sea level, but the maps were probably inaccurate. We saw dim lights below occasionally through cloud breaks but had to remain on instruments.

We tried to contact the field at Chuchow on 4495 kilocycles. No answer. This meant that the chance of any of our crews getting to the destination safely was just about nil. Chuchow was situated in a valley about two miles wide and 12 miles long. Without a ground radio station to home in on, there was no way we could find it. All we could do was fly a dead-reckoning course in the direction of Chuchow, abandon ship in midair, and hope that we came down in Chinese-held territory.

When the gas gauges read near zero, I put the B-25 on automatic pilot and told the men in which order to jump: Braemer, Potter, Leonard, and Cole. If we all jumped in a straight line, it would be easier to find one another when we got on the ground. As Dick Cole left, I shut off both gas valves and squeezed quickly after him through the forward hatch. It was about 9:30 P.M. ship time. We had been in the air for 13 hours. We might have had enough fuel left for about another half hour of flight, but the right front tank gauge showed empty, and fuel gauges, even today, are notoriously inaccurate when registering near the zero mark. We had covered about 2,250 miles, mostly at low speed, but about an hour at moderate high speed had more than doubled the consumption during that time.

As I dropped into the rainy darkness, I suddenly realized that I should have put the flaps down before we bailed out. It would have slowed down the landing speed, reduced the impact, and shortened the glide.

This was my third parachute jump to save my hide. It was impossible to see anything below, so all I could do was wait until I hit the ground. My concern as I floated down was about my ankles, which had been broken in South America in 1926. Anticipating a sudden encounter with the ground, I bent my knees to take the shock. When I hit, there wasn't much impact. I had landed in a rice paddy and fallen into a sitting position in a not-too-fragrant mixture of water and "night soil."

I stood up, unhurt and thoroughly disgusted with my situation and the smell, unhooked my parachute harness, and looked around. I saw a light and approached what looked like a small farmhouse. I knocked on the door and shouted, *"Lushu hoo megwa fugi"* ("I am an American"). This was the Chinese phrase we had been taught aboard the carrier by Lieutenant Commander Stephen Jurika, who had served in the Far East before the war. But I must have used the wrong dialect. I heard movement inside, then the sound of a bolt sliding into place. The light went out and there was dead silence.

It was cold and I was shivering. I stumbled on in the darkness and came to a sort of warehouse. Inside, two sawhorses held a large box that was occupied by a very dead Chinese gentleman. It must have been the local morgue. I left and found a water mill, which got me out of the rain, but I was thoroughly chilled. I lay down but couldn't sleep, so spent most of the night doing light calisthenics to stave off the cold. I stayed there until dawn and then followed a well-worn path toward a small village, where I came upon a Chinese who spoke no English. I drew a picture of a train on a piece of paper. He smiled, nodded, and started off. I followed him to a military headquarters where a Chinese major who spoke a little English gestured for me to hand over my .45-caliber automatic pistol. I refused and explained that I was an American and had parachuted during the night into a rice paddy nearby. He didn't seem to believe me, so I told him that I would take him to the spot and show him the parachute.

The officer, surrounded by about a dozen armed soldiers, escorted me to the rice paddy where I had landed, but the 'chute was gone. I said the people in the house must have heard our plane and could verify that I had knocked on their door the night before. However, when the farmer, his wife, and two children were questioned, they denied everything. The major said, ''They say they heard no noise during the night. They say they heard no plane. They say they saw no parachute. They say you lie.''

The soldiers started toward me to relieve me of the .45. It was not a comfortable situation. I protested and was saved from having to tussle with them when two soldiers emerged from the house with the parachute. The major smiled and extended his hand in friendship, and I was thus admitted officially to China. He led me back to his headquarters for a warm meal and a much-needed bath. I dried out my uniform but the stench remained intact.

Meanwhile, the major's men found all four of my crew. It was a relief to see that they were in reasonably good shape. The only minor injury was suffered by Hank Potter, who had sprained an ankle on the bailout.

When the soldiers found our plane, Paul Leonard and I went to the crash site to see what we could salvage. There is no worse sight to an aviator than to see his plane smashed to bits. Ours was spread out over several acres of mountaintop. I fished around the debris for my belongings and found my oil-stained uniform blouse. Some enterprising scavenger had already stripped it of all the brass buttons. There was nothing left of our personal belongings that was worth carrying away.

I sat down beside a wing and looked around at the thousands of pieces of shattered metal that had once been a beautiful airplane. I felt lower than a frog's posterior. This was my first combat mission. I had planned it from the beginning and led it. I was sure it was my last. As far as I was concerned, it was a failure, and I felt there could be no future for me in uniform now. Even if we had successfully accomplished the first half of our mission, the second half had been to deliver the B-25s to our units in the China-Burma-India theater of operations.

My main concern was for my men. What had happened to my crew probably had happened to the others. If so, they had to be scattered all over a considerable area of China. How many had survived? Had any been taken prisoner by the Japanese? Did any have to ditch in the China Sea?

As I sat there, Paul Leonard took my picture and then, seeing how badly I felt, tried to cheer me up. He asked, "What do you think will happen when you go home, Colonel?"

I answered, "Well, I guess they'll court-martial me and send me to prison at Fort Leavenworth."

Paul said, "No, sir. I'll tell you what will happen. They're going to make you a general."

I smiled weakly and he tried again. "And they're going to give you the Congressional Medal of Honor."

I smiled again and he made a final effort. "Colonel, I know they're going to give you another airplane and when they do, I'd like to fly with you as your crew chief."

It was then that tears came to my eyes. It was the supreme compliment that a mechanic could give a pilot. It meant he was so sure of the skills of the pilot that he would fly anywhere with him under any circumstances. I thanked him and said that if I ever had another airplane and he wanted to be my crew chief, he surely could.

While I deeply appreciated Paul's supportive remarks, I was sure that when the outcome of this mission was known back home, either I would be court-martialed or the military powers that be would see to it that I would sit out the war flying a desk. I had never felt lower in my life.

Looking back over more than nine decades it is difficult to recall names and incidents of my very early childhood with much certainty. Unfortunately, I never knew my grandparents on either side, but my mother was a good photographer and it is through the many photographs in the albums she maintained for me that I am able to bring back memories of distant times and places.

Our branch of the Doolittle family is believed to have originated in France, relocated to England, then migrated to this country in the late 1600s or early 1700s. My grandfather, Augustus Albertus Doolittle, was born in East Canaan, Connecticut, in 1844. He was a carpenter and married my grandmother, Margaret Hobson, in the 1860s.

My father, born in 1869, was Frank Henry Doolittle. It isn't certain whether he was born in Connecticut or Massachusetts. A restless, ambitious man who was smitten with wanderlust, he was an excellent carpenter. In his early thirties, he sailed around the Horn from Massachusetts, arrived in San Francisco, and settled down across the bay at Alameda to practice his craft. He met and married my mother, Rosa Ceremah Shephard, in the early 1890s. I came along on December 14, 1896, an only child.

I regret deeply that I cannot recall much about my mother's family background. I know she was of sturdy pioneer stock, strong-willed yet compassionate, intent upon keeping me on a straight-and-narrow path, but a firm disciplinarian when I strayed. She guided me safely through those early years and managed somehow to see to my needs. I owe her more than I can ever express.

I guess they didn't know what to name me for a while, since my birth certificate recorded me simply as "Doolittle." The "James" and "Harold" were added later and I have no idea where they came from. I have never been particularly happy about my middle name.

In the summer after I was born, my father joined the thousands of dreamers and adventurers who stampeded to the Klondike in search of gold. He took his bag of carpenter's tools with him and sailed by boat to Seattle and then to Skagway, Alaska. Then he trekked over the Chilkoot Pass to the Klondike gold fields near Dawson. Doubtless he prospected, but since gold was elusive, he kept body and soul together with his carpentry skills. However, he lost his tools in a boat accident as he traveled down the Yukon River to Norton Sound.

In 1899, my father worked his way around to St. Michael where he got a job with the Alaska Commercial Co., a supplier of tools and mining equipment for the prospectors. Still hoping to make his fortune, he pushed on to the Seward Peninsula and finally Nome when the news spread that gold had been discovered on the beaches and was easy pickings.

Once he got to Nome, my father wanted us to join him. On one of the last ships to leave before the winter freeze, he sent a letter to my mother asking her to bring me with her the following spring. So in June 1900, my mother, her sister Sarah, and I sailed on the SS *Zealandia* and arrived in Nome two weeks later. It was just one of the 30 steamers that carried nearly 10,000 people to Nome that month.

Contrary to popular conception, the Klondike River and the gold district named for it are in Canada, not Alaska. The real gold rush stampede to Alaska was not to the Klondike. It was to the sandy beaches of Nome, a thousand miles to the west, during that summer of 1900. It could be reached only by dog sled or boat; therefore, most took the latter course so they wouldn't have to climb mountains, run river rapids, or backpack their own supplies to get there.

A Dawson City newspaper warned its readers, "The gold fever is no respecter of persons. Like the dew of heaven it falls with absolute impartiality upon the just and the unjust alike. Its germs once planted in the system, take root and thrive so vigorously that it dominates its victim like an all-consuming passion for drink."[1]

Gold had been found in September 1898 along the Snake River near where Nome now stands. Three Swedes were the first to stake claims and took out about $2,000 in gold that year. The Cape Nome Mining District was organized and claims were staked out and recorded. That autumn about 40 men filed claims to 7,000 acres of prospecting ground. Late in June 1899, when the ice broke in the Bering Sea, several vessels reached the settlement that was growing up along Anvil Creek where about 400 people were living in tents and crude driftwood cabins.

A man named John Hummel, who was ailing and could not work much, is generally believed to have been the first to discover gold along the beach. As soon as the news got out, the miners working a few miles inland along the creeks rushed to the beaches. The strike was unquestionably the greatest poor-man's diggings ever found. Within a short time, 2,000 miners were at work sifting the sand. Within two months, using simple hand rockers to sift the sand, the miners had taken out about $750,000 in gold dust.

When the steamers returned to the States that autumn, stories of the gold find spread around the world. Interest in "the gold sands of Nome" grew rapidly. Many thought the gold in the beach would be inexhaustible because, supposedly, the supply was being constantly renewed by the waves from the ocean bottom. It wasn't true, but the stampede began in the spring of 1900 when the first ships left ports on the West Coast and made their way through the Aleutian Islands and the Bering Sea ice fields to this paradise of riches. The ice on Bering Sea broke early and on May 2, 1900, the *Jeanie*, an old whaler, reached Nome, the first of a large fleet to follow.

The history of man in flight...
THE BANTAM AIR AND SPACE SERIES

The Bantam Air and Space Series is dedicated to the men and women who brought about this, the era of flight—the century in which mankind not only learned to soar the skies, but has journeyed out into the blank void of space.

❏ 28556-4 1: THE LAST OF THE BUSH PILOTS
by Harmon Helmericks $4.95
❏ 28557-2 2: FORK-TAILED DEVIL by Martin Caidin $4.95
❏ 28778-8 4: DIARY OF A COSMONAUT: 211 DAYS
IN SPACE by Valentin Lebedev $4.95
❏ 28780-X 5: FLYING FORTS by Martin Caidin $4.95
❏ 28857-1 6: ISLAND IN THE SKY by Ernest K. Gann $4.95
❏ 28845-8 9: THE ELECTRA STORY: AVIATION'S
GREATEST MYSTERY by Robert J. Serling $4.95
❏ 28872-5 10: ZERO by Masatake Okumiya and Jiro
Horikoshi with Martin Caidin $4.95
❏ 28919-5 11: PIONEER BUSH PILOT by Ira Harkey $4.95
❏ 28993-4 12: MEN FROM EARTH
by Buzz Aldrin and Malcolm McConnell $5.99
❏ 29037-1 13: BLAZE OF NOON by Ernest K. Gann $4.99
❏ 29321-4 14: FLYING FOR THE FATHERLAND: THE
CENTURY'S GRETEST PILOT by Judy Lomax $4.99
❏ 29273-0 15: THE GREAT AIR RACES
by Don Vorderman $4.99
❏ 29240-4 16: TO FLY AND FIGHT by Col. Clarence E.
"Bud" Anderson with Joseph P. Hamelin $4.99
❏ 29260-9 17: BAND OF BROTHERS by Ernest K. Gann $4.99
❏ 29586-1 18: THE LEGENDARY DC-3
by Carroll V. Glines and Wendell F. Moseley $4.99
❏ 23949-X 19: THE SKY BEYOND by Sir Gordon Taylor $4.99
❏ 29697-3 20: ERNEST K. GANN'S FLYING CIRCUS
by Ernest K. Gann $4.99
❏ 29426-1 21: TEST PILOT by Martin Caidin $4.99
